1

LEGACIES
OF THE
COMFORT
WOMEN
OF
WORLD WAR II

LEGACIES
OF THE
COMFORT
WOMEN
OF
WORLD WAR II

Margaret Stetz
and Bonnie B. C. Oh
editors

AN EAST GATE BOOK

M.E. Sharpe
Armonk, New York
London, England

An East Gate Book

Library of Congress Cataloging-in-Publication Data

Legacies of the comfort women of World War II / edited by Margaret D. Stetz and
Bonnie B.C. Oh.
   p. cm.
"An East gate book."
Includes index.
ISBN-0-7656-0543-0 (alk. paper) — ISBN 0-7656-0544-9 (pbk. : alk. paper)
   1. Comfort women–Asia. I. Stetz, Margaret D. (Margaret Diane), 1953–   II. Oh,
Bonnie B.C.

D810.C698 L44 2001
940.54′05′082095—dc21   2001020048

Contents

Editors and Contributors

Editors

Bonnie B. C. Oh is Distinguished Professor of Korean Studies in the School of Foreign Service at Georgetown University, where she is also Faculty Ombuds Officer. She is co-editor of *East Meets West: Jesuits in China, 1582-1773* (1988), a contributor to volumes such as *Japan Examined: Perspectives on Modern Japanese History* (1983), and editor of *Korea Under the American Military Government, 1945-48* (forthcoming).

Margaret D. Stetz is Associate Professor of English and Women's Studies at Georgetown University. Her recent publications include *British Women's Comic Fiction, 1890-1990* (2001) and essays in journals such as *Transformations, Peace Review, Feminist Teacher,* and *Canadian Women Studies*. She received the 2000 "Wise Woman Award" for Women's Studies service and scholarship from the National Association for Women in Catholic Higher Education.

Contributors

Christine Choy is Director of the School of Creative Media at City University in Hong Kong. She is a distinguished director, cinematographer, and producer, whose many films include *Who Killed Vincent Chin?*, a widely screened documentary on the racist murder of an Asian American; *Sa-I-Gu* (with Dai Sil Kim-Gibson and Elaine Kim); and (with Nancy Tong) *In the Name of the Emperor*, about the Nanjing Massacre.

Grant K. Goodman is Professor Emeritus of History at the University of Kansas. A specialist in Japanese intellectual history and cultural relations, he is author or editor of fifteen books, including *Japan: The Dutch Experience* (1986), *Japanese Cultural Policies in Southeast Asia During World War II* (1991), and *Asian History*, 3rd Edition (1993).

Dongwoo Lee Hahm is President of the Washington Coalition for Comfort Women's Issues, Inc. (WCCW), based in Maclean, Virginia. Named "Person of the Year" by the Senior Pastors Association of Greater Washington, she has given numerous speeches and lectures internationally, staged protest rallies, created a video about "comfort women," and produced *Comfort Women Speak* (2000), a volume of testimonies edited by Sangmie Choi Schellstede.

Mona Higuchi is an Asian American visual artist who in 1996 was Artist-in-Residence at the Isabella Stewart Gardner Museum in Boston, where she created *Bamboo Echoes*, an installation dedicated to the "comfort women." Her other recent installations addressing social and political issues include the collaborative works *Kristallnacht* (1998) and *Turbulencia Terrenal* (2000).

Dai Sil Kim-Gibson is an acclaimed filmmaker and writer, as well as a former professor of Religious Studies, whose documentaries include *A Forgotten People: The Sakhalin Koreans* and *Sa-I-Gu* (with Christine Choy and Elaine Kim). In 1999 she published *Silence Broken: Korean Comfort Women* and also directed a documentary with the same title, broadcast in May 2000 on PBS.

John Y. Lee, an attorney in Washington, DC, is Chairman of the Board of the Washington Coalition for Comfort Women's Issues, Inc. He has worked on matters related to war crimes for the Office of International Affairs in the Criminal Division of the U. S. Department of Justice, and he has taught law in both Korea and China. He is the recipient of the U. S. Legion of Merit, the ROK Security Medal, and other civilian service awards.

Jill Medvedow is Director of the Boston Institute of Contemporary Art (ICA), as well as the founder of "Vita Brevis," an arts organization that commissions and presents projects responding to the historical, aesthetic, physical, and psychological landscape. While Deputy Director for Programs and Curator of Contemporary Arts at the Isabella Stewart Gardner Museum from 1991-96, she designed and directed its education programs and supervised those relating to Mona Higuchi's installation, *Bamboo Echoes*.

Therese Park is a Korean-born musician and novelist living in Kansas, where she retired after thirty years as a cellist with the Kansas City Symphony. *A Gift of the Emperor*, her novel about a Korean "comfort woman" in Palau, was published by Spinsters Ink, a feminist press, in 1997. A sequel about the fictional protagonist's post-World War II years is forthcoming.

Chunghee Sarah Soh is Associate Professor of Anthropology at San Francisco State University. A fellow of the American Anthropological Association and recipient of numerous grants, she has published widely on gender and Asian culture and politics in journals such as *Asian Survey, Social Science Japan, Peace Review*, and *Korea Journal*. A second edition of her book *Women in Korean Politics* was published in 1993, and she is at work on a book about "comfort women."

Yuki (Toshiyuki) Tanaka is Professor of International and Cultural Studies at Keiwa College in Japan. He formerly taught in Australia, where his published research on the Allies' indifference to Japanese war crimes made him a notable and controversial figure. He is the author of *Hidden Horrors: Japanese War Crimes of World War II* (1996) and of the forthcoming book *Japan's Comfort Women: Sexual Slavery and Prostitution during World War II and the U.S. Occupation*.

Pamela S. Thoma is Assistant Professor of American Studies and Women's Studies at Colby College. She has published essays on women, race, and culture in journals such as *Frontiers* and *Genders*, and her book *Asian American Women's Writing: Theorizing Transnationalism* is forthcoming.

Taeko Tomiyama is among the most important living Japanese women artists. Famed both for her oil paintings and lithographs, which have been exhibited internationally, she is equally well known as a political activist. She was one of the first visual artists in Japan to produce work that confronted the sexual exploitation of women in World War II, along with other crimes linked to Japanese imperialism, colonialism, and militarism.

Linda Gertner Zatlin is Professor of English at Morehouse College. A co-founder of the Nineteenth Century Studies Association, she is the author of *The Nineteenth-Century Anglo-Jewish Novel* (1981), *Aubrey Beardsley and Victorian Sexual Politics* (1990), and of *Beardsley, Japonisme, and the Perversion of the Victorian Ideal* (1997), for which she received an award from the Society of Art Historians in Britain. She is now preparing a catalogue of the work of Aubrey Beardsley for Yale University Press.

Acknowledgments

The editors would like first to thank the many individuals, organizations, and institutions that made possible the original conference on "comfort women" at Georgetown University in 1996 which inspired this volume. These include our co-sponsors—the Washington Coalition for Comfort Women Issues, Inc. (WCCW) and its President, Dongwoo Lee Hahm, and the Korea Society, with our special thanks to David Kim—along with Georgetown University's School of Foreign Service, Department of English, Women's Studies Program, and Women's Center. We thank, too, many other co-sponsors and contributors for various kinds of help and support, including the Washington, DC office of Human Rights Watch, the Center for Women Policy Studies, Fr. Peter Ruggere of the Maryknoll Office for Global Concerns, Anne Cubilie, Angela Kim, Mindy Schrader Kim, Chris Simpson, Soon-Mi Yoo, Christine Choi, Miran Kim, and Lynn Thiesmeyer. We are grateful for the generosity of Jhoon Rhee and of Ohara Yasunaga and Ohara Chikako. We are also deeply grateful to Mme. Miki Mutsuko and her translator, Fujimoto Noboyuki, as well as to Sangmie Choi Schellstede for her superb translation of the testimony of Kim Yoon-shim.

Our work has been supported by research grants from the School of Foreign Service and the Graduate School of Georgetown University, as well as the Association for Asian Studies, through its Northeast Area Council Small Research Grant.

For invaluable editorial assistance with this project, we thank Kathleen Burns, Lezlie Christensen, Su-Yeon Cho, Chris Davies, and Felicia Messina-D'Haiti.

For permission to reproduce "War Brothels Were Strict, Report Shows," we thank Kyodo News (http://home.kyodo.co.jp), as well as Antonio Kamiya. Pamela Thoma's chapter has been adapted from an article appearing in *Frontiers: A Journal of Women's Studies* by permission of the University of Nebraska Press, © 2000 by *Frontiers: A Journal of Women's Studies*. We would like to thank Anne Hieber and Sarah Bennett of the *Peace Review* (http://www.tandf.co.uk) for help in securing permission to reproduce material from Chunghee Sarah Soh's chapter which appeared there first, and to acknowledge the *Social Science Japan Journal*. A slightly revised version of Yuki Tanaka's chapter, "'Comfort Women' in the Dutch East Indies" appears in *Japan's Comfort Women: Sexual Slavery and Prostitution During World War II and the U.S. Occupation* by Yuki Tanaka (© 2001 Routledge). We thank Routledge for granting permission to use this chapter herein, and we thank Emma Davis of Taylor & Francis/Routledge for her assistance.

We acknowledge Hagiwara Hiroko for her kind assistance in securing the consent of Tomiyama Taeko. The photographs of Mona Higuchi's work are by John Kennard, courtesy of the Isabella Stewart Gardner Museum and the artist. (We also thank Tiffany York, Programs Coordinator at the Gardner Museum, for her assistance.) And we thank David Hagen, photographer at Georgetown University's Lauinger Library.

For their helpfulness and dedication to this project, we are grateful to Patricia Loo and Angela Piliouras of M. E. Sharpe Publishers. We could not have produced this book without the support and assistance of John Oh and Mark Samuels Lasner. And most of all, we express our admiration, respect, and gratitude for the courage of Kim Yoon-shim and all the other "comfort women" survivors, to whom we humbly dedicate this volume.

Introduction

Margaret D. Stetz and Bonnie B. C. Oh

If a "legacy" is usually a gift of property, passed on to one's descendants, then what does it mean to speak of the legacies of the military sexual slaves of World War II, commonly known as "comfort women"? Members, in most cases, of poor families of the rural working classes, the roughly two hundred thousand Asian women who were taken from their communities and put into brothels by the Japanese imperial army owned nothing. They were, indeed, said to have no claims to their very bodies, which were confiscated and used as war matériel. Few of those who might have been entitled, after 1945, to a small share of a family farm or other such income ever came home to receive it, for the severity of the trauma they had suffered left them incapable of returning and of resuming their former identities. Penniless and stranded abroad, those who did wish to come back seldom could find the means to do so. They became the displaced and the dispossessed—the possessors only of memories, and those seemingly too horrible to share. And, in recent years, their efforts to petition the Japanese government for financial reparations, which would symbolize Japan's acknowledgment of legal responsibility for the crimes committed against them, have met with rebuffs. Today, the three hundred or so self-identified survivors are, by and large, living out their old age in poverty.

The question of direct descendants, moreover, to whom the former "comfort women" might pass on a legacy is a problematic one. Many of the sex slaves made to "serve" the Emperor's troops were already dead by the end of the war from a variety of causes. Imprisoned in brothels that were set up at the front lines, in order to provide the Japanese soldiers with "relief" from the fighting, some women died of wounds inflicted during battle. Others succumbed to the effects of untreated illnesses, including sexually transmitted diseases. Some, too, were murdered, whether casually for sport, or as punishment for trying to escape, or, in 1945, in hopes of eliminating them as potential postwar witnesses to the crimes of their captors. In despair or in defiance, many also killed themselves. Those who did survive proved, in numerous cases, either unwilling to bear children or physically unable to do so, as a consequence of the injuries left by repeated mass rapes. They remained outside the community-building institutions of domestic life from which their ordeals had forever alienated them—in some instances, isolated and shunned by their former compatriots, who shrank from them as reminders of the shame of Japanese wartime conquest. Most of the women who did have either biological or adopted children viewed their own life histories as too great a burden to impose upon their descendants and, thus, spoke of these to no one. The feminist political historian Cynthia Enloe writes, for instance, of Amanita Ballahadiu, a survivor from the Philippines, who for "fifty years . . . kept her secret from all but her husband," in order to spare her children.[1]

To consider, therefore, the "comfort women" as having any legacy to give is to begin by assigning value to women who have been designated, in multiple contexts, as without value. They were chosen for systematic rape, in the first place, because they were seen as worthless and, afterward, defined as worthless, because they had been raped. The editors and authors of this volume recognize that to affirm their value now is in itself an act with broad, political implications. It deliberately challenges so-called racial hierarchies that allowed the Japanese imperial army to exploit and then dispose of the women of Korea, the Philippines, Taiwan, China, Indonesia, Malaysia, and Burma as inferior creatures, fit only to be military chattel. It opposes, moreover, hierarchies of class that enabled the peoples of several cultures—both Asian and Western—to ignore for decades the fate of the "comfort women," since these were figures from the ranks of the poor and uneducated. But most of all, to pay homage to "comfort women" and to name them as bearers of an important legacy is to overturn hierarchies of gender that have ranked men above women in general, as well as "pure" women above both rape victims and prostitutes in particular. This volume is grounded firmly in the belief that such hierarchies, just as much as any individual perpetrators, must be held accountable and condemned for their roles in the crimes of war. Without the existence of mutually reinforcing ideologies of race, class, and gender, these women would not have been victimized as they were, both during and after World War II—first through institutionalized rape in military brothels and later through enforced silence.

Even now, those who do not want the stories of the Japanese imperial army's atrocities revealed continue to assert that the testimony of such "low" women cannot be trusted.

In the face of opposition and obstacles, what legacies are the survivors of the "comfort system" now transmitting and to whom? How are their stories—along with the cultural and historical backgrounds to their situations—being collected, circulated, and interpreted, and in the service of what ends? Why should these women, roughly 80 percent of whom were Korean, be looked upon as playing a significant and continuing role in the politics and culture of both Asia and the West, into the beginning of a new century? These questions provide us with our starting point.

We propose, in this volume, to trace the legacy of the victims of military sexual slavery through three channels, by presenting a selection of the work it has inspired among scholars, political activists, and creative artists. The essays offered here demonstrate, moreover, that the worlds that the former "comfort women" and their stories have influenced are not discrete, but rather overlapping and intersecting ones. Indeed, the challenges raised by these war victims are so wide-reaching—challenges not only to the concepts of imperialism, militarism, sexism, classism, and racism, but also to the ways in which history itself has traditionally been recorded and written—that they can only be addressed through multifaceted approaches. Thus, in confronting, exploring, understanding, and taking up these challenges, academics are finding themselves moved to political activism, activists are turning to mediums of artistic representation, and artists are performing the duties of scholarly researchers and analysts.

The legacies of the "comfort women" have encouraged, if not required, such acts of fusion and of crossing over, in style as well as in substance. In this volume, readers find the accounts of work about, with, and on behalf of "comfort women" written in languages that range from the detached, scholarly, or legalistic to the impassioned and personal, often within the same essay.

Perhaps it will come as no surprise that such disciplines as women's studies, Asian studies, cultural studies, international law, and military and political history are being affected and altered by the stories of the "comfort women," which require scholars not only to understand what happened and why it happened, but to acknowledge the importance of the individuals to whom it happened—women whose seeming insignificance and irrelevance to global matters was taken for granted for almost fifty years. Those changes are represented throughout this volume, in the many essays that treat the subject of "comfort women" through the lenses of feminism, New Historicism, legal studies, and cultural criticism. Readers may, however, be surprised to discover that the arts, too, have begun to bear the impress of the legacy of the "comfort women," even as they have worked to extend that legacy. In finding the means to embrace subjects related to "comfort women," media such as film, painting, and fiction are also extending their own technical, emotional, and political reach; so, too, are cultural institutions, such as American museums, in ways that are described in the third section of this volume.

As Octavia Butler has written, in a futuristic novel about civil warfare and sexual violence in U.S. society, "All that you touch/ You Change./ All that you Change/ Changes you."[2] The legacies of the "comfort women" are indeed being shaped by the contributors to this volume; but so, too, are they shaping, in turn, both the practice of the contributors themselves and the various professional fields, intellectual disciplines, and artistic media in which these contributors participate.

Even the genre or medium of the scholarly conference has become implicated in this movement. It was a personal commitment to contribute to a growing legacy that led the editors of the present volume, in September 1996, to stage "The Comfort Women of WWII: Legacy and Lessons," the first academic conference in the United States on the subject of "comfort women." It brought together from Seoul, South Korea, a survivor of sexual enslavement with some of those who have tried to record, disseminate, and contextualize the facts of her past sufferings, as well as to instigate redress for them. On the opening day of that conference, held at Georgetown University in Washington, D.C., Christine Choy—the Asian American filmmaker, feminist, and professor of film studies at New York University—showed her documentary about the Nanjing (a.k.a. Nanking) Massacre, *In the Name of the Emperor*. The 1995 film addressed not only the massacre itself, but also its aftermath, including the importation of Korean women to serve in the so-called "comfort stations" maintained for the occupying Japanese army. In the question period that followed this screening, a white American male academic in the audience stood up to ask, "How are we to make sense of this uniquely horrible exploitation of women's bodies? Was it attributable to some flaw in the Japanese character? What made Japanese men so different, that they were able to do this?"

Questions such as these showed us why a longer and more sustained process of education on the topic than a mere conference could provide would be necessary. Embedded in these plaintive inquiries was the wish of the speaker—and of many of those who encounter information about this crime of sexual violence for the first time—to distance himself and to distance other cultures from it. If these atrocities could be attributed to some national, indeed to some racial, taint that made Japanese men peculiarly monstrous, then all other peoples in general and all other men in particular could see themselves as innocents.

But the subject of the "comfort system" cries out against such simplistic, reassuring, and self-serving formulations. It demands to be understood not only in terms of specific cultural and political circumstances of Japan in the first half of the twentieth century, but also as a manifestation of assumptions about men's right to power over women's bodies that have shaped and continue to shape the policies of every nation and every culture, in wartime and in peacetime. Cynthia Enloe, who is a feminist activist as well as a scholar of political theory, has said, "Reports about soldiers' abuses of women are not enough. What these abuses mean for women is the real story."[3] Throughout this volume, the contributors' essays focus again and again on confronting what these abuses have meant for the Asian women victims of World War II and also what they might mean for all women today. Ultimately, the legacies of the "comfort women" reach beyond the particulars treated in this volume, to link up with the present-day situation of women around the globe, especially with those who are raped by combatants during times of armed conflict, or who are forced to provide sex for standing armies in the many "camptowns" surrounding military bases throughout the world.

If the effect of nearly fifty years of public silence on the subject of these war crimes was isolation and alienation for the victims, the result of breaking that silence has been a burgeoning network of alliances. Not only have the surviving women themselves formed links with one another and with a variety of human rights groups and feminist organizations worldwide, but the supporters of their struggles for official acknowledgment, apologies, and reparations from the Japanese government have come together in ever-expanding coalitions. These coalitions continue to move across the lines of nationality, as well as of profession and discipline. In the essays that follow, readers find the legacies of the "comfort women" embodied in the efforts of Korean, Japanese, Australian, and U.S. scholars of Asian history and politics, feminist theorists, human rights workers, documentary filmmakers, visual artists, and novelists to address a common project: giving visibility to the events of the past, listening to and valuing those who have survived, obtaining justice in the present, and ensuring a future free of organized and politically sanctioned sexual violence against women.

Notes

1. Cynthia Enloe, *Maneuvers: The International Politics of Militarizing Women's Lives* (Berkeley: University of California Press, 2000), p. 83.
2. Octavia Butler, *Parable of the Sower* (New York: Four Walls Eight Windows, 1993; New York: Warner Books, 1995), p. 3.
3. Cynthia Enloe, "Spoils of War," *Ms.* (March/April 1996): 15.

Part I

Historical and Cultural Contexts

Chapter 1

The Japanese Imperial System and the Korean "Comfort Women" of World War II

Bonnie B. C. Oh

Introduction

During World War II, hundreds of thousands of women, about 80 percent of whom were from Korea, but also from other parts of Asia, were forced into sexual slavery by the Japanese army to "serve" soldiers on the front lines. Generally known as "comfort women,"[1] these victims were stationed in "comfort stations" throughout Asia and the South Pacific. Virtual prisoners in these stations, they were subject to such daily degradations as physical and verbal abuse, repeated rapes, hard labor, and sometimes they even were murdered. Yet until recently, their experiences were unknown—even to women's rights groups, to the international human rights community, or to the academic world. Only since the late 1980s has there been a drive to make this story visible. The United Nations, as well as community-based activist organizations around the world,[2] has taken up the cause to win official apologies and reparation from the Japanese government. The efforts are still continuing on behalf of the small and ever-dwindling number of surviving victims.

Recent disclosure of the existence of the "comfort women" systems during World War II in the Japanese Empire has created an impression that such practices were unique to Japan, and that some particular quality of Japanese "uniqueness" led to the establishment and sanctioning of the "comfort women" project. But wartime sexual violence against women is as long as human history and as widespread as to cover the entire

3

human geography. No period in human history and no race or nation has been exempt from it.[3] So pervasively and so commonly has sexual violence against women in wartime occurred that until recently it has not been considered a crime. It has been systematically disguised as "prostitution." Only in the second half of the twentieth century, with the spread of feminist-inspired thinking, has rape been thought of as a legitimate subject of discussion among men as well as women, and wartime rape seen as a war crime and as a crime against humanity to be taken up by governments, nongovernmental organizations (NGOs), and international organizations.[4]

Obviously, war crimes (including sexual violence against women) are *not* a uniquely Japanese phenomenon and not derived from a peculiar Japanese-ness or national character.[5] Nonetheless, there are at least two points that render the Japanese "comfort women" system unique: the "official," governmental initiative in establishing the mechanism and apparatus that the government authorities systematically and methodically carried out, and the extreme brutality and inhuman treatment inflicted on "comfort women."

Two ideological bases underlie the "comfort women" issue in general. The first of these, according to Professor Yuki Tanaka, is xenophobia, which is closely related to the Japanese emperor ideology. The second is the contempt with which women have been held in Japanese society and the exploitation of their sexuality by Japanese men.[6] In the case of Korean "comfort women," the additional factors of imperialism and colonialism must be considered. Japanese authorities did not think too seriously about making an ideological leap from organized prostitution of women already in sex work to the sexual slavery of innocent girls, for the subject matter was poor Korean girls and young women, the least significant members of a colony.

It is not my intention here to dwell on Japanese uniqueness or on the universality of similar systems of "military prostitution." Rather, I will focus on the imperial origins of Korean "comfort women" during World War II after a brief, general observation of related topics such as the "tradition" of organized prostitution in Japan and the subordinate position of women in Japanese society.

The "Tradition" of the "Comfort Women" System

The idea of traveling military prostitution was not new for the Japanese. In the late nineteenth and early twentieth centuries, Japanese prostitutes traveling with the military were called *karayuki*,[7] and were found in many regions of Asia that later became a part of the Japanese Empire. In fact, they were in the vanguard group of Japanese, mostly businessmen, who paved the way for the Japanese military who came on their heels. Yamazaki Tomoko found that the foreign currency that the *karayuki* remitted home was an essential capital for Japanese modernization since the Meiji Restoration. The amount was enormous: over Y200,000. Fukuzawa Yukichi, the leading intellectual and advocate of westernization, encouraged the emigration of women as prostitutes, particularly to regions undergoing rapid economic development.[8] Even in the civil sector, "in pre-war Japan, prostitution was state organized, with the women licensed and subjected to medical inspections" and thus the idea of exporting "women for sexual service was . . . not a new idea for the Japanese."[9]

Elsewhere in this volume, Linda Zatlin points out that "there was nothing new in the power relations codified by the "comfort women" system; such relations already existed in the accepted and institutionalized system of prostitution"[10] in traditional Japan. The Tokugawa regime (1603–1868), for example, dealt with prostitution with openness and enacted laws that regulated it. These official policies led to the development of the famous Yoshiwara district in Edo (the historical name for Tokyo) and the erotic art known as the *ukiyoe* (floating world),[11] which saw its heyday at the end of the seventeenth and early eighteenth centuries. "Glamorized by artists and writers, the wealth of erotic literature and art disguised the slave-like conditions in which the women worked."[12] After the establishment of the modern Meiji government in 1868, a series of laws and ordinances of the 1870s, such as the Ministry of Popular Affairs Notice of 1871 and the Finance Ministry Proclamation 127 of 1872, prohibited bondage and restricted prostitution to a voluntary contract system. But, in reality, much of the tradition of organized prostitution lingered on, well into the twentieth century. The only major difference between the "modern" and traditional systems seems to have been that under the new system, the state required physical examinations to control sexually transmitted diseases.[13]

War, Sex, and the Emperor Cult

Given such open acceptance of systematized and legalized prostitution, it is not surprising that there should have been an organized brothel system in the Japanese military. As the Japanese imperial expansion progressed through the 1930s, the Japanese armed forces embarked on wars of consolidation of the conquered areas, which required protracted commitment. Japan became engaged in the Fifteen-Year War (1931–1945, the period from the Manchurian Incident to the end of World War II), a prolonged war situation. The length of this period aside, war in general is a patriarchal game and is a problem associated with a male-dominated, militaristic society.[14] Wartime is when values of patriarchal order are pushed to the extreme, when brutal force and physical strength are admired and rewarded, and when those men who are in uniform and engaged either in combat or in confined, regimented situations become preoccupied with sex. Wartime is also a time when men regard women as real hindrances to carrying out warfare and act to remove them. Failing that, they resort to punishing them—inflicting violence (most often sexual violence) on them that is, to women, the ultimate shame and defilement, while to men, it is a source of conquest and even satisfaction. Add the conditions of modern warfare, and fighting men often become "deranged."[15] Women of Japan and in the colonies and occupied areas at this time were subject to twin patriarchal commands of "providing comfort" to fighting men and producing male children to replace soldiers killed in battle.

In addition to these circumstances of modern warfare in general, in 1930s Japan, under the militarists' control, there existed a kind of national paranoia, which in turn led to xenophobia. Scholarly debates still go on as to why Japan had slid into militarists' rule in the 1930s, while in the 1920s, Japan had appeared to be headed in the direction of democracy in its domestic politics and internationalism in its foreign relations. To simplify the interpretations of Akira Iriye, a historian of U.S.–Japan–East Asian relations, at least two theories can be cited. One is the failure of a viable, alternative international system to replace imperialism in Asia after its demise following World War I.[16] And the other is the simultaneous expansion of both the United States and Japan across the Pacific at the turn of the century.[17]

The Japanese militarists who took power in the 1930s believed that the West "betrayed" and discriminated against Japan. Japan had learned from the West and modernized according to the Western model since 1868 and joined the Western "imperialist club."[18] But after the Japanese defeated imperial Russia (in the Russo–Japanese War of 1904–1905), a Western power, it appeared to the Japanese that the Western bloc was attempting to stop their further expansion. Japan seemed to ignore the fact that Japanese imperialism, coming later, coincided with the rise of a virile brand of nationalism, which was combined with socialism and communism among peoples of threatened Asian countries. By the fourth decade of the twentieth century, these Asian countries were better prepared to oppose domination from any external power than before, regardless of the race of the predators. As Japan embarked on expansion in China in the 1930s, for example, it did not anticipate such forceful nationalist reaction from the Chinese. The ultranationalist leaders of Japan blamed the West for placing obstacles on its road to expansion. With determination and resolve, the newly risen imperial Japan took on the mighty Western imperialist countries and attempted to garner help from fellow Asians in the Japanese scheme to expel Westerners from Asia. The fear of being betrayed by and isolated from the West led to xenophobia, which, in turn, evolved into an ardent emperor cult, and the resolve to guide the rest of Asia developed into the Greater East Asian Coprosperity Sphere, the declared aim of the Pacific War.

Japan, since 1868, had developed a profound contempt for other Asian nations. Japan hated the other Asians for failing to respond successfully, as it had done in a spectacularly victorious manner, to the Western encroachment. As a country in Asia, Japan could not but feel a sense of shame, especially because it had benefited culturally from other older Asian countries, such as China, India, and even Korea. To these Asian countries of ancient civilization, Japan owed much for its own philosophical and religious development, as it had become a culturally sophisticated country. But after the Meiji Restoration, Japan was not like other Asian countries; it alone had became modernized and "civilized" in the new world, and it hated other Asian nations for failing to come up to its level. Whether the Japanese hated other Asians or not, or whether other Asians liked it or not, Japan would steer the other Asian nations, forcibly if necessary, into its struggle to secure Asia for Asians, at whatever cost and through whatever means to establish a coprosperity under Japan's hegemony.

By the mid-1930s, imperial Japan, led by extreme militarists and with the divine emperor as leader, was positioned to "guide" all its Asian neighbors. It was convinced of the superiority of its race and the absolute moral correctness of its mission in the military conquest of other parts of Asia. For many Japanese, including most of the general population, World War II in Asia was indeed a holy war for imperial Japan to redeem Asia from the Western imperialists.

The entire region under attack by the Japanese was placed under the spell of the divine emperor cult, with which the Japanese attempted to brainwash their colonized peoples. But the process of assimilation (or Japanization) was particularly intense on the Korean peninsula. Japanese survival depended on the success or failure of these pursuits, and where and when this policy failed, the Japanese did not hesitate to use whatever means necessary to achieve their aim. Armed with these multilayered beliefs and dire determination, Japanese soldiers, especially those outside their homeland, displayed utter disdain toward non-Japanese, whom they considered subhuman. Thus, they felt no compunction about committing numerous inhuman brutalities. The rape of women of the conquered areas, such as in the cities of Shanghai and Nanjing, was one of these assorted activities.

The Official Establishment of the "Comfort Women" System

What actually prompted Japanese military authorities to establish the "comfort houses" in China was the fierce and angry reaction from the local populace against the Japanese rape of women of Shanghai in 1932. This official action made the Japanese "comfort women" establishment unique in the history of wartime violence against women. Generals Okabe Naosaburo and Okamura Yauji ordered the establishment of "army comfort houses" in Shanghai in March of that year. Both of the generals were on the staff of the Shanghai Expeditionary Army.[19] If the generals' intentions were to reduce rape, this worked only for a short time. Within five years, in 1937, during the "Rape of Nanking,"[20] Japanese soldiers committed mass rape of Chinese women by the tens of thousands, sadly rendering credence to the popular designation of that incident. It will remain as one of the most heinous crimes in the annals of human history.

Following the capture of Nanjing in the winter of 1937, the Japanese military authority established "comfort houses." Orders to open "comfort houses" were issued for all Asian war zones, starting with central China in December 1937 and northern China in 1938. In Japanese-occupied China, the chain of command for the order was through the Japanese military establishment—from the chief of staff of the north China area army, who was directly responsible to the emperor, to each expeditionary army commander to the camp overseers who managed day-to-day operations of "comfort stations." "Each such army received orders about military operations from the general chief of staff of the Imperial Army, which was authorized by the emperor for such particular matters [as 'comfort stations']."[21]

In Korea, this vertical chain of command was through the colonial administration. The governor-general and the Japanese army exercised great control over "comfort women" policies. The military authorities would be the first to make requests to the Office of General Affairs, which would in turn forward them to the governor-general. On receiving the request, the governor-general would then announce the recruitment of "comfort women" for the provinces. From that point on, it was a straight line: from the provincial governor down to *kun* (county) to *myon* (township) and to villages.[22] Both of these top Japanese officials, the chief of staff of the North China area army in China and the governor-general of Korea, reported directly to the emperor.[23] Every soldier was aware of this command structure and believed that it was the emperor, a divine entity, who was directly concerned about such human affairs as the soldiers' need for "comfort women." Naturally, they felt grateful for a special favor from the emperor. Indeed, the soldiers considered the "comfort women" as special "gifts from the emperor."[24]

The official institutionalization of the "comfort women" structure demonstrates the licentious male attitude toward sex, which in itself is not a peculiar characteristic of Japan. But it became a Japanese military man's unique obsession when it was combined with Japanese superstition and with quasi-psychological rationalizations. On a personal level, Japanese soldiers about to embark on a battle believed that having sex shortly before fighting protected them from injury and death. On the other hand, the military hierarchy believed that allowing sex to soldiers boosted their morale, promoted their discipline, and aroused courage, as well as relieved stress from combat. Another practical consideration was to curtail the spread of venereal diseases by providing soldiers with safe sex partners.

Korean "Comfort Women"

Eighty percent of an estimated 100,000 to 200,000 "comfort women" of World War II were Korean girls and women.[25] In addition to the obvious fact that there were plenty of poor Korean young women, especially in impoverished rural areas under Japanese colonialism, who could be "recruited," enticed and deceived with the promise of well-paying jobs, kidnapped, conscripted, and even sold, there were also hidden and complex reasons for choosing them. After the Japanese women and women of Okinawa, Korean women were preferred above all others. As will be discussed below, there was clearly an element of racism with significant implications.

The *karayuki* of the Russo–Japanese War of 1904–1905 mostly had been Japanese women who were already in prostitution. As areas under Japanese colonial rule or occupation increased in the 1930s and 1940s, so did the need for military prostitutes. The *karayuki* alone could not meet the demand, and the Japanese authorities began to include women from the colonies and occupied countries as military "comfort women."[26] The ordinary women of Japan were also needed at home to fulfill the other of the twin patriarchal obligations, the bearing and rearing of future soldiers, as well as to perform a variety of tasks, such as tending farms and working in factories. Japanese women already in prostitution continued to participate, but there were not enough of them, and a small number of them were "reserved" for high-ranking officers. The medical examinations also revealed that Japanese prostitutes were already carrying varieties of sexually transmitted diseases, while very few of the young Korean "recruits" had them.[27]

Another reason for the preference for Korean girls seemed to be based on a notion of racial hierarchy, which was determined by the skin color and by the geographical proximity of their native land to Japan. Whether the race and skin color factors were conscious determinants or not, Japanese soldiers reportedly preferred Korean women next to the Japanese and Okinawans. Then came the Taiwanese, Chinese, the Filipinas, and so on. Ironically, the most preferred were the first to be "chosen" and the most victimized. This explains why as many as 80 percent were Koreans. The women were thought to be chosen to serve the emperor by providing "comfort" to soldiers fighting for the emperor in the holy war. It is not surprising that some innocent young Korean women—like the fictional Soon-ah, the protagonist of Therese Park's novel *A Gift of the Emperor*—became persuaded, at least initially, that they were indeed chosen and that they were serving the emperor.[28] All the women so chosen were given Japanese names or were known by numbers.

In the hysteria of the "Japanization" of Korea in the early 1940s, when Koreans were required to change their names to Japanese-style names, to speak Japanese exclusively, to recite the loyalty oath, and to visit Shinto shrines daily to pay homage to the emperor, Korean schoolchildren were often confused about their identity. Had I not been se-

instructed by my father in the Korean *han-gul* (Korean alphabet) and history before and during the early part of my elementary-level school years, I, too, would have thought that I was Japanese. Slogans such as "Japan and Korea Are One" and "Two People, One Root" were everywhere, and Koreans were supposed to be proud of the heritage of the superior race of Japanese to whose ancestry they belonged. But when it came actually to rendering service to the Japanese state, Koreans were not Japanese and, therefore, were the first to be victimized.

Methods of Recruitment

The recruiting method of "comfort women" progressively deteriorated as in the case of the Korean laborers. In the early to mid-1930s, most young women were recruited with the enticements of traveling abroad, of high-paying jobs, and even of educational opportunities. In some destitute rural families, young women, out of filial piety, volunteered to earn a good salary to help their poor parents and to send brothers to school. In the early stage, some women indeed worked as nurses' aides in military hospitals and infirmaries and as laborers in munitions factories. After the outbreak of the war with China in 1937, the Japanese authorities employed unscrupulous Koreans to recruit Korean young women. Low-ranking local police, village authorities, and paid recruiters participated in the recruitment of Korean girls.[29] They all deceived young women, made them sign up, and ordered them to show up at the police stations or government offices. If women who had signed up did not appear, local authorities would resort to "slave raids,"[30] searching houses, interrogating parents and relatives, rounding them up, and shipping them out. In the final phase of the war in the 1940s, with the National General Mobilization Ordinance, parents were duped, and many young school girls were literally taken from classrooms[31] or picked up from streets.[32]

Kim Yoon-shim, a victim of the "comfort system" who gave testimony in September 1996 at the conference on "comfort women" held at Georgetown University, Washington, D.C., has told how her curiosity as a fourteen-year-old got her into a lifelong ordeal, which still continues. As she has recounted, "I was playing jump-rope in front of my house when an automobile pulled over. I had never seen a car before. When the driver offered me a ride, I, curious and naive, climbed in with my friend. Immediately, that car rolled on with us in it and then kept on going and going, never returning me to my village." (See more about her testimony elsewhere in this volume.) She was not to return until six years later. The age of Korean "comfort women" ranged from the early teens to the early twenties.

In the treatment of the Korean "comfort women," similar racism as in the case of soldiers' preference was evident. More Korean women than Japanese, who were drafted for the allegedly same Women's Voluntary Service Corps, were sent to the "comfort stations." Even among "comfort women," Japanese women or those Korean young women who could speak good Japanese were sent to more secure areas and made available for higher-ranking officers, whereas other Korean girls were sent to the front lines and housed in makeshift shacks.[33] Also, there was considerable disparity in the fees paid to Japanese, as opposed to Korean "comfort women." Many Korean "comfort women" never received any payments.[34]

In addition to the Koreans, women were also recruited from Taiwan, another Japanese colony, and other Japanese-occupied territories such as China, the Philippines, and Indonesia.[35] Some Dutch women in Indonesia were forced into servitude. Japan also attempted to force Australian nurses as well.[36]

Life as "Comfort Women"

The women drafted as "comfort women" had a regimented schedule. Each woman had to serve twenty to forty men a day, at a rate of a man every thirty minutes, or sometimes even ten to fifteen minutes per soldier. In the morning, rank-and-file soldiers would queue up outside a woman's room. Afternoons would be reserved for middle-ranking officers, and the evening hours for higher-ranking officers. Commanders of a military unit or the camp where the "comfort station" existed monopolized the overnight stay privileges.[37]

The majority of the Korean women, like Kim Yoon-shim, never knew where they were, at least in the beginning. They often arrived in the middle of the night. They were frequently moved about with the troops, but were not allowed outside the barbed-wire-fenced military compound. When they were sent out to wash soldiers' uniforms or, to do hard labor, or, on rare occasions, when they were allowed outside, they were always escorted and guarded by armed soldiers. Wherever the Japanese troops went, "comfort houses" were set up. Records show that they existed in semicircle shape from north China and Hong Kong to French

Indochina to Southeast Asian countries to the Philippines to the Micronesian islands in the Pacific to the Okinawan islands, and to the north to Sakhalin and Hokkaido. Toward the end of the war, in anticipation of a decisive battle on the mainland, "comfort houses" were organized even in Japan and Korea.[38]

When the war ended, most "comfort women" were simply abandoned. Again, to quote Kim Yoon-shim, "For a few days, no soldiers lined up outside the doors and things were extremely quiet. When we peeked outside, the whole military establishment had disappeared." In the jungles of Java and Sumatra, some women simply never came out. Nobody knows how many perished, unable to make it out. Many never attempted to return home, not knowing how to do so, or they remained hidden for fear of shame and humiliation back home.

Silence, Secrets, and Politics of "Comfort Women"

Having been products of societies where Confucianism, which emphasized chastity as a woman's most important virtue, was the dominant mode, former "comfort women" felt ashamed and were reluctant to disclose their past. Thanks to research by Kim Il-myon,[39] Yoshimi Yoshiaki,[40] Yuki Tanaka, George Hicks, and others, it is now an established fact that the Allied forces were fully informed by and, in some cases, received the sexual services of interrogated "comfort women" themselves, but did little to assist the women in their recovery from trauma and their return to normal life. Among the photos exhibited in conjunction with the conference on "comfort women" held in 1996 at Georgetown University, one particularly stands out in my mind. That is a picture of a Japanese–American intelligence officer photographed with several Korean "comfort women" in a Southeast Asian country. When I met him in the course of planning the conference, he pointed himself out in the picture, but when we invited him to talk publicly about his experience related to the "comfort women" whom he had investigated, he refused.[41]

Ustinia Dolgopol, who edited the special report of the International Commission of Jurists on "comfort women," has explained that, in documents, the "comfort women" were categorized as "camp followers," a term that does no justice to the way women were treated. Among the feeble excuses that the Allies gave for not disclosing the existence of "comfort women" were that they regarded "rape convictions" as "difficult to secure," and that, out of "thoughtful consideration," they believed it would be better for the women if the issue were not pursued due to the shame the women would endure.[42] Another factor of the Allied forces' deliberate oversight was that they themselves had condoned the existence of prostitution stations for their own troops although, unlike those set up by the Japanese military, these were not officially organized or regulated by the military or staffed via forced recruitment.[43] Thus, despite the fact that the Allies were well informed about the "comfort women" situation, it was not included in the war settlement between Japan and the Allied forces.

In the Japan–Korea Basic Treaty signed in 1965, the South Korean government under Park Chung-hee did not include discussion of the "comfort women." Park's priority was Korea's economic development. He used the fund of $300 million in grants and $200 million in soft loans from the Treaty for the overall economic modernization of the nation as a whole, rather than for individual compensations.[44] But the unspoken and underlying reason was clear—it was not a subject fit for public discussion.[45] It was also the story of mostly working-class, un-educated, now elderly women, who had little influence in society, let alone any leverage to influence national policies. Finally, in the atmosphere of dictatorial regimes under former generals, which lasted until 1987, no open, grass-roots deliberation of *any* subject, let alone a taboo subject, could take place.

In the late 1980s, just as the three-decades-long dictatorial rule was breaking up, several factors converged in South Korea, such as the rise of feminist scholarship and organizations, that led to a considerable change in the old attitudes toward viewing rape and enforced prostitution as offenses against chastity, rather than as crimes. The maturing of feminist scholarship in the West and in Asia from the 1970s onward created an atmosphere, more hospitable than before, for the issues of rape and the related matter of "comfort women" to be discussed. The feminist perspective and analyses made it possible to confront the subject of wartime rape and to encounter it in new ways. Through the concerted efforts of feminist academics and activists, rape, which used to be a taboo, became a subject that could be spoken about, and the victims of rape themselves could be speaking subjects on the international stage.[46] On "comfort women" issues specifically, Professor Yun Chong Ok disclosed her many years of research, and the South Korean Church Women's Alliance initiated activism in condemning sexual violence against women as a basic human rights issue.[47]

In 1988, women's organizations in the Republic of Korea (South Korea) learned of the institution of "comfort stations" in the Japanese military and demanded an investigation. Two summers later, in 1990, in Japan, a Socialist Party member of the Diet, Motooka Shoji, demanded in the Diet's Budget Committee that the government look into the circumstances of military "comfort women." Outraged by the Japanese government's response that the "comfort women" were prostitutes who had worked voluntarily for private entrepreneurs and that the government and the military would not accept any responsibility in the matter, the Korean Women's Association sent an open letter to the Japanese government and requested an apology, a memorial to "comfort women," and a thorough inquiry. In November of the same year, the Korean Council for Women Drafted for Sexual Slavery by Japan was formed in the Republic of Korea. Thus the issue of the "comfort women" exploded into full public view both in South Korea and Japan.

Ironically, however, a good number of Japanese had known about the "comfort women" long before these disclosures in the late 1980s. The first research on "comfort women" was undertaken by a Japanese male journalist, Senda Kako, as early as 1962. His book[48] was published in 1973 and had become a "hidden" best-seller among scholars and intellectuals without attracting much attention from the public. In the 1980s, several books on "comfort women" were published in Japan, but it was still not an issue of public attention. The matter started to gain more interest after the radio interview of a Japanese "comfort woman," Shirota Suzuko, in 1986. A year later, Yun Chong Ok started to work with some of the concerned Japanese.[49] Thereafter, the number of groups interested in the "comfort women" issue dramatically increased. A Washington, D.C.–based organization, The Washington Coalition for "Comfort Women" Issues (WCCW), was organized in December 1992.[50]

During his visit to Japan in 1990, South Korean President Roh Tae Woo brought up the "comfort women" issue and requested a list of draftees, which the Japanese provided. The list, however, was a simple enumeration of names and included no other details. A month later, Motooka Shoji, the Japanese Diet member, raised the question of whether or not "comfort women" were included in Korean forced drafts and claimed that he had concrete evidence. But in April 1991, the Japanese government (responding to its own politician's allegations and to the open letter from the Korean women's organization of the previous year) denied the charges and reiterated its earlier position that there was no possibility of any apology, any memorial, any disclosure, or any compensation by the Japanese government. The Korean "Comfort Women" Problem Resolution Council, which Professor Yun headed, refuted the Japanese disclaimer and presented its six-point demands to Japanese prime minister Kaifu Toshiki. The six points included the recognition of the forced draft of Korean women as "comfort women," a public apology, the full disclosure of all the barbarities, a memorial for the victims, compensation for the survivors or their bereaved families, and, last, the inclusion of the "comfort women" accounts in history education in Japan.[51]

In August 1991, Kim Hak Sun, a former "comfort woman" in the Republic of Korea, testified in public for the first time that she had been forcibly taken as a "comfort woman" by the Japanese military. Ms. Kim's disclosure was corroborated and confirmed by Yoshida Seiji, the former director of the Japanese Labor Mobilization of Yamaguchi Prefecture during World War II. Confronted with the intransigence of the Japanese government, Kim Hak Sun and two other former Korean "comfort women" in the Republic of Korea filed suit against Japan in the Tokyo District Court for damages and other compensation. And, finally, the government of the Republic of Korea formally requested the Japanese government to conduct an investigation into the "comfort women" system.

It took another year and eight months, numerous disclosures by Japanese academics, such as Yoshimi Yoshiaki of Chuo University, and by newspapers, such as *Asahi Shimbun*, by women's groups, by former Japanese military personnel, and by Grant Goodman, an American university professor who submitted a long-neglected document,[52] as well as the United Nations taking up the issue,[53] before the Japanese government finally admitted in August 1993 that the government and military authorities had an unspecified role in the military brothels. Still it denied any legal responsibility for the victims and continued to contend that the brothels were neither a "system," nor a war crime, nor a crime against humanity. The United Nations took up the "comfort women" matter for the third time in August 1993, this time at its Sub-Commission on the Prevention of Discrimination and Protection of Minorities. In November 1993, the U.S. Congress finally took notice of the situation, and twenty-four of its members wrote to the Japanese prime minister, Hosokawa Michiro, urging a thorough investigation of the sexual slavery of the "comfort women."

The year 1994 witnessed several important developments: public demonstrations for the "comfort women's" cause in several U.S. cities, coinciding with the visit of Emperor Akihito of Japan; the UN appointments of two rapporteurs—Ms. Radhika Coomaraswamy of Sri Lanka specifically as Special Rapporteur on Violence against Women to investigate crimes against "comfort women," and Linda Chavez of the United States as Special Rapporteur on Sex Slavery during Wartime; and Japanese prime minister Murayama Tomiichi's announcement of the establishment of a "private fund" for "comfort women." But the Japanese government still officially rejected reparations or individual compensation for the victims.[54] At the end of the year, the International Commission of Jurists concluded, in a special report, that "it is indisputable that these women were forced, deceived, coerced and abducted to provide sexual services to the Japanese military . . . [Japan] violated customary norms of international law concerning war crimes, crimes against humanity, slavery and the trafficking in women and children."[55]

The year 1995, which marked the fiftieth anniversary of the conclusion of World War II, began auspiciously for the "comfort women" cause. The Japan Federation of Bar Associations announced its findings and recommendations concerning "comfort women" issues. This prestigious organization of Japanese lawyers stated that the "comfort women" system had been created and administered by the Japanese state and the imperial army and implemented by related authorities, and that immediately after the war the Japanese government had issued orders to destroy or burn all evidence on "comfort women." The Federation of Bar Associations further recommended that the Japanese government pay individual compensation and take other measures. In March, the UN Commission on the Status of Women (NGO) workshop adopted a resolution supporting "comfort women." Between May and August 1995, Japanese prime minister Murayama Tomiichi offered what the *Washington Post* described as a "near apology" for wartime atrocities against China, Korea, and other Asian nations and to "comfort women." In August, the second version of the private fund plan was established at the recommendation of the Japanese government, and the fund-raising campaign began in Japan.[56] This version was to offer payments to individual "comfort women" survivors but to reject *governmental* responsibility for the system of military brothels and charges that the "comfort women" system was a war crime or a crime against humanity as defined in customary norms of international law. The "comfort women" themselves and their organized supporters strongly criticized the private fund plan. The private fund, called the Asian Women's Fund, was headed by Mrs. Miki Mutsuko, widow of former prime minister Miki Takeo, and a target figure was set at $20 million.

The United Nations Fourth World Conference on Women, held in Beijing in September 1995, adopted resolutions supporting "comfort women," despite intense counterlobbying by the Japanese government's representatives. In January 1996, Radhika Coomaraswamy, the UN Special Rapporteur on Violence against Women, presented a detailed report on crimes against "comfort women" to the United Nations Commission on Human Rights. And in February, the United Nations sent a statement to the Japanese government advising it to take legal responsibility for its actions. But the UN Commission on Human Rights, bowing to intense pressure from Japanese representatives, adopted a "compromise" resolution that only "takes note" of the Coomaraswamy report. Observers from NGOs who were supporters of the "comfort women" criticized the compromise resolution as calculated to evade Japanese state responsibility for war crimes and crimes against humanity.

In Spring 1996, Mrs. Miki Mutsuko resigned as chair of the Asian Women's Fund, protesting her own government's delay in proffering apologies and the lack of sufficient public interest in the fund.[57] Only $3 million were raised, a mere fraction of the original target amount of $20 million. As a replacement for Mrs. Miki, the Japanese government appointed a senior LDP politician, Bumbei Hara, who was reputed by some to have led and organized the government-wide destruction of Japanese state records of war crimes during World War II, including those concerning "comfort women." When the international conference on "comfort women" was held at Georgetown University in 1996, Mrs. Miki, in the keynote address on September 30, delivered a candid speech critical of the Japanese government for not taking official responsibility and for not offering restitution from the government treasury. Mrs. Miki said that she considered the "comfort women" matter a fundamental human rights issue and stated that the women who suffered during war represented human suffering of tragic proportions. She linked their stories with "national struggles for global prestige and national security issues" involving life-and-death conflict. She added that the "comfort women" tragedy came out of the conflict of these enormous historical forces.[58]

The Japanese Embassy in Washington, D.C., boycotted the conference, and the South Korean Embassy was cool toward it, alleging that a conference on issues such as "comfort women" would incite ill feelings between the two neighboring countries, which are attempting to bury the past and to look ahead to friendly future relations.[59] But obviously, the conference had a far greater impact than expected. On 3 December 1996, the U.S. Justice Department "banned sixteen Japanese citizens from traveling in the United States, charging that the men conducted horrific medical experiments (Unit 731 in Manchuria) or forced thousands of women to serve as sex slaves for members of the imperial army during World War II." The men cited were the first suspected Japanese war criminals ever placed on a government "watch list" created in 1979 under the (Elizabeth) Holtzman Amendment, which prevents the admission of aliens suspected of acts of persecution under the authority of Nazi Germany or its wartime Axis allies. The conclusive evidence needed to identify individual Japanese war criminals only recently became available.[60] John Y. Lee, Esq., a Korean American lawyer, who serves as the chair of the board of the WCCW, contributed to providing the information to the Justice Department. Since most of the Japanese involved in Unit 731 experiments in Manchuria were medical personnel, who were better educated and, therefore, older than young military draftees, they had already died; thus, the majority of the sixteen cited were those involved in "comfort women"–related activities.[61]

The Japanese government spokespersons expressed surprise and reportedly said that highlighting the "comfort women" issue seemed particularly astonishing, because the Japanese had issued formal apologies to many women and paid damages in some cases. This was only partially correct. Apologies were issued, but they were *personal* apologies from the prime ministers[62] and payments were made out of the private fund; only seven Filipina former "comfort women" had accepted them.[63] Korean, Chinese, and Taiwanese "comfort women" had refused, and the governments and NGOs of these countries continue to press Japan to offer formal, official apologies and to pay restitution out of official funds.

At the beginning of 1997, just before the scheduled meeting of South Korean president Kim Young Sam and Japanese prime minister Hashimoto Ryutaro, it was reported that the Japanese had secretly contacted Korean "comfort women," met with them at an undisclosed hotel, and offered them money. It was suspected that a few hard-pressed former Korean "comfort women" might have accepted the offer, although they denied that they had.[64] A diplomatic impasse between the two neighbors was averted, only after the Japanese government announced that it would refrain from further clandestine activities. Since the successful consolidation of power by Prime Minister Hashimoto Ryutaro, conservative nationalism has been on the rise, and shrill voices have been heard in Japan against apologies and compensation for World War II atrocities committed by Japan.

Conclusion

The "comfort women" have been hidden victims for over half a century. Having been victims of sexual violence, a taboo in Confucian cultures where women's chastity is upheld as more important than life, many of these women have blamed themselves and kept their sufferings even from family members and from the community, fearing the tainting of the family name and ostracism from society. Feminist scholarship, independent scholars' research in South Korea, Japan, and other Asian nations, and the work of numerous NGOs and of the UN Commission on Human Rights have resulted in accomplishing what only a decade or so ago was inconceivable: a raised consciousness of "women's rights as human rights"[65] and a changed atmosphere in the world at large, as well as in the native countries of former "comfort women," both of which have encouraged these women to speak out about the unspeakable horror they experienced. Once the disclosures were made, there was no stopping the emergence of organizations and activities to assist the surviving "comfort women." A number of previously unthinkable goals have been attained—the official acknowledgment of the Japanese government of the existence of the "comfort women" system, apologies, albeit only personal ones so far, from the prime ministers to the "lowly" former "comfort women," some agreement—though still not a governmental one— to compensate these women, and the U.S. government's banning of former perpetrators of the crime. But there is still much to be done.

The "comfort women" ordeal has not ended. They continue their isolated existences in poverty and poor health. They have neither regained their honor nor had their pains eased, for the Japanese government continues to delay issuing its official apologies or to compensate them from the government treasury. The "comfort women" continue to endure insulting comments made by irresponsible Japanese officials and by neo-conservative nationalists, who claim that many Korean women were merely sex workers for money during World War II.[66] As late as the end of January 1998, the top aide to Japanese prime minister Hashimoto suggested that many women became "comfort women" for money, and that the Japanese military's use of the women was justified by the mores of the times.[67] Prime Minister Hashimoto apologized personally to President Kim Young Sam to avert a diplomatic crisis. But for the surviving former "comfort women," such comments cause added pain.

Within a month of the inauguration of South Korean president Kim Dae-jung, a lifelong fighter for democracy and human rights, the South Korean government announced on 30 March 1998 its plan to compensate 155 Korean victims of Japanese wartime sexual slavery with lump sums from a fund of over 4.8 billion won. The payments were to be made with the expectation that the fund would be reimbursed by Japan. Under the plan, each woman would receive about 38 million won (about $30,000), with about 31.5 million won coming from the government and the rest from private donations. The courage of the former "comfort women" in "coming out," however, has gained them more than compensation. They have commanded worldwide respect for themselves and have helped to raise the world's consciousness about wartime violence against women and to categorize it as a crime against humanity. Many of us who have been engaged in the "comfort women" issue and have conducted research on the subject are often chided and criticized for wasting time, effort, and resources on some old, insignificant women, of whom only a small number are still alive and who will soon disappear entirely. But aside from highlighting the need for continuing efforts to assist the surviving "comfort women," the study of the "comfort women" can contribute to new knowledge—hence, the need for academic research and understanding of the problems that have not been addressed in a variety of fields. Some of these areas are the study of women of Asia, particularly the women of Korea; the impact of imperialism and colonialism on colonized (and on the host) societies; and, finally, the Japanese imperial system and emperor cult in pre–World War II Korea. Understanding these will be necessary to educate both ourselves and future generations, so that similar incidents will never occur in the future.

Notes

1. The term "comfort women" is commonly considered to be a euphemism, but it is actually a form of officialese. See George Hicks, *The Comfort Women: Japan's Brutal Regime of Enforced Prostitution in the Second World War* (New York: W.W. Norton, 1994), p. 18. The Japanese word for them is *ianfu*, and the Korean word is *wianbu*. Both of these translate as "comfort women." South Koreans prefer to use *Chongsin dae*, which means "volunteer corps." A dozen other words were used. See

Shin Young-sook and Cho Hye-ran, "On the Characteristics and Special Nature of the Korean Military 'Comfort Women' under Japanese Rule," *Korea Journal* (*The Impact and Legacy of Japanese Imperialist Rule*) (Seoul, Korea: Korean National Commission for UNESCO) 36:1 (Spring 1996): 51.

2. Hyunah Yang, "Revisiting the Issue of Korean Military 'Comfort Women': The Question of Truth and Responsibility," *Positions: East Asia Cultures Critique* 5:1 (Spring 1997): 54.

3. Hicks, *Comfort Women*, pp. 29–32.

4. Margaret Stetz, "Wartime Sexual Violence against Women: A Feminist Response," (paper presented at the conference "The 'Comfort Women' of World War II: Legacy and Lessons," 30 September 1996 at Georgetown University, Washington, DC) and revised for this volume.

5. Yuki Tanaka, the Japanese-born Australian scholar who is also a contributor to this volume, challenges culturally based notions of uniqueness in Japanese war crimes. See Yuki Tanaka, *Hidden Horrors: Japanese War Crimes in World War II* (Boulder, CO: Westview Press, 1996), p. 4.

6. Ibid., p. 199.

7. Also romanized as *garayuki(sang)*. See Shin and Cho, "On the Characteristics and Special Nature of the Korean Military," p. 51.

8. Yamazaki Tomoko, *Sandakan Brothel No. 8: An Episode in the History of Lower-Class Japanese Women*, trans. Karen Colligan-Taylor (Armonk, NY: M.E. Sharpe, 1999), pp. xx–xxv.

9. Fujime Yuki contends that the licensed prostitution system *did not originate* in Japan and he questions the traditional view that the system was uniquely Japanese and predated Western contact. Instead, it began in the West during the Napoleonic era. See "The Licensed Prostitution System and the Prostitution Abolition Movement in Modern Japan," *Positions* 5:1 (Spring 1997): 135–136; Hicks, *Comfort Women*, p. 27.

10. See Linda Zatlin, "'Comfort Women' and the Cultural Tradition of Prostitution in Japanese Erotic Art," later in this volume.

11. Ibid.

12. Hicks, *Comfort Women*, p. 27.

13. Fujime, "Licensed Prostitution System," p. 137; Tanaka, *Hidden Horrors*, p. 199.

14. Tanaka, *Hidden Horrors*, p. 109.

15. Hicks quotes a Japanese medical officer, *Comfort Women*, p. 28.

16. Akira Iriye, *After Imperialism: The Search for a New Order in the Far East, 1921–1931* (New York: Atheneum, 1969), passim.

17. Akira Iriye, *Pacific Estrangement: Japanese and American Expansion, 1897–1911* (Cambridge, MA: Harvard University Press, 1972), passim. See also, Akira Iriye, *Across the Pacific: An Inner History of American-East Asian Relations* (New York: Harcourt, Brace, 1967), passim.

18. Whether Japan should be part of Asia or the West (joining the Western imperialist club) had been a much discussed topic since the beginning of the Meiji period (1868–1912). One of the most famous westernizing intellectuals of the time, Fukuzawa Yukichi, wrote a treatise, "A Debate on Leaving Asia," which became the basis of the early Meiji policy of Japan going the way of the West. Since that time, Japan was supposed to have gone through cycles of leaving Asia and entering Asia,

with intervals of twenty-five to thirty years, much like the U.S. cycle of isolationism and internationalism. See Hashikawa Bunzo, *Jungyaku no Siso: Datsua Ron Igo* (Tokyo: Keiso Shobo, 1973), pp. 6–9.

19. Center for Research and Documentation of Japan's War Responsibility, *The First Report on the Issue of Japan's Military "Comfort Women,"* (Osaka, Japan: Center for Research and Documentation of Japan's War Responsibility, 1993), p. 2.

20. "Nanking" is used here, instead of the current term "Nanjing," as the reference to the incident is popularly known with that Anglicized name of the city.

21. Dai Sil Kim-Gibson, "Korean and Other Comfort Women" (paper presented at "The 'Comfort Women' of World War II: Legacy and Lessons," Georgetown University, Washington, DC, September 1996), p. 45; *The First Report on the Issue of Japan's Military "Comfort Women,"* p. 11.

22. Shin and Cho, "On the Characteristics and Special Nature of the Korean Military," p. 59.

23. The governor-general in Korea had been outside the regular government organization of Japan since even before the formal annexation of Korea by Japan in 1910. See Kim Chang Rok, "The Characteristics of the System of Japanese Imperialist Rule in Korea from 1905 to 1945," *Korea Journal* (Spring 1996): 20–49. In a war situation, the Japanese chief of staff in China reported directly to the emperor.

24. Therese Park's novel, published in 1997, is titled *A Gift of the Emperor* (Duluth, MN: Spinster's Ink, 1997). Another novel on the subject was published in 1997—Nora Okja Keller's *Comfort Woman* (New York: Viking, 1997)—and reviewed by Michiko Kakutani for the *New York Times,* 25 March 1997.

25. Tanaka, *Hidden Horrors*, p. 99. Tanaka hypothesizes that the number is closer to 100,000. He uses the following computation: The Japanese military plan devised in July 1941 called for one woman for every thirty-five soldiers, and there were 3.5 million Japanese soldiers sent to China and Southeast Asia.

26. See Shin and Cho, "On the Characteristics and Special Nature of the Korean Military."

27. Hicks, *Comfort Women*, p. 48.

28. As Theresa Park records in her novel *A Gift of the Emperor*, young high schools girls would reverently make a deep bow to the gigantic portrait of the emperor, hung in the front of the classroom, and raise their hands indicating their willingness to serve him.

29. Different methods of recruitment and participation of Koreans among recruiters provided opportunities for detractors of the "comfort women" issues to refute that "comfort women" were forced to serve.

30. Hicks, *Comfort Women*, p. 55.

31. Professor Yun Chung Ok, the first South Korean university professor who conducted research and disclosed the existence of the "comfort women" system, recounted how she was saved by her parents' adroitness in detecting the school authorities' true intentions and kept her from school. See Hicks, *Comfort Women*, p. 4.

32. Of 160 former "comfort women" registered with the South Korean government, 46.9 percent report that they were deceived, 34.3 percent taken by force, and 12.5 percent mobilized through government directives. See Kim-Gibson, "Korean and Other Comfort Women," 48; Chung Ching Sung, "Korean Women Drafted for Military Sexual Slavery by Japan," in *True Stories of the Korean Comfort Women*, ed. Keith Howard (London: Cassell, 1995), p. 206.

33. Kim-Gibson, "Korean and Other Comfort Women," p. 48.

34. Chung, "Korean Women Drafted for Military Sexual Slavery by Japan," p. 21.

35. Elsewhere in the volume, Yuki Tanaka deals with the subject of Indonesian "comfort women."

36. Tanaka, *Hidden Horrors*, p. 103.

37. Testimony of Kim Hak Sun, *"Comfort Women"* (McLean, VA: WCCW, 1995), videocassette.

38. Kim-Gibson, "Korean and Other Comfort Women," p. 45.

39. Kim Il-myon was one of the first to publish a comprehensive study on "comfort women," *Tenno no Guntai to Chosenjin Ianfu* (The emperor's forces and Korean "comfort women"), (Tokyo: San-ichi Shobo, 1976).

40. Yoshimi Yoshiaki, *Jugun Ianfu Shiroshu* (Reference material for military "comfort women"), (Tokyo: Otsuki Shoten, 1992).

41. This officer lives quietly in a Washington suburb. For Australian forces' activities, see Tanaka, *Hidden Horrors*, p.104; for more on U.S. troops, see Hicks, *Comfort Women*, pp. 222, 227.

42. Ustinia Dolgopol, *Women's Voices, Women's Pain* (Johns Hopkins, Baltimore, MD: University Press, 1995), chapter 5.

43. Yoshimi, *Jugan Ianfu Shiroshu*, pp. 202–208.

44. Yang, *Revisiting the Issue of the Korean "Comfort Women,"* p. 55.

45. Even in 1996, some South Korean officials in Washington attempted to dissuade us from staging the "The 'Comfort Women' of World War II: Legacy and Lessons" conference at Georgetown University.

46. See Stetz, "Wartime Sexual Violence against Women: A Feminist Response," elsewhere in this volume.

47. Marian L. Palley, "Feminism in a Confucian Society," in *Women of Japan and Korea*, eds. Joyce Gelb and Marian Palley (Philadelphia: Temple University Press, 1994), 290–292.

48. The final version was not published until 1992. See Senda Kako, *Jugun Ianfu to Tenno* (Military "comfort women" and the emperor), (Kyoto: Kamogawa Shippan, 1992).

49. Hicks, *Comfort Women*, pp. 117, 119–120.

50. Known as the WCCW, this organization was one of the cosponsors of the 1996 "The 'Comfort Women' of World War II: Legacy and Lessons" conference at Georgetown University, and two of its board members have contributed essays to this volume.

51. Hicks, *Comfort Women*, pp. 181–185.

52. Grant Goodman, a retired professor of Japanese studies at the University of Kansas, happened to have a paper in his possession, which he obtained in Manila, the Philippines, in 1945 while serving as a translator. Having learned of an uproar about the "comfort women" in Japan in 1995, he sent a copy to a Japanese publication. See Goodman's essay later in this volume.

53. The issue was first raised by the UN Commission on Human Rights in February 1992 and again in May 1992 for the UN Working Group on Contemporary Forms of Slavery.

54. Dong Woo Lee Hahm, *(WCCW) Chronology of Dates and Events: "Comfort Women" Issues*, a flier prepared for distribution at the conference, "The 'Comfort

Women' of World War II: Legacy and Lessons," 30 September 1996, at Georgetown University, p. 5.

55. Ustinia Dolgopol, ed., *Unfinished Ordeal: Special Report of the International Commission of Jurists on "Comfort Women"* (Geneva, Switzerland, 1994).

56. Hahm, *Chronology*, p. 6.

57. As reported in the *New York Times*, 12 May 1996.

58. Mutsuko Miki, "A Keynote Address: The 'Comfort Women' of World War II: Legacy and Lessons, 30 September 1996." See the full text printed in *Mid-Atlantic Bulletin of Korean Studies* 35 (Winter 1996): 11–13.

59. The officials of the two embassies were citing the joint sponsorship of the 2002 soccer championship events as examples of future friendlier relations between Korea and Japan in their personal conversations with the author during August 1996.

60. As reported in the *Washington Post*, 4 December 1996.

61. Representative Elizabeth Holtzman of New York introduced, during the first session of the 95th Congress in 1978, two bills to exclude aliens who had persecuted any person on the basis of race, religion, national origin, or political opinion, and to deport such aliens who have been admitted into the United States. After deliberation, the bills passed both the House and the Senate and became Section 212 (a)(3)(E) and Section 241 (a)(4)(D) of the Immigration and Naturalization Act. The imposition of sexual slavery is considered an extreme form of the kind of harm and suffering covered in this legislation. See John Y. Lee, *News from WCCW* (February 1997), p. 2.

62. The prime minister of Japan, Hashimoto Ryutaro, issued a statement at the beginning of 1996, which said, in part, "As Prime Minister of Japan, I thus extend anew my most sincere apologies and remorse to all the women . . . as 'comfort women.'" A copy of the statement was obtained from the Japanese Embassy and displayed at the registration desk of the "The 'Comfort Women' of World War II: Legacy and Lessons" conference at Georgetown University, but Margaret Stetz and I were not allowed to distribute it to the conference attendees.

63. Maria Rosa Henson of Manila, the Philippines, was the first to accept a Japanese reparation payment of $19,000 from a private fund, according to the *New York Times* of 12 November 1996.

64. This controversy continues to cause diplomatic problems between South Korea and Japan. A 24 July 1997 website reported that Usuki Keiko, a forty-nine-year-old Japanese woman, was barred from entering South Korea for having made clandestine deals with surviving South Korean "comfort women." See *Chosun Ilbo*, 24 July 1997.

65. The title of the speech on Item 9 by Ambassador Geraldine Ferraro, then head of the U.S. Delegation to the UN Human Rights Commission, was, "Further Promotion and Encouragement of Human Rights and Fundamental Freedom: Women's Rights Are Human Rights," 10 April 1996.

66. Numerous websites exist claiming that "comfort women" voluntarily joined the corps for monetary gain.

67. See the *Washington Post*, 26 January 1997, p. A27.

Chapter 2

"Comfort Women" and the Cultural Tradition of Prostitution in Japanese Erotic Art

Linda Gertner Zatlin

The twentieth-century Japanese system of providing women for the sexual relief of its troops during World War II in order to relieve the tensions of the battlefield was not new. Its antecedents were the licensed brothel districts that had operated in Japan for over three centuries and, from the 1860s to the 1930s, the brothels in Southeast Asia staffed by Japanese women exported for that purpose. Indigenous Japanese attitudes toward sex, the middle-class culture that developed under the Tokogawa regime, the growth of the book trade from which sprang popular visual art, and the formalized system of prostitution had, beginning in the early seventeenth century, extended male privilege for the middle and upper classes. To examine each of these threads in relation to the others is to gain a sense of their interlocking nature and to see more distinctly the ways these social forces, particularly the art that explored the world of the prostitute, buttressed the patriarchy.[1]

Like the provision of female bodies, the power relations codified by the "comfort women" system already existed in the accepted and institutionalized system of prostitution. When the Tokogawa regime assumed control of Japan in 1603, it made overwhelming changes to the structure of society in its drive to maintain control of the populace. One change stratified the classes. Another legislated prostitution, which the regime formally codified by licensing brothel areas in major cities, such as the Yoshiwara district in Tokyo. While the shogunate closely scrutinized these areas, it permitted men to believe that within the districts they could escape the regulations governing much of the public aspects of their lives. Like the "comfort women," women for these earlier brothel districts were generally recruited from the countryside, from among farmers and the lower classes. A girl as young as six years old was generally kidnapped; conversely, she could be purchased outright or on a loan contract from parents who could not afford to raise her and who usually were unaware of the situation in which she would find herself. Placed by a recruiter in the care of an older courtesan, she was trained until she was old enough to assume her own place in a brothel. Unless she could find a man who would marry her or pay off her debts, she worked all her life to repay her "benefactor," the recruiter or the brothel owner who purchased her. Particularly beautiful girls commanded higher prices as courtesans, but like the "comfort women," courtesans were responsible for the costs of daily living and, out of concern for public decorum, their physical movements were restricted to the fenced district. The major new element in the system of "comfort women" was the transferral of the notion of male privilege to a specifically military context. Indeed, the Japanese recorded the manner in which "comfort stations" were run, because they were "regarded . . . as a normal amenity."[2]

The "normal[ity]" of the "comfort system" can be seen as arising from Japanese traditions, which were at least three centuries old. For the medieval Japanese, sexual congress seems to have been a joyful exploration during which body, mind, and spirit were united. Attitudes toward sex in Japanese culture were unique in Far Eastern civilization. Unlike Buddhist Tantrism and Chinese Taoism, in which the practice of theurgic erotic rites can lead to enlightenment, Japanese attitudes were formed by indigenous phallic worship cults, which emphasized fertility, and the Shinto religion, which stressed procreation and life in this world.[3] The Japanese tended, therefore, to perceive religion and sexual desire as belonging to a single realm. When the Tokogawa government took over, phallicism and Shintoism "provided both a form of worship with strong sexual overtones and a climate of opinion which encouraged an open sexual activity."[4]

This attitude toward sex would find its place in the middle-class culture, called *ukiyo*, which developed under the Tokogawa regime. *Ukiyo* culture exalted sexuality at the expense of the contemplative and the spiritual. The middle class diverted itself through a search for anything new or entertaining. Fashionable life consisted of wearing expensive, dazzling clothing; attending exciting Kabuki drama; reading witty, sexually allusive fiction and poetry that demanded no intellectual effort; as well as owning sumptuous prints, or *ukiyo-e*, which celebrated this manner of existence. Underlying the pursuit of this prevailing taste was a sense of transience, described as early as 1661 by the novelist Asai Ryoi:

> Living only for the moment, turning our full attention to the pleasures of the moon, the snow, the cherry blossoms and the maple leaves, singing songs, drinking wine and diverting ourselves just in floating, floating, not caring a whit for the pauperism staring us in the face, refusing to be disheartened, like a gourd floating along with the river current, this is what we call the floating world.[5]

The shogunate's rigid rules, which required the unthinking loyalty of its nobility and the blind obedience of those in the lower classes, gave rise to a determined optimism and a refusal to confront anything but that which could entertain.

Forbidden a place in the political sphere, unable to mix socially with the aristocracy, the wealthy and reasonably educated merchant class developed in *ukiyo* an escapist culture, in which a search for pleasure dominated. Its center was the Yoshiwara, the most famous licensed brothel district in Tokyo. As with licensed districts in other cities, the Yoshiwara was close to the theater and sumo districts, wherein courtesans, Kabuki actors, and wrestlers could freely entertain, even as they banded together and created their own hierarchy within their physical and emotional estrangement from inhabitants of accepted society.[6] Here was the equivalent of Belle Epoque café society, in which artists could find stimulation. Here, too, middle-class men could mix with aristocrats as they partook of a varied, cultured, and expensive ritual in which intercourse was the culmination of eating, drinking, dancing, singing, reciting poetry, and talking—in short, a male fantasyland far away from one's home and the responsibilities of family or what could be perceived as the pressures of a critical spouse and crying children. The *geisha*, a female companion whose attention did not necessarily include sexual favors, was "intelligent, sophisticated, and extremely accomplished."[7] She presided over both the private ceremony of sex and the more public festivals unique to and held entirely within the district.[8] A major symbol of this escapist culture, she was fittingly celebrated in *ukiyo* books and prints.

Japanese attitudes toward women were contradictory. Some women were objects of both disdain and esteem; consequently, their position in Japanese society was complicated, and opinion about their role divided. Women who succeeded in the arts, such as the poets whose pictures reappear in books from the sixteenth and seventeenth centuries, or writers, such as Lady Murasaki, seem to have assumed a place in society as men's equals. In fact, Lady Murasaki's accomplishments may have originated the inclination to treat women as having potential to succeed in a society ruled by men.[9] While women in the arts were not the objects of condescension, the lives of ordinary women, adequate wives and accomplished *geisha*, were uniformly burdened by restrictions and not infrequently unpleasant.[10] Moreover, according to Jack Hillier,

> The attitude [toward women] certainly differed according to age and marital status. Marriage did imply a situation akin to "property owning"— the laws were very strict against seducing another man's wife; but there was also a sort of reverence in later years for the matriarch. Women in the brothels—the higher class [more expensive] brothels—had to be "won," and one gains the impression there was a more "romantic" relationship between the man and his paramour, and hardly a situation where the woman was settled "property." In prints, we take it for granted that when man and wife are presented the man is clearly superior, always at the head and in the lead, although with peasant families there seems less insistence on the distance between them. In novels . . . quite frequently the whole gist of the story lies in the treatment of women or woman, and [it is] the deviations from the norms (as in our own novels, after all), the causes of the crises, the separations and the reunions, that constitute the chief interest.[11]

Shunga, the type of *ukiyo-e* depicting sexual pleasure, reproduces the class and age-based treatment of women, the superiority of men, as well as the Japanese concept of romance and the family.

Japanese visual art naturally incorporated some of the complex cultural controls that regulated human behavior.[12] Following a code of elegance, for example, was essential in both social and sexual situations. Elegance of pose, pattern, and overall design became the notable feature of *ukiyo-e* and *shunga*. Most important, the concept of furtiveness about sex (and therefore pornography) was unknown (at least until Commodore Perry's arrival), portrayals of sex encompassing more of human relations than the sexual flourished, and lovemaking became an "art to be practiced with extreme care."[13] This attitude found its visual expression in *shunga*. While illicit sex, often next to a sleeping husband, appears hurried, the attainment of an orgasm is usually portrayed as a sensual process, an art dedicated to sustaining sensations through kissing, gradual disrobing, and varied types of caressing before intercourse. As stimulation for the consumer, these prints treat various sexual positions with an emphasis on mutual satisfaction.

The two earliest *ukiyo* illustrated books were published in 1660, and like the earliest prints, the first book printed was an album of erotic illustrations set in the Yoshiwara, establishing the importance of this subgenre.[14] Such a book may well have developed from painted hand scrolls, or *makimono*, small enough when rolled to be carried in the sleeve of a kimono and hidden from public view. By 1765, the book publishers' target had been for a hundred years the newly literate and monied middle class in newly created urban areas. This group had a particular interest in the theater and brothels, a concern that led, most likely around 1690, to the independent publication as prints of book illustrations that focused on these two areas.[15] The prints had several major thematic concerns: the world of the theater, the daily life and beauty of courtesans, and the varieties of lovemaking.[16] It is the last of these on which we will focus. Not infrequently, for example, an entwined couple in a print looks at a couple on a screen or in a scroll embracing in a different position. Kunisada makes the arousal of his lovers explicit with his title, "The Uses of Shunga," for *An Appraisal of Sensual Pleasure* (Shiki no nagam, c.1826). Holding hands, the couple enjoys a position different from those on the erotic scroll spread out in front of them. Likewise, Sugimura's young man and woman eye each other with desire, presumably after examining the scroll that lies in front of them (untitled design, c.1687), and Sugimura apparently intends that their ardor will be increased by the scroll and that of the human spectator by the presence of the woman outside the room behind the window.[17] Erotic scenes painted on screens offered equal variation, as in Sugimura's design for *Pillow of Compatible Temperaments of the Three Worlds* (Sanze aisho makura, 3 vols., 1687).

Erotic books proliferated as the demand grew: one-fifth of the illustrations by Moronobu, the earliest *shunga* artist known by name, show sexual scenes, while one-fourth of the two hundred books for which Sukenobu designed pictures are similarly voluptuous. These books were often called "pillow pictures," or *makura-e*, because a pillow in a room represents a bed or sleeping room, and because the books could be commissioned as bridal gifts for purposes of instruction and reinvigorating marital pleasure through variation of physical position.[18] Scenes executed from the seventeenth through the nineteenth centuries delineate various types of intercourse, male and female homosexuality, copulation with animals as well as skeletons, masturbation, and a voyeur.[19] (And while the depictions of such scenes are usually erotic, they can as easily be humorous. Humor about human sexuality functions to bridge distances of intimacy, and the Japanese made fun of sex by parodying erotic scenes and by naming scenes allusively after sumo holds.) The prominent placement of genitalia in *makura-e* arose from the accentuation on a prolonged sensual ritual. The actual size of the genitals necessitated artistic enlargement, according to a conversation between an Abbot and a student about the male genitalia, recorded in a thirteenth-century manuscript: "Let my master consider the erotic pictures of the older masters; the phallus is always depicted large, far in excess of the actual size. As a matter of fact, if it were drawn in its natural size, it would be hardly worth looking at."[20] While illustrations of sexuality can be subtly suggested, as in *shunga* executed by Utamaro and Hokusai, they more frequently make male and female genitalia prominent, as in a section of a scroll executed before 1650.

After 1800, *shunga* began to take on a greater brutality, violence, and sadism than the often "gentle and amiable" early works.[21] Like the increasingly horrific portrayals of the grotesque in *ukiyo-e*, the dramatic upswing in representations of violence, including scenes of rape, can be attributed to the increasing turbulence in nineteenth-century Japanese society. Given the economic and social impossibility of a woman subsisting in mainstream Japanese society after she made a rape public, there were powerful motivations to suppress documentation. But because the violence more often than not is directed at women, it is more accurate to say that the *shunga* that depict violence reproduce the Japanese man's hostility toward woman. And it may easily be argued that this hostility culminated during World War II in the rape of a teenaged girl either in front of her parents or at "comfort stations." Such methods of "breaking" in a virgin equaled defilement in a culture deeply concerned with female chastity. Military society viewed her solely as a prostitute and, as George Hicks records, began the process that would destroy a girl's self-esteem and render her emotionally incapable of sustaining a married relationship after the war.[22]

Dissimilar to the treatment of violence in art and life is that of voyeurism, a theme widespread and accepted in Japanese visual and literary art. Japanese novelists have occupied themselves with this subject from the earliest, Murasaki Shikibu in eleventh-century Genji stories, through Ihara Saikaku in the seventeenth century, to Mishima Yukio in the twentieth. This stress has made the Japanese appear obsessed by voyeurism: The secretiveness of the sexual act was both emphasized and intruded on by the presence of a witness, normally hidden from the lovers.[23] In *The Life of an Amorous Woman* (Koshoku ichidai onna, 1686), for example, Saikaku spends a chapter tracing the exploits of an eavesdropper in a brothel, recording the sensations of the sounds and conversations emanating from the surrounding rooms.[24] Like the novelists, the masters of *shunga*, including Moronobu, Sugimura, Harunobu, Utamaro, and Hokusai, frequently resorted to the theme of the observed lovers. They often heightened the emphasis on voyeurism by depicting the erotic stimulus on the secret viewer, as did Sukenobu. One of his designs for *Ehon Mitsuwa-gusa*, 1721, for example, shows an old man who comes to barter for domestic junk. He arrives just as the husband, outlawed for a transgression, seizes an opportunity to return and make love to his wife at the threshold to his house. By entitling this scene "The Anguish of the Old Clothes Man," Sukenobu shows that he intends for the veteran trader's agony of having to watch without taking part to heighten the print's eroticism.

In addition, perhaps the many nonsexual scenes, in which the roof as well as part of the exterior walls of a house are cut away to reveal women playing musical instruments or reading (occurrences Westerners would consider private), owe their composition to crowded living conditions in Japan as much as to artistic convention. Only part of a home and a few inhabitants are depicted in these woodcuts, for example, in Masanobu's illustration for *The Young Genji* (Wakakusa genji monogatari, 1707). In the foreground, Genji spies on a young woman and her companion while they play a game of Go. While the abruptly severed rooftop defines the limits of the pictorial space, the viewer is forced to peer over this normally restraining barrier in order to see the poet and her friend. In prints structured in this manner, the designer actively invites the viewer's complicity to invade the privacy of a home's communal areas.

Not only were Japanese houses erected close to each other, but moveable screens, or *shoji*, which formed the walls in houses and brothels alike, made privacy difficult. *Shunga* designers could turn the potential lack of privacy to their advantage, as did Kunisada, whose "Plum-Loving: Fragrance Transmitted in the Bedroom" (for *Kaiko keichu den senko*, 1840s) portrays an illicit affair. Leaning over the low screen, the female lover tells the maid who is needed to serve sake to hide her eyes and ears so that she is not implicated in the affair. While the screen physically divides the maid from the couple at the right, it is low enough that the maid could see the lovers without much effort; moreover, she cannot help but hear what transpires between them. Kunisada teaches the viewer to regard such a barrier to voyeurism as transient.[25] If a low screen creates a negligible barrier, neither is a high screen, or *shoji*, an impermeable obstruction to watching. From *The Bridge of Heaven (*Ama no ukibashi, c.1830s, attributed to Yanagawa Shigenobu), an untitled print shows the couple in the foreground being aroused by the sounds of the couple in the partially exposed room at the left. Designers such as these used screens or moveable walls to encourage voyeurism for sexual stimulation.

Even after the restoration of the emperor in 1868, a regime determined to be accepted by the West and therefore less permissive about sex, voyeurism was an accepted treatment in art and literature. And voyeurism was easily transferred to wartime conditions. During World War II, "comfort stations" were set up in former hotels, as in Malaya, or more usually were hastily built barrackslike wooden huts whose architects had little concern about tightly fitting doors, as in the Shanghai suburbs.[26] The women were forced to service men in rapid succession, ensured by a time regulation of thirty minutes per visit, and to judge from reports of communal (observed) rape during the breaking-in process as well as the line for "service" in one photograph that Hicks includes, privacy was impossible.[27] No longer just an erotic act by which the male gaze could penetrate a woman's "hidden chamber," watching became unavoidable.[28] Defined more broadly and widely implemented within the military, the act of voyeurism abounded.

Between 1868 and World War II, despite the less permissive official attitude to sex, *shunga* remained popular, and it is therefore helpful to examine the inferences that can be drawn from these woodblock prints, first on the level of the art and, by implication, of the designers. *Shunga*'s attitude toward sex is that it is worthy of observation, or that it is so much a part of everyday life that it is likely to be observed. The prints call attention to the love-play portrayed and invite the human spectator to recreate the story or pictures. *Shunga* that depict a voyeur thus integrate the spectator into the scene. He or she gazes at the sexually engaged couple. Although a few leer at a scene of lovemaking, many more show signs of arousal, in Japan exhibited by biting a kimono sleeve or a handkerchief or by the crispation of one's toes. Some voyeurs move toward the couple, indicating that they will join the love-play, neither making fun of the sexual activity nor displaying and thereby heightening embarrassment. Instead, by making the voyeur an intrinsic part of the scene and an element of contrast and balance to the composition, designers emphasize both the voyeur's presence and the response elicited by spectating.

A second level of inferences focuses on the purchaser of erotic woodblock prints. *Shunga* that include voyeurs require imaginative participation from the consumer. That is, the viewer must actively collaborate with the designer to complete the scene by imagining what will occur next. Prints with a trespasser watching sexual activity offer a clear point of entry into the scene for the consumer, who may perceive the scene as a tableau of human behavior or whose fantasies may be thereby further aroused. This stimulus can depend on one or two different fantasies. Either a human spectator may imagine replacing first the figure of the voyeur, such as a bath attendant, a passerby, an eavesdropper, a maid, and then one of the participants in love-play. Or the consumer may partake of the solitary satisfaction that Hokusai shows in one design for *Manpuku Wago-jin*: Unable to bear the sexual tension caused by the scene she overhears, a woman satisfies herself (3 vols., c.1821).[29] The act of viewing an integrated observer doubles the viewer's erotic frisson by the invasion of the voyeur's privacy.

From the inception of the genre, voyeurs in *shunga* are unrestricted by gender.[30] The voyeur may be a man who watches a woman dressing, as in Harunobu's design of "The Voyeur" (1768), or a woman peering around a screen at embracing lovers, as in Moronobu's print from an untitled *shunga* album. It may be a maid, on hand to refill the tobacco pipe in one page of Sukenobu's album, *Bamboo Curtains* (1719), whose very title promises voyeurism. Or it may be the eponymous protagonist of Harunobu's *The a-la-mode Libertine Maneemon* (Furyuku enshoku maneemon, 1769), which features a voyeur who, with the aid of a magic potion, becomes a miniature man, or homunculus, able to spy on lovers whose various intimacies form the album pages. The portrayal of male and female voyeurs allows the consumer of either gender to identify with the integrated voyeur. The lack of gender-specific role distributions in *shunga* could suggest that these prints were intended to be viewed by both sexes, possibly during their coition, as is suggested by some of the prints themselves.

Shunga includes no coy veiling of the sex organs, and no parading of the female body for male titillation. While *shunga* depict men as superior and as having their choice of women, the woman appears to participate in sex on an equal basis, and she is not objectified as a rule, although there are instances in which she is. In fact, as with figures of voyeurs, objectification of the body is not gender specific, and the genitalia of both sexes are often displayed and exaggerated in order to arouse a viewer.

As in nonerotic *ukiyo-e*, designers emphasized the design of the page, of the clothing, and of the disposition of the bodies to create a harmonious whole. A Japanese consumer could openly purchase erotic prints but, while there is no documentation of aesthetic appreciation, *shunga* offered a representation of pure sensuality that required attention to texture and elegance of line.[31] *Shunga* reveal erotic excitement as well as tranquil moments: Couples drink tea or sake, smoke or eat, and they converse, write, or paint during or between sessions of intercourse. The situations depicted in *shunga* do not reduce the human relationship to sexual activities and, it could be argued, are therefore more representative of reality, in which human beings engage in activities in addition to sex. Because the purpose of *shunga* seems to have been to stimulate and provide variety to one's sex life, this art urged the viewer to recreate a scene with a partner, and therefore prepared the way for a perception of sex that seems to have remained the same until the Meiji Restoration.

The social inference remains to be considered. This art is not social document. Nonetheless, for more than three centuries, it has projected at the least male artists' fantasies about sex. Despite the expressions of mutual satisfaction in *shunga*, the modern viewer cannot ignore the fact that this art sprang from the licensed brothel districts and therefore that the women depicted were courtesans. These women may have been kidnapped and sold into sexual slavery as children, or they might have been sold by parents who could either not afford to support the young girls or who were tricked by agents of brothel owners. Once in a brothel, these young girls were apprenticed to older courtesans who trained them in the ways of pleasing a man. When they came of age, they took their places in the licensed quarter. Therefore, while the art places a euphemistic facade onto the life and sexual activity of courtesans, a courtesan's background cannot be forgotten nor the fact that she traded on physical charms, which disappeared with age. Unless she had been fortunate enough to marry a suitor or to save money (a difficult feat when a courtesan was responsible for clothing and feeding herself and her trainees), her old age was frequently unprotected and penurious—a situation not faced in *shunga*.[32] While there was most likely no collusion between the artists and the brothel owners in terms of formal advertisement, *shunga* must nonetheless be considered a method of acclimatizing a particular attitude toward sex within Japanese culture—in other words, *shunga* very likely contributed to and reinforced those cultural mores in Japan that denigrated women. Thus, the formalized system of prostitution as much as the erotic visual art to which it gave birth can be viewed as significant elements of the Japanese cultural preparation for its exportation of the brothel system and the conscription of "comfort women."[33]

Beginning in the 1860s and extending into the 1930s, an outgrowth of the indigenous brothel system formed the vanguard of Japanese colonial and commercial expansion. From the 1860s, local traffickers systematically recruited poverty-stricken farm women from northwestern Kyushu and smuggled them out of the country into brothels in nascent Japanese colonies across Southeast Asia. Called *karayuki-san*, a contraction of the terms for "going to China" or "going to the Chinese people," these young women believed that they would support their families at home by performing honorable work abroad. Therefore, many willingly allowed themselves to be shipped to Borneo, Malaya, Manchuria, and mainland China, among other countries, where they were sold to brothels. The amount of money the approximately twenty thousand registered prostitutes sent home became an economic lifeline for the Japanese government. Despite their economic value, like the courtesans at home, *karayuki-san* faced an impoverished old age. Those whom the Japanese government repatriated received neither training in a skill or a trade, nor funds for housing, food, or clothing; they existed during their final years at a mere subsistence level. Many died before they were repatriated, others drifted into prostitution wherever they found themselves. In addition, the *karayuki-san* were the prototype for the Japanese military to conscript foreign women on a large scale during World War II. Between 1930 and 1945 as many as two hundred thousand, overwhelmingly foreign, women relieved Japanese troops in "comfort stations" across Southeast Asia.[34]

Organized opposition to prostitution in Japan had surfaced almost concurrently with the establishment of the *karayuki-san* in Southeast

Asia: after the 1872 decree freeing courtesans from the slavery of conscripted sex. As with women's liberation movements the world over, the
decree was in reality opposed by the state which, in the case of Japan,
hid under the concept that prostitution was an individual choice, en-
abling licensed prostitution to emerge again. Nonetheless, for the last
twenty years of the century, religious groups, mostly Christian but also
Buddhist, worked to eliminate legalized prostitution. In 1900, this opposition movement was strengthened by a law that permitted prostitutes
to stop working in brothels of their own free will and, in 1911, by a fire
that destroyed the Yoshiwara, from whose ashes arose a national movement against state-endorsed prostitution.[35] Thus, despite the cultural tradition of *shunga*, the acceptance and glorification of prostitution and
male promiscuity were not universal and monolithic during the first half
of the twentieth century. On the other hand, because there was resistance and opposition to sexual slavery within Japan, especially by proto-
feminists, because Japanese women were needed to cultivate the fields,
and because the government was concerned about the morale of its troops
should Japanese women be found in foreign brothels, the military during World War II found it even more appealing to go outside of the
country to seize women who could be conscripted as prostitutes. Such a
development, however, does not argue against the positive influence of
feminism within Japanese culture and politics. It merely points to the
limits of feminist accomplishments thus far, both in Asia and in the
West, in the struggle against patriarchy around the world.

Notes

1. In different form, some of the information in this chapter appeared in my
book, *Beardsley, Japonisme, and the Perversion of the Victorian Ideal* (Cambridge:
Cambridge University Press, 1997). I am grateful to Yumiko Hulvey for reading and
commenting on this chapter and to Patricia Pringle for her suggestions about *bunraku*
and *karayuki-san*.

2. George Hicks, *The Comfort Women Japan's Brutal Regime of Enforced Prostitution in the Second World War* (New York: Norton, 1994), p. 83.

3. On the sect of Tantrism, which flourished in Japan, and on Shinto, see H.
Paul Varley, *Japanese Culture*, 3rd ed. (Honolulu: University of Hawaii Press, 1984),
pp. 47–48 and 8–13, respectively; on phallicism, see Edmund Buckley, *Phallicism
in Japan* (Chicago: University of Chicago Press, 1895), passim; and Dr. Genchi
Kato, "Religious Ideas in Japanese Phallicism," in *The Story of Phallicism*, ed. L.
Alexander Stone. 2 vols. (Chicago: Pascal Covici, 1927), I: 259–286, passim.

4. Tom and Mary Anne Evans, *Shunga; The Art of Love in Japan* (London:
Paddington Press, n.d.), p. 44. According to Richard Lane, *Images from the Floating*

World: The Japanese Print (Secaucus, NJ: Chartwell Books, 1978), pp. 47, 140–141, and Evans, *Shunga*, p. 11, the attitude of the Tokugawa regime toward *shunga* was permissive.

5. Lane, *Images*, p. 11. Seeking beauty in impermanence, *ukiyo* culture intensified an ancient component of Japanese values; Varley, *Japanese Culture*, p. 43; see also pp. 75, 77, 89, which stress that the Japanese seek beauty in nautre, "in the fragile, the fleeting, the perishable."

6. See Cecilia Segawa Seigle, *Yoshiwara: The Glittering World of the Japanese Courtesan* (Honolulu: University of Hawaii Press, 1993), passim; and Evans, *Shunga*, pp. 60–69, for lively evocations of the Yoshiwara; see Ivan Morris's introduction to Ihara Saikaku, *The Life of an Amorous Woman* (Koshoku ichidai onna 1686), ed. and trans. Ivan Morris (New York: New Directions, 1969), pp. 3–15, Appendix III, for a discussion of the period and for the hierarchy of courtesans and their prices, given also by J. E. de Becker, *The Nightless City, or The History of the Yoshiwara Yukwaku.* 1905, 5th ed. (Rutland, VT: Charles E. Tuttle, 1971), pp. 45–51, and Seigle, *Yoshiwara*, pp. 7–8, 229–232. Seigle's history of the Yoshiwara is detailed and unromanticized.

7. Evans, *Shunga*, p. 69. See also Seigle, *Yoshiwara*, passim, who chronicles changes in the status of courtesans over the centuries.

8. de Becker, *Nightless City*, pp. 191–244.

9. Hillier, personal communication, 1990. On Murasaki's literary accomplishments, see Donald Keene, *The Pleasures of Japanese Literature* (New York: Columbia University Press, 1988), pp. 81–87. I have been unable to find any discussion linking art and women's place in Japanese culture.

10. Evans, *Shunga*, pp. 54–69; de Becker, *Nightless City*, passim.

11. Hillier, personal communication, 1989.

12. Sarah Lubman, "The Art of Love: Sexuality and Anxiety in Medieval Japanese Literature," *Journal of Asian Culture* 12 (1988): 105–137; p. 130 discusses the manifestations of some controls as they appear in medieval Japanese literature.

13. Evans, *Shunga*, p. 48.

14. At that time, books in Japan included romances, novels, folktales, haiku, and critiques, which are Japanese analogues of English "flash" books containing courtesans' pictures, the district in which each lived, and the charge for services. The predominant subgenre was erotica in the form of pictures of love-play, aimed at an educated and sophisticated class of connoisseurs.

15. Jack Hillier, *The Japanese Print: A New Approach* (Rutland, VT: Charles E. Tuttle, 1975), pp. 13–15, 24, 27.

16. Lane, *Images*, p. 42.

17. Evans, *Shunga*, p. 103, describes this book as educational in the sense that it is a "work of sexual astrology, cataloguing men and women by their date of birth and astrological temperament and plotting the conditions and outcomes of their sexual conjunctions." See also other illustrations for Utagawa Kunisada, *Kaiko anchu den senko.* 1840s. *An Appraisal of Sensual Pleasures* (Shiki no nagame), c.1826. I have translated titles of books only when there is an English equivalent that makes sense.

18. Richard Lane, "Japan," in *Erotic Art of the East: The Sexual Theme in Oriental Painting and Sculpture*, ed. Philip Rawson (New York: G.P. Putnam's Sons, 1968), p. 308; Evans, *Shunga*, p. 75. In addition, connoisseurs could seriously study the art of sex in these pictures, according to Lane, *Images*, pp. 30, 42. Seigle notes that

through the seventeenth and eighteenth centuries the Yoshiwara neither generated nor particularly enjoyed *shunga*.

19. While homosexuality, male and female, in Japan was more accepted than in the West, it was nonetheless still *sub-rosa* and, according to Seigle, personal communication, 29 January 1994, "the degree of tolerance changed with history. During the ascendancy of Buddhism, and in times of national strife and civil wars, homosexual practices were more accepted. This would cover the periods from the late twelfth century to the late sixteenth century." Seigle, *Yoshiwara*, p. 156, states that there was no tradition of lesbianism among women and that *shunga* depicting women using artificial devices were "usually products of highly imaginative non-Yoshiwara male artists." *Shunga* portray a smaller amount of homosexuality than existed in the culture, but those depictions would have been suppressed in the West even more rigorously than heterosexual *shunga*.

20. Lane, "Japan," p. 303.

21. Jack Hillier, *The Art of Hokusai in Book Illustration* (London: Sotheby Park Bernet, 1980), p. 161. I am not claiming that *shunga* depicted social reality, although this type of *ukiyo-e* was a part of the exposition of daily activity (*fuzoku*); Hillier, personal communication, February 1994, believes that depicting social reality was not a conscious motivation of *shunga* designers.

22. Hicks, *Comfort Women*, passim.

23. In contrast to Saikaku, Lady Murasaki subtly suggests sexual congress by focusing on the "morning after" poem a man would send a woman with whom he had spent the night. On voyeurism in twentieth-century Japan, see Ian Buruma, *A Japanese Mirror: Heroes and Villains of Japanese Culture* (New York: Viking Penguin, 1984), chapters 1–6.

24. On Saikaku's novels, see Keene, *The Pleasures of Japanese Literature* (New York: Colombia University Press, 1988), pp. 90–93, and Shuichi Kato, *A History of Japanese Literature*, 3 vols. (Tokyo: Kodansha International, 1983), vol. II: pp. 104–112.

25. Varley, *Japanese Culture*, p. 71.

26. Hicks, *Comfort Women*, pp. 13, 46.

27. Hicks, *Comfort Women*, pp. 84, 70, 99.

28. The popularity of hidden gazing probably began during the Heian period, when Murasaki Shikibu wrote *The Tale of Genji* and social custom prohibited face-to-face contact between unrelated or unmarried men and women.

29. In their entry for 2 September 1889, the Goncourts, vol. 15, p. 131, remember this print as "l'admirable image obscène d'Hokusai." See Edmond and Jules de Goncourt, *Journal*; *Mémoires de la Vie Littéraire*, eds. Fasquelle et Flammarion, 22 vols. (Monaco: Les Éditions de l'Imprimerie Nationale de Monaco, 1956), 15: 131.

30. Hillier, personal communication, July 1988.

31. Although Japanese wives controlled the family purse strings by giving the husband a weekly allowance for his necessities, there is no documentation that suggests that women purchased erotic prints.

32. Other art forms such as *bunraku*, plays that dramatize stories utilizing life-sized puppets, more easily portray the feelings of courtesans caught between duty and passion. Patricia Pringle, "The Social and Historical Background of the Love Suicides at Sonezaki," in *An Interpretative Guide to Bunraku* (Hawaii: University of Hawaii at Manoa, 1992), pp. 9–16 details the dramatization of a true story of a 1703

love-suicide pact between a courtesan who loved a man without the means to purchase her contract from her brothel owner and marry her.

33. *Positions* 5.1 (Spring 1998) is devoted to the subject of "comfort women." Of
particular interest in the context of this essay is the section devoted to postwar art
executed by former "comfort women" (pp. 275–278) and by Japanese artists (pp.
279–285).

34. Tomoko Yamazaki, *Sandakan Brothel No. 8, An Episode in the History of
Lower-Class Japanese Women*, trans. Karen Colligan-Taylor (Armonk, NY: M. E.
Sharpe, 1999), pp. xvi–xxv, 183–194.

35. Hiroko Sato, "The Anti-Prostitution Movement in Modern Japan," in *The
Japanese Woman. Annual Report of the Center for Women's Studies* (Tokyo: Tokyo
Woman's Christian University, 1995–1996), pp. 24–25.

Bibliography

Of Japanese works, only illustrated books are listed below; choice collections of individual prints, including those I cite, are in collections at
the British Museum, the Bibliothèque Nationale, the Art Institute of
Chicago, and the Museum of Fine Arts, Boston.

Buckley, Edmund. *Phallicism in Japan*. Chicago: University of Chicago Press, 1895.
Buruma, Ian. *A Japanese Mirror: Heroes and Villains of Japanese Culture*. New
    York: Viking Penguin, 1984.
de Becker, J. E. *The Nightless City, or the History of the Yoshiwara Yukwaku*. 1905.
    5th ed. Rutland, VT: Charles E. Tuttle, 1971.
Evans, Tom, and Mary Anne. *Shunga, The Art of Love in Japan*. London: Paddington
    Press, n.d.
Goncourt, Edmond and Jules de. *Journal, Mémoires de la Vie Littéraire*. Ed.
    Fasquelle et Flammarion. Monaco: Les Éditions de l'Imprimerie Nationale de
    Monaco, 1956. 22 vols. 15: 131.
Harunobu, Suzuki. *The a-la-mode Libertine Maneemon* (Furyu enshoku maneemon).
    2 vols. c.1769.
Hicks, George. *The Comfort Women Japan's Brutal Regime of Enforced Prostitu-
    tion in the Second World War*. New York: Norton, 1994.
Hokusai, Katsushika. *Manpuku Wago-jin*. 3 vols. c. late 1820s.
Kato, Dr. Genchi. "Religious Ideas in Japanese Phallicism." *The Story of Phallicism*.
    Ed. L. Alexander Stone. 2 vols. Chicago, IL: Pascal Covici, 1927, I: 259–286.
Kato, Shuichi. *A History of Japanese Literature*. 3. vols. Tokyo: Kodansha Interna-
    tional, 1983.
Keene, Donald. *The Pleasures of Japanese Literature*. New York: Columbia Univer-
    sity Press, 1988.
Kunisada, Utagawa. *Kaiko anchu den senko*. 1840s.
———. *An Appraisal of Sensual Pleasures* (Shiki no nagame). c.1826.
Lane, Richard. *Images from the Floating World: The Japanese Print*. Secaucus, NJ:
    Chartwell Books, 1978.
———. "Japan." *Erotic Art of the East: The Sexual Theme in Oriental Painting and
    Sculpture*. Ed. Philip Rawson. New York: G. P. Putnam's Sons, 1968, 277–375.

Lubman, Sarah. "The Art of Love: Sexuality and Anxiety in Medieval Japanese Literature." *Journal of Asian Culture* 12 (1988): 105–137.

Masanobu, Okumura. *Stories about Genji* (Wakakusa genji monogatari). 1707.

Moronobu, Hishikawa. *Love's Pleasures* (Koi no tanoshimi). 1683.

———. untitled shunga album. Early 1680s.

Positions: East Asia Cultures Critique 5.1 (spring 1997).

Pringle, Patricia. "The Social and Historical Background of *The Love Suicides at Sonezaki." An Interpretative Guide to Bunraku.* Hawaii: University of Hawaii at Manoa, 1992, 9–16.

Saikaku, Ihara. *The Life of an Amorous Woman* (Koshoku ichidai onna). 1686. Ed. and trans. Ivan Morris. New York: New Directions, 1969.

———. *The Man Who Lived for Love* (Koshoku ichidai otoko). 1682. Trans. Kengi Hamada. Rutland, VT: C. E. Tuttle, 1964.

Sato, Hiroko. "The Anti-Prostitution Movement in Modern Japan." *The Japanese Woman. Annual Report of the Center for Women's Studies.* Tokyo Woman's Christian University, 1995–1996, 24–25.

Seigle, Cecilia Segawa. *Yoshiwara; The Glittering World of the Japanese Courtesan.* Honolulu: University of Hawaii Press, 1993.

Shigenobu, Yanagawa. *The Bridge of Heaven* (Ama no ukibashi). c.1830s.

Sugimura Jihei. *Pillow of Compatible Temperaments of the Three Worlds* (Sanze aisho makura). 3 vols. 1687.

———. untitled shunga album (Series II, no. 4). c. mid-1680s.

Sukenobu, Nishikawa. *Bamboo Curtains* (Tama sudare). 3 vols. 1719.

———. *Ehon Mitsuwa-gusa.* 1721.

Tales of Ise (Ise monogatari). 1607.

Utamaro, Kitagawa. *Hana Fubuki.* 1802.

———. *Poem of the Pillow* (Uta-makura). 1798.

Varley, H. Paul. *Japanese Culture,* 3rd ed. Honolulu: University of Hawaii Press, 1984.

Yamazaki, Tomoko. *Sandakan Brothel No. 8, an Episode in the History of Lower-Class Japanese Women.* Trans. Karen Colligan-Taylor. Armonk, NY: M.E. Sharpe, 1999.

Chapter 3

"Comfort Women" in the Dutch East Indies

Yuki Tanaka

Japan's Invasion in the Dutch East Indies and Military Violence against Women

For the Japanese imperial forces that entered the war against the Allied nations in early December 1941, the conquest of the Dutch East Indies (the present Indonesia) was a high priority. This area had a number of major oil fields, particularly in southwest Borneo, Java, and Sumatra. In order to secure these oil fields, as well as those in northwest Borneo, occupied by the British at the time, the Japanese forces started invading northeast Borneo soon after the destruction of Pearl Harbor.

The Seria and Miri oil fields and the refinery in Lutong were first captured in mid-December, and by the end of January 1942, the whole of Borneo was in Japanese hands. By late February, Sumatra Island was also seized by the Japanese. On 1 March, Japanese forces landed at three different places in Java—Merak, Eretan Wetan, and Kragan.[1] On 8 March, three days after the Japanese forces entered Batavia (the present Jakarta), the Dutch forces, led by General Ter Poorten, officially surrendered to the enemy. This was the beginning of a three-and-a-half-year-long occupation of Indonesia by the Japanese imperial forces. Java and Sumatra were put under the control of the army, and the rest of the islands were administered by the navy.[2]

Japanese troops seemed to have committed sexual violence, in particular, against the Dutch women, at various places immediately after they invaded. For example, when they entered Tjepoc, the main oil center of central Java, "the women were repeatedly raped, with the approval of the commanding officer."[3] The following are some extracts from the testimony on this particular case given by a Dutch woman after the war, which was subsequently presented at the Tokyo War Crimes Tribunal as one of numerous pieces of evidence of war crimes that the Japanese committed against the Allied civilians:

> On that Thursday, 5 March 1942, we remained in a large room all together. The Japanese then appeared mad and wild. That night the father-in-law and mother-in-law of Salzmann . . . were taken away from us and fearfully maltreated. Their two daughters too, of about fifteen and sixteen, had to go with them and were maltreated. The father and mother returned the same night, fearfully upset, the girls only returned on Friday morning, and had been raped by the Japanese.
>
> On Saturday afternoon, 7 March 1942, the Japanese soldiers (odd soldiers) had appeared in the emergency hospital where the women and children were seated together. The ladies were here raped by the Japanese, in which connection it should be mentioned that this happened where the children were not present. These ladies were myself, Mrs. Bernasco, Mrs. Mebus, Mrs. Dietzel, Mrs. de Graaf, Mrs. van Bakerghem, Mrs. Verbeek, [and] Mrs. Warella.
>
> This occurred from 7 to 17 March 1942; generally the Japs came at night, but by way of exception, also during the day. It was a mass, continuous merciless rape. The first afternoon that this happened, as mentioned, three enlisted men came, and everything took place under threat. After this happened, we managed to tell the Chinese doctor Liem. He went to the Commandant, whereupon that afternoon, Mrs. Dietzel, myself and one or two others had to appear before the Commandant. The Commandant said that we would be given an opportunity to point out the Japs who had misconducted themselves, and that they would be shot dead before our very eyes.
>
> However, nothing happened and after an hour we were sent back to the emergency hospital. That evening, at 8 o'clock, we were transferred to a classroom in a school near by. According to what we were told, this was done for our own safety, since the Japs would not come there.
>
> Between ten and twelve o'clock that night, when we were all asleep, a whole mass of Japanese soldiers entered with the above mentioned Commandant at the head. The Commandant sat on a table in our classroom and then watched how each of the women was dragged away, one by one, to be raped. He himself did not join in this.[4]

As only a part of this testimony was read at the Tokyo War Crimes Tribunal, it is not clear what happened to these women after this incident. However, Lieutenant Colonel Damste, a Dutch prosecutor who submitted this testimony to the Tribunal, claimed that "the same as happened when the Japanese entered the oil town of Bahkpapan"[5] in southwest Borneo.

According to a Dutch government report, the rape of Dutch women was also committed by the Japanese in Tarakan, Menado, Bandung, Padang, and Florence during the invasion and the early stage of the occupation.[6] It is also reported that at Blora, a place near Semarang on Java, about twenty European (presumably Dutch) women were imprisoned in two houses.

Fifteen of them, including mothers and their daughters, were raped several times a day for three weeks by the Japanese troops passing by. This was finally ended by a high-ranking Japanese officer who happened to visit.[7]

There is hardly any official record about sexual violence against Indonesian women committed by the Japanese at the time of the invasion. Thus it is very difficult to speculate how prevalent the rape of Indonesian women was by the Japanese troops in various places in the Dutch East Indies, where many Dutch women became the victims of sexual violence.

It seems that the initial Japanese behavior toward Indonesians was relatively civilized. This could mainly be attributed to the initial impression of Indonesians that the Japanese occupation would liberate Indonesia from Dutch colonial rule. In almost every town and city where the Japanese troops made their triumphant entry, crowds of local Indonesians lined the streets, greeting the victors with Japanese flags and *merah-putih* (Indonesian flags) and singing *Indonesia Raja*, the present national anthem.[8]

This was a totally different situation from that experienced in China, where there was strong, deep-rooted, and widespread local resistance against the Japanese military occupation. The peaceful honeymoon period between the Japanese invaders and the Indonesian population lasted only a short period, as the local people soon realized that the Japanese had no intention of giving them autonomous political power. Yet it may not be wrong to speculate that Japanese sexual violence against the local Indonesian women was not a serious and widespread problem in *the early stage* of the Japanese military occupation of the Dutch East Indies.

Exploitation of Existing Prostitutes by the Japanese Troops

Unfortunately, there is very little firsthand information available as to the operations of "comfort stations" in the Dutch East Indies. There seem to be a number of relevant archival documents housed in the Dutch National Archives, but apart from a small number of War Crimes Tribunal documents that have so far been released, most of them are closed until 2025. In January 1994, the Dutch government published a short study report on this issue both in Dutch and in English.[9] This report has only a very short bibliography and has no footnotes. Nonetheless, when we combine this limited number of archival documents with other available information in Japanese and Indonesian, the following general picture of the "comfort women" issue in the Dutch East Indies emerges.

According to the above-mentioned Dutch official report, there were between two hundred and three hundred "European women" working in the "comfort stations" in the Dutch East Indies during the war. Sixty-five of them were "most certainly forced into prostitution."[10] As this report uses the word "European" for both Dutch and Eurasian (i.e., Indo-Dutch) women, and as there were numerous Eurasian women who were exploited as "comfort women" by the Japanese, two to three hundred "European women" in this particular context probably means that they were white Dutch women. As we will see later, there were some Dutch professional prostitutes working—mainly in Java—before the war, and it can be presumed that some of these women were the professionals who continued business for the Japanese, even after the Japanese invasion. Some others might have been the so-called volunteers who reluctantly agreed to serve the Japanese in order to avoid the harsh living conditions they faced as captives of the Japanese.

The cases of enforced prostitution using Dutch civilian women increased from mid-1943. Apart from the above mentioned rape cases, there is little evidence of any practice by the Japanese in the early invasion between 1942 and early 1943 of forcibly using young Dutch women in "comfort stations."

This does not mean, however, that the Japanese troops who invaded the Dutch East Indies did not set up "comfort stations" in the early stage of occupation. The following part of the memoirs written by a former NCO, Nakamura Hachiro, clearly testifies to the fact that the Japanese established "comfort stations" not long after their invasion into the territory:

(One day in March 1942, at Meulaboh on the west coast of Sumatra) I was ordered by my troop commander to set up a "comfort station." I consulted with a medical officer who was assisting the settlement of our troops in this area and decided to establish the facility. An appropriate place was found quite easily. We decided to use a vacant hotel which had been used by the Dutch travellers. It was a new western-style building which had seven rooms, and I thought it was too good for a "comfort station." My next task was the recruitment of women. This was not difficult either *as there were many jobless women remaining in the town after the Dutch Forces left.* However, it would cause a serious problem if they had V.D. Therefore, our medical officer conducted V.D. inspection on the women who turned up for the job. We selected only four who passed the medical check-up and put them in the hotel. The fee was set and thus I could start operating the "comfort station."[11] (Emphasis added)

The above memoirs indicate that there were many professional prostitutes in the Dutch East Indies before the war, and the newly arrived Japanese troops used these women as "comfort women." In this particular case, it seems that some of these women were Indonesians.

However, the memoirs of a Japanese journalist, Kuroda Hidetoshi, reveal the fact that white Dutch women were also used by the Japanese as "comfort women," in particular at officers' "comfort stations," from the early stage of the Japanese occupation. Between November 1942 and May 1943, Kuroda traveled to various places in Southeast Asia, with a group of Japanese journalists and writers, at the request of the Imperial Military Headquarters in Tokyo. He was to travel this region and report back to the Japanese populace about "the liberation of Asian nations from the Western Imperialism."

When they visited Batavia in mid-November 1942, a public information officer took Kuroda and other members of the traveling group to one of these officers' "comfort stations" in the city, where Dutch women were working as "comfort women." According to Kuroda, the army also had officers' "comfort stations" staffed solely with Indonesian women. He states that the navy had Eurasian and Indonesian "comfort women" and did not have Dutch women at their officers' "comfort stations." Kuroda believes that this was probably because Java was controlled mainly by the army, and that the army monopolized the Dutch women. Kuroda was also informed by an army medical officer in Batavia that many high-class army officers, such as staff officers of the Headquarters, had Dutch concubines.[12]

It was not only army officers who exploited both Dutch and Indonesian women. According to another journalist, Goto Motoharu, a well-known Japanese writer, Oya Soichi, operated the "White Horse Riding Club" and the "Black Horse Riding Club" at a large mansion in Batavia where he lived. Oya was one of a few civilian writers who were sent to Batavia with the first Japanese army contingent to the Dutch East Indies, in order to engage in local propaganda activities. In truth, these clubs were "prostitution clubs," the one using Dutch and Eurasian women and the other staffed by Indonesian women. It is presumed that they were operated for Japanese civilians of high social status, such as bureaucrats and businessmen living in Batavia. For a long period, the officers of the army headquarters believed that they were genuine "horse riding clubs," as there were several horses at this mansion. When army officers found out the real purpose of these clubs, they also joined the clubs.[13]

Indeed, prostitution had been a widespread business in the Dutch East Indies well before the Pacific War broke out. It seems there were a vast number of Indonesian, Eurasian, and Dutch prostitutes in major cities like Surabaya, Batavia, and Semarang in Java. They were involved in the business mainly to serve young and unmarried Dutch men. Surabaya, where the Dutch naval base and garrison were located, was notorious for extensive prostitution. In fact, until well into the second decade of the twentieth century, many Dutch and Indonesian soldiers had concubines in their own army barracks. For example, in 1911, 2,372 out of the 10,320 Europeans in the colonial army had concubines, the majority of the women being Indonesians.

The existence of European prostitutes in Java was also recorded as early as the late nineteenth century. In Surabaya, Batavia, and Semarang, there were already well-known brothels owned by Europeans, employing white women to cater only for European men.[14]

During the Dutch colonial time, it was quite a common phenomenon for divorced Indonesian women to leave their villages and work as prostitutes in nearby towns or cities for a few months each year over a long period.[15] Some of them worked as "house maids" for Dutch men, which included sexual service as well.

As a Dutch medical doctor wrote in 1941, "A switch from the life of a prostitute to the normal life through marriage occurs very easily without deep conflict or radical change and is to be attributed to the great tolerance of the Javanese."[16] These "semiprofessional prostitutes" often went back to their own villages, and if they remarried they were accepted back into the village community. Thus prostitution was a widespread business and was not regarded as an "immoral occupation" by the Indonesians in the colonial period. Perhaps such tolerance toward prostitution was partly due to the general poverty that Indonesians suffered under Dutch colonial rule. Prostitution was accepted as a means for women's survival.

Prior to the war, there were also small numbers of Japanese prostitutes *(karayuki-san)*, who were brought in from Singapore or elsewhere by Japanese brothel owners operating in Java.[17]

So, when the Japanese troops entered the Dutch East Indies in March 1942, there were large numbers of prostitutes—Indonesian, Eurasian, and European (mainly Dutch) women—who had lost Dutch clients, due to the defeat of the Dutch forces and the subsequent internment of Dutch soldiers and civilians by the Japanese. It is therefore strongly believed that a vast proportion of these semiprofessional and professional prostitutes were used by the newly arrived Japanese troops as "comfort women" and employed at both military "comfort stations" and civilian brothels/ clubs catering to Japanese government bureaucrats and businessmen. It is also presumed that Japanese brothel owners, who had been operating businesses in Java before the Japanese occupation, were commissioned by the army to procure "comfort women" and to run some of the newly established "comfort stations." As has been mentioned, many of these prostitutes, in particular the Dutch women, seem to have become concubines of high-class officers of the Japanese army.

Procurement of Dutch Women

The Japanese started using coercion, as well as deception, to procure Dutch "comfort women" from mid-1943. This sudden increase of the enforcement of prostitution on the young Dutch internees was undoubtedly related to the fact that, by this time, VD problems among the soldiers had become a grave concern for the Japanese military leaders in the Dutch East Indies. In order to reduce the high VD rates among their men, the Japanese senior military officers believed that young, unmarried women free of sexual disease should be recruited into military prostitution. The timing of the use of coercion seems also to be related to the rapidly worsening living conditions of Dutch civilians under the Japanese military administration.[18] There is no doubt that the Japanese tried to take advantage of these harsh living conditions in the internment camps to lure many young women into prostitution.

According to the Tokyo War Crimes Tribunal records, about eighty thousand Dutch civilians in the Dutch East Indies were interned during the war. Of these, 10,500 died by the end of the war. The high death toll (approximately 13 percent) indicates the hardship these civilians experienced for the three and a half years under Japanese military rule.[19]

The internment of these civilians did not happen immediately on the Japanese invasion of the Dutch East Indies. Until September 1942, apart from about 4,500 people who were regarded as "hostile civilians" detained in nineteen different internment camps in Java, Allied civilians were free to move around, so long as they carried the Alien Resident Registration Identification Card issued by the Japanese military government in Java.

After September 1942, all men between sixteen and sixty years old were separated from their families and put into camps. The women, children, and old people were forced to live in designated places. Their freedom was further restricted in 1943, when the war situation turned unfavorably against Japan and as local resistance movements became stronger. By October 1943, 46,784 women, children, and elderly people were interned in a number of camps in six different regions of Java. The private assets of these civilians were frozen. They were forced to rely on extremely meager provisions of food, clothing, and medicine at the internment camps.[20] It seemed to be around this time that the Japanese started to exploit the harsh conditions facing the Dutch civilians, in order to lure young women into becoming "comfort women."

For example, in March 1943, eight women in Chiapit Internment Camp on the outskirts of Bandung were taken out of the camp under the false pretense that they would be taken to a Chinese restaurant and allowed to live outside the camp. However, they were taken to an officers' club instead and ordered to work as "comfort women." Despite persistent pressure by Japanese officers, six of these eight women refused the demand, and two days later they were released. Two women, however, gave in and became "comfort women" at this officers' club. There were similar cases in Cirebon and Jember.[21]

In September 1943, a Japanese man, Aoji Washio, started operating a military brothel called the Sakura Club, near Pasar Baru in Batavia, by using Dutch women, as requested by a Japanese army officer. Aoji was living with a Dutch prostitute who had been a brothel owner in Java prior to the Japanese invasion. This Dutch woman obtained permission to visit Cideng Internment Camps and recruited eleven young women by offering them jobs as "bar maids" to serve the Japanese customers. However, once these women were brought into the Sakura Club, they were forced to act as prostitutes, after being threatened that they would be handed over to *Kempeitai* (Japanese military police) if they refused to cooperate. Nine other Dutch women working at this club were brought from other camps in Java. Two of them were from Semarang; one of them was just fifteen years old.[22]

In November 1943, the Japanese Ministry of the Army changed its policy of dealing with the civilian internees from the Allied nations. The Ministry removed the responsibility from the local military governments and decided to put all the internees of the Japanese occupied territories under the direct control of each regional army commandant.[23]

The internees of the Dutch East Indies were placed under the control of the 16th Army, and until about April 1944, reorganization of the camps was carried out by transferring some of the internees from one camp to another.[24] It seems that, in this process, a number of women were forced to choose between moving to a different camp or working at a "comfort station." There were at least two such cases in Bandung. The Japanese also tried to separate about one hundred women during a transfer of internees from a camp in Surabaya to Gedagan Camp in Semarang. However, due to fierce opposition from the internees, this plan was abandoned.[25]

The enforced procurement of "comfort women" from the internment camps in the Dutch East Indies became more frequent between late 1943 and mid-1944. This was due probably to the fact that internment camps were now put under the direct control of the army, making it easier for the army officers in charge of "comfort stations" to hunt for suitable women among the civilian internees.

There was a "comfort station" called the Magelang Club in Magelang. In December 1943, a group of Japanese, including the resident (equivalent to a "governor" in the Dutch colonial administration) of Magelang and a *Kempeitai* officer, visited Muntilan Internment Camp in the vicinity. They ordered the camp leaders to call up all the internees who were between sixteen and twenty-five years old. About one hundred young internees were gathered in front of the camp office, and they were ordered to walk, one by one, before the Japanese. The Japanese selected about fifty of them and ordered the camp leaders to take a list of their names. In fact, the Japanese made sure that the camp leaders actually typed up the names of these internees on a piece of paper. The camp leaders were not given any reasons for such a request, but suspicions were gathering quickly among the camp leaders and the mothers of young girls.

The camp leaders and an internee doctor, after conferring with their mothers, picked out most of the young girls from the list of about fifty people and put them in the camp hospital on the pretense that they were seriously ill.[26]

On 25 January 1944, the Japanese, together with about fifty Indonesian policemen, arrived at the camp in a bus and ordered the camp leaders to show them the name list. This time, there was a civilian among the Japanese who was believed to be a brothel manager. The camp leaders told the Japanese that the name list had been destroyed, but the Japanese searched the camp office and found it. The Japanese scolded the camp leaders and ordered them to call up the fifty or so listed internees for immediate inspection at the church.

The camp leaders could not do anything but obey this order. The Japanese lined up the women in the church and inspected each person by lifting her skirts and checking her legs. The camp leaders and the doctor went inside the church building and complained to the Japanese. Eventually the Japanese selected seven women, who presumably had had prior sexual relationships with some of the Japanese camp administrative staff, and eight other young girls. They were ordered to pack up their belongings within half an hour. The Japanese did not explain where they would be taken, but told them that they would be looked after very well. The mothers of those eight young girls panicked and hid the girls in the camp buildings. As these girls did not turn up even half an hour later, Indonesian policemen were instructed to go into the compound and bring out the girls. The police brought out the girls, who were crying frantically, and dragged them to the gate. A crowd of a few hundred internees who were gathering near the gate tried to stop the girls from being taken away. Soon, a scuffle broke out between the police and these internees. The Japanese and Indonesian policemen responded to the internees' action by drawing swords and driving them away. The Japanese eventually took the seven women and eight girls out of the camp.[27]

Three days later, however, the Japanese came back to the camp and proposed to the camp leaders a plan to call for "volunteers" to replace some of the girls who had been taken away. It is said that this was an idea originally put forward to the Japanese by one of the internees, who was a former professional prostitute. Soon a few women "volunteered." As these women were those who were reputed to have been former prostitutes, there was no protest from the internees this time. At the police station, in the presence of the camp leaders, the Japanese carried out a further selection of the girls and women, including the "volunteers." As a result, four internees (one of whom was a fourteen-year-old girl) were sent back to the camp. The remaining thirteen women, including four unmarried girls, were taken on 28 January 1944 to Magelang, where they were examined by a Japanese doctor, raped, and forced to work as "comfort women." A month later, the mothers and relatives of these women and girls received parcels of tinned food and biscuits from the Japanese.[28]

Similar incidents happened at internment camps on other islands of the Dutch East Indies at about the same time. For example, at Padang camp in Sumatra, the Japanese attempted to "recruit" some women as "bar maids," on several occasions between the latter half of 1943 and early 1944. In fact, as early as February 1943, the Japanese tried to procure some women from this camp, but the Japanese attempt led to an uprising at the camp. Surprisingly, in this case, *Kempeitai* took the internees' side, and the Japanese abandoned the plan. However, in October 1943 the camp leaders were forced to agree to transfer a few hundred women from the camp to a building in the town of Padang. The camp leaders insisted that the detailed conditions of the work that these women were to be engaged in should be set out in writing, and that any form of forced prostitution should be excluded from these conditions. In addition, they set another condition that some of the camp leaders should be allowed to accompany the women when they were transferred.[29]

Once these women were taken out of the camp, however, the Japanese requested thirty "volunteers" for work as "bar maids" at a "comfort station" in Fort de Kock. Four women responded to this request and "volunteered." Another seventeen women who subsequently "volunteered" were taken to a Japanese officers' "restaurant" on Nias Island, but for unknown reasons, they were all returned to Sumatra a few weeks later. The Japanese selected a further twenty-five women who had not volunteered and tried to take them to Fort de Kock. The accompanying camp leaders managed to stop the bus that was to transport the women. However, the Japanese eventually succeeded in persuading eleven of these women to go to Fort de Kock. It seems that these women could not bear to return to the camp with its malnutrition and disease. In the end, the Japanese procured fifteen women altogether for a "comfort station" in Fort de Kock. The rest of the women were returned to the camp. In December 1943, the Japanese attempted once again to "recruit" women, but this time no one came forward.[30]

Enforced Prostitution at "Comfort Stations" in Semarang

It appears that the most detailed case of enforced military prostitution using Dutch internees occurred in Semarang. On 17 May 1943, the South Army Cadet School was established in Semarang. This school was set up for the purpose of training young Japanese soldiers, with a relatively high academic background, for eight months. On the completion of training, they were sent to the front lines as second lieutenant–class officers. Due to heavy casualties in the battlefields of Southeast Asia, it became necessary for the South Army to produce many such "lower-class" officers within a relatively short period.[31]

Around October 1943, some teaching staff of the Cadet School contemplated setting up "comfort stations" in Semarang, by procuring young women from the internment camps in the area. The main reason for the establishment of "comfort stations" in the area was the high VD rate among the cadets at the school. Two of the instructors at the Cadet School, Colonel Okubo Torno and Colonel Ikeda Shozo, submitted the plan to the head of the Cadet School, Lieutenant General Nozaki Seiji. They thought that by using young and unmarried Dutch women who were the least likely to be carrying VD as "comfort women," the VD problem could be limited and treated at the station. Nozaki agreed with this plan, so long as he could obtain the permission of the 16th Army Headquarters in Batavia, as well as from the authorities of the military government. In early February 1944, when Nozaki visited the headquarters in Batavia for discussions on other matters, he consulted with the chief of staff, Kokubo, and another staff officer, Lieutenant General Sato Yukinori, about this plan of setting up "comfort stations" in Semarang. Kokubo and Sato told Nozaki that permission would be granted if a formal request were submitted, but they insisted that the Dutch women had to be volunteers in order to avoid any possible legal problems. Upon returning to Semarang, Nozaki instructed his junior officers to discuss the matter with the administrative staff of the military government and to submit a request to headquarters.[32]

Major Okada Keiji, who was Okubo's aide-de-camp, went to the 16th Army Headquarters in Batavia and submitted a formal request for permission to set up five "comfort stations" in Semarang. On the way back to Semarang, Okada visited Bandung and inspected some "comfort stations" in which Dutch women were working as "comfort women" to study how such facilities operated. A few days later, permission to set up four "comfort stations" was sent from headquarters to the Cadet School, on condition that the "comfort women" would be all "volunteers."[33]

In late February 1944, Major Okada instructed Captain Ishida to be responsible for "recruiting" young Dutch women from internment camps in the vicinity of Semarang. Seven women's camps were targeted for this purpose. Ishida met fierce opposition from the camp leaders of the first three carnps he visited—Sumawono Camp in Ambarawa, and Bankong and Lampersari Camps in Sompok. Consequently, he failed to "recruit" anyone. Ishida was a Christian, and was therefore quite reluctant to carry out the job that was imposed on him. In fact, he asked Okada if he could be released from this duty, but Okada insisted that Ishida continue the work. It seems that Okubo, Ikeda, and Okada soon realized that they could not leave this job to Ishida on his own. They decided to use more coercive methods by commanding other Japanese staff to accompany Ishida. When Ishida visited four other camps—Halmaheila, Ambarawa No. 6 and No. 9, and Gedangan—Japanese civil administrators of the Semarang region and other Japanese civilians who were commissioned to be the managers of these new "comfort stations," accompanied him. Ishida was probably a person of weak character, and he left the actual selection of the women to the other Japanese, despite his strong belief that the exercise violated human rights and the Geneva Convention. The selected women were never informed about the work they would be engaged in, and they were given no choice but to be forcibly taken away from the camps.[34]

At Halmaheila Camp the women, aged between fifteen and thirty-five, were summoned for roll call. Each of them was ordered to walk in front of the Japanese, and eventually eleven were selected. Three of them were found to be too weak and sickly. So eight were taken away. These women were told that they would be employed as office clerks, nurses, or workers at a tobacco factory. A few days later, one of them, a sixteen-year-old girl, was returned to the camp. The reason given was that she was too young.[35]

At Ambarawa No. 6 and No. 9 Camp, ten and six women were selected, respectively, from among those who were unmarried and between seventeen and twenty-eight years old. The leaders of these camps protested furiously against the Japanese actions, but their efforts were in vain. It seems that none of these women were informed about their destination.[36]

At Gedangan Camp, several women were selected from the internees between sixteen and thirty years old. However, when these girls were about to be taken away, a large group of internees tried to stop them, and a riot similar to that at the Muntilan Internment Camp broke out. Eventually, the Japanese had to satisfy themselves with a few volunteers who showed a willingness to cooperate with the Japanese. Here, too, some of the volunteers seem to have been former professional prostitutes. According to one testimony, one of the women took her two children (aged two and four years) with her to a "comfort station."[37] It could be the case that she "volunteered" in order to feed her children and herself, so as to survive.

It is almost certain that at least twenty-three women from Halmaheila Camp, and Ambarawa No. 6 and No. 9 Camp, were forcibly taken out of the camps. According to the Dutch government report, a total of thirty-six Dutch women were put into four "comfort stations"—the Officers' Club, the Semalang Club, the Hinomaru Club, and the Seiun-so. Some of these women were brought first to the Semalang Club (formerly the Hotel Splendid), and then Major Okada distributed these women to a few different stations. Others were taken directly to particular stations. All of them were ordered to sign a contract, which was written in both Japanese and Indonesian. When they refused to sign the paper that they could not read, they were severely beaten. Some of them eventually submitted and signed the paper, but others never gave in and kept refusing to do so.[38]

On 1 March 1944, these four "comfort stations" were officially opened. When the women refused to serve the Japanese, they were threatened with torture and death for themselves and their families. They were eventually beaten, kicked, and raped on the opening night. Some of these women were raped by Okada himself, as well as by some of the "comfort station" managers. One of the medical officers, who conducted periodical VD examinations of these women, also raped them.[39]

According to testimonies, one woman tried to commit suicide by taking massive doses of quinine, but failed. She was later sent to a mental hospital. Another woman also tried unsuccessfully to kill herself by slashing a vein. A few women tried to escape from the "comfort stations," but they were soon captured and brought back. One girl was unconscious for two days due to the shock of being raped. Some became pregnant and had abortions.[40]

They experienced immense trauma at the time and the psychological legacy of such torturous treatment continues to plague these women even half a century later. These after effects are clearly described in the following testimony of Jan Ruff-O'Herne, one of the women selected from Ambarawa No. 6 Camp, who was nineteen years old at the time:

> The house was now filling up with Japanese military. We could sense their excitement, hear their laughter. We sat there waiting, huddled together 'til the time had come and the worst was to happen. Then they came.
>
> Lies was the first girl to be dragged out of the dining room and into her bedroom. Then, one by one, the girls were taken, crying, protesting, screaming, kicking and fighting with all their might. . . .
>
> After four girls had been taken, I hid under the dining table. I could hear the crying coming from the bedrooms. I could feel my heart pounding with fear. I held tight to the wooden crucifix tucked into the belt round my waist. . . .
>
> Sitting crouched up under the table, I saw the boots almost touching me. Then I was dragged out. A large, repulsive, fat, bald-headed Jap stood in front of me, looking down at me, grinning at me. I kicked him on the shin.
>
> He just stood there, laughing. He pulled me roughly by the arm. I tried to free myself from his grip, but I could not. My fighting, kicking, crying, protesting, made no difference.
>
> "Don't! Don't!" I screamed. . . . He pulled me toward him and dragged me into the bedroom. I was fighting him all the time. Once in the bedroom he closed the door. I ran to a corner of the room, pleading with him in a mixture of English and Indonesian, trying to make him understand that I was here against my will and that he had no right to do this to me. . . .
>
> I stooped down and curled myself up in the corner like a hunted animal that could not escape from the hunter's net. . . .
>
> The Jap stood there, looking down at me. He was in total control of the situation. He had paid a lot of money for opening night and he was obviously annoyed and becoming angry. . . . Taking his sword out of the scabbard, he pointed it at me, threatening me with it, yelling at me. . . .
>
> I told the Jap that he could kill me, that I was not afraid to die and that I would not give myself to him. . . .
>
> The Japanese officer was getting impatient now. He threw me on the bed and tore at my clothes, ripping them off. I lay there naked on the bed as he ran his sword slowly up and down, over my body. I could feel the cold steel touching my skin as he moved the sword across my throat and breasts, over my stomach and legs. . . .
>
> He threw himself on top of me, pinning me down under his heavy body. I tried to fight him off. I kicked him, I scratched him but he was too strong. The tears were streaming down my face as he raped me. It seemed as if he would never stop.
>
> I can find no words to describe this most inhuman and brutal rape. To

me, it was worse than dying. My whole body was shaking. I was in a state of shock. I felt cold and numb and I hid my face in the pillow until I heard him leave.

In the daytime, we were supposed to be safe, although the house was always full of Japanese coming and going, socialising [sic], eyeing us up and down. There was little privacy and consequently we were often raped in the day as well. But my fear was worse for the evening to come. As it was getting dark, it would gradually build inside me until finally it was burning up my whole body.[41]

But worst of all I have felt this fear every time my husband was making love to me. I have never enjoyed intercourse as a consequence of what the Japanese did to me.

Fifty years of nightmares, of sleepless nights. Fifty years of pain that could never go away, horrific memories embedded in the mind, always there to be triggered off.[42]

While the sexual abuse of most of these women occurred at the four exclusive officers' "comfort stations," some of the women were occasionally sent to "comfort stations" specializing in service for rank-and-file soldiers. For example, Erie van der Plorg, a twenty-one-year-old internee from Halmaheila Camp, testified that every Sunday she was sent out to a soldiers' "comfort station" and was forced to serve a large number of Japanese on that day.[43]

On 1 April 1944, all the women and girls forcibly taken out of the camps and put into "comfort stations" in Semarang were suddenly transferred to the Bogor women's camp. Shortly before this, Colonel Odajima Kaoru, a senior officer in the POW Management Bureau in the Ministry of the Army, had visited Java from Tokyo to inspect the internment camps in the Dutch East Indies. During his inspection tour of Java, he had been informed about these Dutch women and girls by one of the camp leaders of the Ambarawa No.9 Camp. Odajima promptly sent letters to the headquarters of the 16th Army in Batavia, the headquarters of the Southern Army in Singapore, as well as to the Ministry of the Army urging that they close down the "comfort stations" in Semarang. Having received a letter from Odajima, the headquarters of the 16th Army immediately issued an order to close down all four newly established "comfort stations" in Semarang.[44]

As soon as these women and girls arrived at the Bogor camp, they were told never to tell anyone of what had happened to them. They were threatened that if they did, they and their families would be killed. Shortly after their arrival at Bogor, their mothers and siblings were also transferred to the same camp to be reunited with them.[45]

This case of enforced prostitution of Dutch women in Semarang was investigated by the Dutch military forces after the war. As a result, in February 1948 twelve Japanese were tried at the War Crimes Tribunal conducted by the Dutch Forces in Batavia. Colonel Okubo committed suicide in 1947, before the court hearing actually started. Colonel Ikeda was indicted on crimes carrying the death penalty. However, during the court hearing he feigned psychosis, and his trial was delayed. Eventually he was sentenced to fifteen years' imprisonment, instead of execution. Major Okada was sentenced to death, and another officer received a sentence of ten years' imprisonment. Two medical officers were sentenced to sixteen and seven years in prison, respectively. Captain Ishida received a sentence of two years' imprisonment. Four "comfort station" managers were sentenced to between five and twenty years' imprisonment. One Japanese army NCO and one civilian officer of the military government were found not guilty.[46]

For some unknown reason, the trial of Lieutenant General Nozaki Seiji, head of the Cadet School, who was most responsible for the entire matter, was conducted separately in February 1949, a year after the trial of his juniors. The prosecutors requested the death sentence, but the verdict was twelve years' imprisonment. It is interesting to find the following statement by Nozaki in the interrogation report prepared by the Dutch military prosecutors. He said,

> I must admit that such an undesirable situation arose as the result of me neglecting my own duty to properly supervise junior officers. When I received an order to close down the "comfort stations" I was truly ashamed of myself. I went to see the commander of the Southern Army and sincerely apologized for bringing disgrace on the Army Cadet School.[47]

Here it is clear that, for Nozaki, the most serious crime was to disgrace the army's reputation. The violation of human rights of the Dutch internees did not concern him at all.

The Dutch Military Authorities' Indifference to Indonesian "Comfort Women"

During the investigation of the above-mentioned war crime committed by the Japanese in Semarang, the Dutch military authorities interrogated a number of Eurasian women who were also forced into prostitution by the Japanese. According to these interrogations, on 14 April 1944, two weeks after the closure of the "comfort stations" in Semarang, about one hundred local young women, including twenty or thirty Eurasians and a few Chinese women, were ordered to report to the Semarang police headquarters on 16 April. According to one of the testimonies, some of these women were randomly picked up by the police while they were working at restaurants or walking in the street.[48]

At the police station, a Japanese officer made a speech and told the women through an interpreter that, because many Japanese soldiers were now suffering from diseases, VD inspections would be conducted on the women. The women were told that, if they were found to be carriers of VD, medical treatment would be provided. If they were not carriers, the women would be allowed to return home.

They were then taken by car to the Hotel Splendid (the place that had been used as one of the "comfort stations," the Semalang Club). There they were ordered to go into an inspection room one by one where, in front of a Japanese medical doctor and a few Japanese soldiers, each woman was told to take off her underwear and lie on the bed, with her legs apart. If she refused, the soldiers forced the woman to comply. Then the doctor inserted a metal instrument and roughly opened her vagina. Many women screamed and cried, and it scared the other women waiting for their turns outside the inspection room. It seems that the purpose of this inspection was not a VD checkup, but to find out whether these women were virgins or not.[49]

In the end, twenty women were told to remain, and the rest were allowed to leave. Eight of these selected women were Eurasians, one was Chinese, and the rest were Indonesians. That night, they were forced to stay in four different rooms in Hotel Splendid, and each was given fifty guilders. Some women realized what the Japanese were going to do with them and refused to accept the money. However, they were beaten and forced to take the money. Some of them tried to escape that night, but the building was guarded by Japanese soldiers.

It is interesting to note that the Japanese never produced any contracts for these women to sign, while they insisted that the Dutch internees enter into a formal contract. It is obvious that the Japanese were not bothered about any legal problems, so far as the "recruitment" of Asian women was concerned, whereas they clearly knew that enforced prostitution would be a violation of the Geneva Convention when they demanded signatures from the Dutch women.[50]

The following day, these women were taken by three Japanese soldiers to Surabaya by train. They were detained in a house in Surabaya, where the Japanese soldiers kept a continuous watch on them. A Japanese man, who was believed to be a brothel manager, lived in the house. They were waiting to be transferred to Flores Island. The boat sailed from Surabaya, but had to return twice before successfully reaching Flores. The first time, the boat was attacked by Allied airplanes, and the second time it was followed by an Allied submarine. All in all, they stayed in Surabaya for more than a month. During this time, two women managed to escape, and one became ill. Eventually, seventeen women were taken to Flores.[51]

They were put into a "comfort station" in Flores and forced to serve the Japanese from morning to midnight every day until the war ended in August 1945. In the morning, rank-and-file soldiers visited them; in the evening, NCOs turned up; and at night, officers came. On average, each woman was forced to serve twenty soldiers, two NCOs, and one officer every day. The "comfort station" manager received one and a half guilders from each soldier, two guilders from an NCO, and the officers' rate was between three and eight guilders, depending on the time he spent with the woman. On payment, each man was given a ticket, which had to be handed to a "comfort woman." Each "comfort woman" was expected to collect at least one hundred tickets a week, and if she failed, she was physically punished by the manager. Each man was given a condom along with the ticket and was instructed to use it without fail. But many did not want to use condoms and, if a woman refused to serve him without using a prophylactic, physical violence was often inflicted on her. It seems that the women rarely received payment, although sufficient meals were provided every day. A medical officer visited the station once a week and conducted a VD inspection.[52]

According to the testimony of one of these women, there was a group of Eurasians at another "comfort station" that was brought from Bandung. One member of the group, a sixteen-year-old girl, told her that they were soon to be taken to Timor.[53]

Despite the fact that sufficient evidence about enforced prostitution was collected through the interrogations of these women, there is no evidence that the Dutch military authorities charged the Japanese for the violation of the human rights of these Indo–Dutch, Indonesian, and Chinese women. It is believed that these interrogations were conducted in order to gather relevant information useful in the criminal cases of the white Dutch victims. As much as the Japanese were unconcerned about the exploitation of non-Europeans, so too the Dutch were equally indifferent to victims who were not white and Dutch.[54] In fact, there are some testimonies by Indonesians that strongly support the speculation that, from 1943, at about the same time that Dutch women internees were taken out of the camps as "comfort women," a vast number of young Indonesian women were also "recruited" as "comfort women."

According to a Javanese woman, Siti Fatimah, a daughter of Singadikarto, the subdistrict head of Subang in west Java, she was told that she would be sent to Japan to study in Tokyo. In 1943, when she was sixteen years old, she and four other girls from her home subdistrict were put on a ship at Tanjung Priok. They joined a few hundred Indonesian girls who had been deceived by the Japanese and believed that they were going to Tokyo. The ship went instead to the Flores Island.

As soon as they arrived, the Japanese attitude toward the girls suddenly changed. They were put into a camp and were forced to render sexual services to the Japanese soldiers. Each girl had to serve at least two soldiers every day.

Three months later, they were transported to the north of Buru Island, where they were put into a military compound. Here too, they were sexually abused every day until the end of the war.

In both Flores and Buru, many girls died as the result of maltreatment by the Japanese. Others suffered psychological problems as the result of sexual abuse. Soon after 15 August 1945, Fatima and some other girls asked the Japanese to return them home, but their request was refused. Together with a few other girls, Fatima ran away from the compound and sought help from the local Buton fishermen. She later married one of the fishermen and never returned to Java.[55]

Sukarno Martodiharjo, a seaman for a Japanese shipping company in Batavia during the war, recalled an incident in which about two hundred Indonesian girls were loaded onto boats one night in March 1945. The girls, who looked to be schoolgirls aged between fifteen and nineteen, were boarded onto five different cargo ships, part of a convoy at the port of Tanjung Priok. This convoy was to sail to Singapore and Bangkok.

Sukarno was on board one of the vessels and, despite orders not to speak to the girls, managed to talk to a few of the girls during the voyage. He found that the girls were selected to be sent to Tokyo to study Japanese and to be trained as nurses or midwives.

During the first few days of the voyage, they were very cheerful and full of hope about going to Japan. They sang Japanese school and military songs. One of the girls to whom Sukarno was able to talk was Sumiyati, a seventeen-year-old daughter of the head of one of the sub-districts in Kediri.[56]

A few days after they left Java, some girls started crying. One of them even tried to commit suicide for a reason that Sukarno did not know at that time. Sumiyati told him that they had been deceived by the Japanese. They had found out that what the Japanese had told them was a lie and just propaganda.

At Singapore, the girls on two of the other ships were taken off board. The convoy continued to sail on to Bangkok. When the ships arrived at Bangkok, all the other girls from Java were met by a group of Japanese and taken away. This was the only instance that Sukarno saw of the transportation of Indonesian girls from Java to other places in Southeast Asia, but he heard from a colleague seaman that similar transportation was carried out by a different convoy at another time.[57]

After the war, Sukarno continued to work as a seaman. In September 1947, he traveled from Singapore to Bangkok for sightseeing, while his ship was harbored at Singapore. In Bangkok, he unexpectedly met Sumiyati on a city street. Sumiyati told him that she and fellow Indonesian girls were taken to a "comfort station" somewhere near Bangkok and forced to serve the Japanese soldiers day after day until the end of the War. At the "comfort station," fifty Javanese girls were strictly supervised by a Japanese woman.

After the war, they wanted to go back to Java, but they had no money to do so. They were not paid by the Japanese, except for a small amount of money that they were given on days when they were allowed to go into the city for leisure. They were all ashamed of being forced to work as prostitutes and could not face their parents even if they were to be able to do so. When Sukarno met Sumiyati in Bangkok, she was married to a Thai man who was a poor factory worker. At that time, she told him that about fifteen fellow Indonesians were living in Bangkok. She also told him that when the war finished, some of the girls at the same "comfort station" were taken away somewhere by the Japanese.[58]

According to Pramudya Ananta Tur, a well-known dissident Indonesian writer who collected many relevant testimonies including the above-mentioned two cases, many of the Javanese girls who became victims of Japanese military prostitution were the daughters of prominent local chiefs, such as subdistrict heads, village heads, policemen, and school headmasters. The military government had released deceptive information that the girls would be offered an opportunity to study in Japan, and it was passed on to local public servants through provincial Javanese residents (i.e., governors). Thus, those public servants who collaborated with the Japanese were put into the difficult situation of having to show their loyalty to Japan by sending their own daughters first.[59] It is not known how many Indonesian girls were "recruited" in this way nor exactly where they were sent.

Doug Davey, a member of the Australian Ninth Regiment, which acted as the British–Borneo Civil Affairs Unit, was in Borneo in August 1945. There he found some Javanese women who had been transported to Borneo by the Japanese. They were living in the ruins of the Japanese "comfort station" at Beaufort (the present Weston) on the Padas River in the Northwest. The Australian forces took them to a small island off the Borneo coast for medical treatment and rehabilitation, with the intention of sending them back to Indonesia. But the women were afraid of going home, because of the shame associated with their experience. One committed suicide.[60]

It is possible that these women were also deceived by the Japanese in the same way. The Australian troops, who landed at Kupan in the southwest of Timoa Island shortly after Japan surrendered, also found twenty-six Javanese women who had been brought there as "comfort women." The Japanese tried to camouflage this by making them wear Red Cross armbands.[61] It seems that the Australian forces had no intention of finding out which Japanese were responsible for crimes against these Indonesian women.

It can be presumed from these testimonies that a vast number of Indonesian girls were taken out of Java and put into "comfort stations" in various places in Southeast Asia, stretching from Thailand to New Guinea, from North Borneo to Timor.[62] This means that such extensive transportation of "comfort women" must have been a plan that was designed and implemented at a high level by Japanese military bodies such as the headquarters of the Southern Army and, most likely, in collaboration with the 16th Army, which controlled the entire country of Java. Yet, due to a lack of interest by the Dutch and other Allied nations' military authorities, the unprecedented scale of sexual abuse by the Japanese of Indonesian women was consigned to oblivion.

Since 1993, in response to the Indonesian government's request, more than twenty thousand Indonesian women have come forward and claimed that they were victims of sexual violence committed by the Japanese troops stationed in various places in the Dutch East Indies during the war.[63] They were not all "comfort women"; many of them seem to be victims of rape. Some of these women may have been "semiprofessionals" working at "comfort stations" or as concubines serving Japanese officers. At the peak time, two hundred twenty thousand Japanese soldiers and military employees were stationed throughout the Dutch East Indies. Numerous "comfort stations" were operated to cater to these men. From the available information that I have examined in this chapter, there is no doubt that a large number of Indonesians and Eurasians were forcibly pressed into prostitution at these military brothels and ill-treated by the Japanese.

The Dutch army extensively sexually exploited Indonesian women during its colonial period prior to the Pacific War. Its men stationed in the Dutch East Indies suffered high rates of VD as a result.[64] It followed that, when the Japanese invaded, the sexual abuse of the Indonesian and Indo–Dutch women by the Japanese was probably not viewed as a serious crime against humanity. It is in this climate, and because of previously accepted sexual "norms," that we see that racial and gender factors are closely intertwined. Due to racial discrimination against the Indonesian and Indo–Dutch women and sexual discrimination against women in general, the Dutch military authorities were unable to see the serious criminal nature of the "comfort women" issue. The same can be said about postwar attitudes of other Allied forces. They all failed to pursue legal prosecution against the Japanese who committed crimes against numerous Asian women, despite the fact they had accumulated ample evidence.[65]

Notes

1. Harada Katsumasa, ed., *Showa: Niman Nichi no Zen Kiroku*, Vol. 6, *"Taiheiyo Senso"* (Tokyo: Kodansha, 1990), pp. 142–143.

2. For details of the Japanese military occupation of the Dutch East Indies, see Shigeru Sato, *War, Nationalism and Peasants: Java Under the Japanese Occupation, 1942–1945* (Armonk, NY: M. E. Sharpe, 1994); in particular, see Part I, "The Military Administration for Total Mobilisation" [sic].

3. The International Military Tribunal for the Far East (Tokyo, 1946, hereafter IMTFE), p. 13,639.

4. Ibid., pp. 13,639–13,642.

5. Ibid., pp. 13,638.

6. *Report of a Study of Dutch Government Documents on the Forced Prostitu-*

tion of Dutch Women in the Dutch East Indies during the Japanese Occupation (1994, hereafter The Dutch Government Report), p. 4.

7. Ibid., p. 4.

8. Ajia Minshu Hotei Junbi-kai, ed., *Nippon no Shinryaku* (Tokyo: Otsuki Shoten, 1992), p. 228.

9. See note 6. This report was presented to the Lower House of the Dutch Parliament by the Dutch Minister of Foreign Affairs on 24 January 1994. There are a couple of basic faults in this report, so far as its references to Japanese history are concerned. First, the report claims that prostitution was illegal in prewar Japan. On the contrary, Japan had a long history of regulated prostitution throughout the nation before World War II. Second, the 7th Army of the Japanese Imperial Forces at Singapore was not directly under the authority of the headquarters in Tokyo, but under the control of the South Army.

10. The Dutch Government Report, p. 2.

11. This particular part of Nakamura Hachiro's memoirs, in his book *Aru Rikugun Yobishikan no Shuki* (Gendai-shi Suppan-kai, 1978), was reproduced in Takasaki Ryuji, ed., *Hyakusatsu ga Kataru Ianjo: Otoko no Honne* (Nashinoki-sha, 1994), pp. 74–75.

12. An extract from Kuroda Toshihiko, *Gunsei* (Gakufu Sjoin, 1952), appeared in Takasaki Ryuji, ed., *Hyakusatsu ga Kataru Ianjo*, pp. 72–73.

13. An extract from Goto Motoharu, *Kaigun Hodo Senki* (Shin Jinbutsu Oraisha, 1975), appeared in Takasaki Ryuji, ed., pp. 73–74.

14. John Ingleson, "Prostitution in Colonial Java." *Nineteenth and Twentieth Century Indonesia: Essays in Honour of Professor J.D. Legge*, D.P. Chadler and M.C. Ricklefs, eds. (Monash: Centre of Southeast Asian Studies, Monash University, 1986), pp. 126, 134.

15. Ibid., p. 137.

16. Tio Biauw Sing, *De Syphilis in het Regentschap Bandoeng*, p. 51, cited by John Ingleson, "Prostitution in Colonial Java," p. 136.

17. John Ingleson, "Prostitution in Colonial Java," p. 138.

18. For details of the worsening living conditions in the internment camps, see for example, Nell van den Graaff, *We Survived: A Mother's Story of Japanese Captivity* (Queensland: University of Queensland Press, 1989), in particular, chapters 4–10. At the International Military Tribunal for the Far East in Tokyo, a British officer, Lieutenant Colonel Nicholas Read-Collins, testified about the appalling physical and mental conditions of the Dutch female internees whom he met and interviewed during his trip to Java shortly after the war. His testimony appears in IMTFE, pp. 13,528–13,553. He stated, for example, that in Batavia, "the main diseases were malnutrition, edema from beriberi, dysentery and a variety assortment of nervous disorders." He also claimed that "practically every woman bore the marks of tropical ulcers and some still had an extreme wasting of various parts of the body, of the arms and of the legs, and in one instance I saw a woman whose legs had been eaten away to the bone by a tropical ulcer." See IMTFE, p. 13,541.

19. IMTFE, pp. 13,487–13,488.

20. For details of the changes to the Japanese policies of the internment of the Dutch civilians during the war, see Utsumi Aiko, "Sumaran Ianjo Jiken," *Indonesia* 5/6 (1995): 5–6.

21. Ibid., p. 7; The Dutch Government Report, p. 12.

22. The Dutch National Archives (Algemeen Rijksarchief) Collection, Algemene Secretarie 5200 (hereafter AS 5200). A Japanese freelance journalist, Kajimura Taichiro, who resides in Berlin, translated this document into Japanese in 1992, with assistance from Koen Mathot. I obtained a copy of the Japanese translation through a Japanese publishing house, Otsuki Shoten, to which the translation manuscript was submitted for consideration for publication. Unfortunately, however, the Japanese translation of this document has not yet been published. The document contains interrogations of the Japanese suspects in war crimes committed against Dutch women, those of some victims of Japanese sexual violence, as well as of camp leaders and other internees of several internment camps in Java. It also contains actual court proceedings of war crimes tribunals on "comfort women" cases, conducted by the Dutch military forces in Batavia. The page numbers of the Japanese translation are believed to be different from those of the original documents, and therefore I do not specify any page numbers when referring to this document in footnotes.

23. Chaen Yoshio, ed., *Horyo ni kansuru Sho-hoki Ruishu* (Tokyo: Fuji Shuppan, 1988), pp. 85–90.

24. Utsumi, *Indonesia*, p. 6.

25. AS 5200.

26. AS 5200 and the Dutch Government Report, pp. 13–14. There are some discrepancies in the details of the account of this event among testimonies given by some camp leaders and internees of the Muntilan Internment Camp. I reconstructed the whole event by relying on a few camp leaders' testimonies, which seem to be the most reliable information collected by the Dutch military authorities after the war.

27. Ibid.

28. Ibid.

29. The Dutch Government Report, pp. 19–20.

30. Ibid., pp. 20–21.

31. Utsumi, *Indonesia*, p. 9.

32. AS 5200.

33. Ibid.

34. Ibid.

35. Testimony of E. van der Plog, the Japanese translation of which was published in *Kikan Senso Sekinin Kenkyu* 6 (1994): 69–71.

36. AS 5200; Jan Ruff-O'Herne, *50 Years of Silence* (Sydney, Australia: ETT Imprint, 1994), pp. 64–72.

37. AS 5200.

38. Ibid. According to Jan Ruff-O'Herne, who was taken to a "comfort station" directly from Ambarawa No. 6 Camp, the paper that they were ordered to sign was written only in Japanese, and a Japanese army interpreter orally translated the gist of its content into English for the Dutch women. This information was given to me by Ruff-O'Herne in her letter addressed to me in August 1997. However, several other Dutch victims, who were interrogated by the Dutch military authorities after the war, testified that the paper was written both in Indonesian and Japanese. Incidentally, Ruff-O'Herne and some others from the same internment camp refused to sign the paper and never signed.

39. AS 5200. Jan Ruff-O'Herne was also raped by this doctor at each medical inspection time. See Ruff-O'Herne, *50 Years of Silence*, pp. 94–96.

40. AS 5200; Ruff-O'Herne, *50 Years of Silence*, pp. 93–94, 102–103.

41. Ruff-O'Herne, *50 Years of Silence*, pp. 82–89.

42. An extract from the testimony of Jan Ruff-O'Heme, published in *The Age*, 11 December 1992.

43. Testimony of E. van der Plog. See note 35.

44. AS 5200; Utsumi, *Indonesia*, pp. 11–12.

45. Ruff-O'Herne, *50 Years of Silence*, p. 108.

46. AS 5200; Utsumi, *Indonesia*, p. 14. The Japanese translation of the results of this Dutch War Crimes Tribunal was published in *Kikan Senso Sekinin Kenkyu* 3 (1994): 44–50.

47. AS 5200.

48. Ibid. Initially the Japanese treated the Eurasians in the same way as the Indonesians rather than the Dutch, and thus they were not put into the internment camps. However, as anti-Japanese sentiment became stronger among the Indonesians, the Japanese suspicion of the Eurasians' loyalty to Japan also grew stronger. As a consequence, they took harsh attitudes toward them from early 1943, although the Eurasians were still free to move around. See H.J. Benda, J.K. Irikura, and K. Kishi, eds., *Japanese Military Administration in Indonesia: Selected Documents* (New Haven, CT: Yale University Press, 1965), p. 72.

49. Ibid.

50. Ibid.

51. Ibid.

52. Ibid.

53. Ibid.

54. As far as I know, there are two exceptional cases that the Dutch military authorities brought to the War Crimes Tribunal, in which enforced prostitution involving non-Dutch "comfort women" was dealt with. One of them is the case of a "comfort station" in Balikpapan. A Japanese man called Ishibashi Nakazaburo, the manager of the "comfort station," was charged with kidnapping several Indonesian women and forcing them to render sexual services to the Japanese. However, three Indonesian "victims," who appeared in court as witnesses, actually testified against the Dutch prosecutors, claiming that, thanks to Ishibashi, they had a good life during the war. Thus Ishibashi was found "not guilty." For details of this case, see Utsumi, *Indonesia*, p. 2.

Incidentally, "comfort stations" in Balikpapan were set up by Nakasone Yasuhiro, former Japanese prime minister, who was then a young paymaster of the Japanese navy troops stationed in Balikpapan. This fact is stated by Nakasone himself in his recollection, "*Niju-san ai de Sanzen-nin no So-shikikan*," in Matsuura Takanori, ed., *Owari-naki Kaigun* (Bunka Hoso Kaihatsu Senta Shuppanbu, 1978), p. 98.

The other case was the rape and enforced prostitution of five Indonesian women by the Japanese troops in Pontianak. Between October 1943 and June 1944, about fifteen hundred civilians—Indonesians, Chinese, and Indians—were arrested as suspects of an underground resistance movement, and the vast majority were eventually tortured and killed. During this period, some wives of the suspects were raped by members of the Japanese Naval Special Police Force, and then they were forced to work at a navy "comfort station" for the following eight months. For this crime, Captain Okajima Toshiharu and twelve other members of the Naval Special Police Forces were found guilty. Okajima and two others received death sentences. The sentence was made in conjunction with verdicts on counts of torture and murder of the fifteen hundred civilians, not just for rape and enforcement of prostitution. For details of this tribunal, see the Japanese Diet Library Collection, Microfilm Document No. 5594.

55. Paramudya Ananta Tur, "Mencari Jejak Para Perawan Yang Digondol Jepang: 1942–1945" (unpublished paper). Only a small proportion of this Indonesian manuscript was translated into Japanese and published in *Kikan Senso Sekinin Kenyku* 16 (1997). For details of Siti Fatima's testimony, see the Japanese translation, pp. 62–65.

56. Ibid., p. 59.

57. Ibid., p. 60.

58. Ibid., p. 61.

59. Ibid., pp. 58–59.

60. Interview with Doug Davey, conducted by the author in August 1992.

61. The Australian War Memorial holds several photos of these Javanese "comfort women," who were found in Timor when the Australian forces landed at Kupan (Negative Nos. 120082–120087). However, apart from short captions for each photo, there is no other information available on these women.

62. Recently, a Japanese broadcasting corporation based in Nagoya, Chukyo-TV, produced a documentary film on the Indonesian "comfort women" and broadcast it in May 1997. One of several former Indonesian "comfort women" who were interviewed in this film testified that she was taken to New Guinea. This film, titled *Koe Tozasarete Soshite*, was directed by Ms. Owaki Michiyo.

63. This information is provided in the above-mentioned documentary film, the source of which is the Indonesian government itself.

64. For details of high VD rates among the Dutch forces stationed in the Dutch East Indies before the Pacific War, see Ingleson, "Prostitution in Colonial Java," pp. 133–136.

65. The U.S. forces also collected substantial information on "comfort women" during the war. (See Grant Goodman's essay elsewhere in this volume.) After the war, however, the United States did not take any legal action against the Japanese who were responsible for institutionalizing the "comfort women" system by exploiting vast numbers of Asian women. For detailed analysis of the reasons for the lack of the U.S. forces' interest in this issue, see Yuki Tanaka, "*Naze Bei-gun wa Jugun Ianfu Mondai o Mushi shitanoka*" in *Sekai* 625 (Sept. 1996): 174–183; and *Sekai* 626 (Oct. 1996): 270–279.

Chapter 4

Prostitutes versus Sex Slaves

The Politics of Representing the "Comfort Women"

Chunghee Sarah Soh

Introduction

The issue of the wartime "comfort women" for the military of Imperial
Japan leapt to the attention of the world community, nearly half a century after the end of World War II, with a series of United Nations Commission on Human Rights (UNCHR) hearings that began in 1992. The
UNCHR series of formal hearings on the "comfort women" issue described below provided a major turning point in transforming the nature
of the "comfort women" debate, from a class action suit (brought about
by a small number of Korean plaintiffs—including three former "comfort women"—against the Japanese government in December 1991) to
an international human rights issue supported by legal experts and feminist activists across nations.

In February 1992, UNCHR first heard the critical statements delivered
by Totsuka Etsuro against the Japanese government concerning the "comfort women" issue. Mr. Totsuka, a Japanese lawyer, spoke as a representative of East Asia for the International Educational Development (IED), a
nongovernmental organization (NGO).[1] In May 1992, representatives of
the IED and the Korean Council for Women Drafted for Military Sexual
Slavery by Japan, a Korean NGO formed in 1990 (hereafter referred to as
the Korean Council), raised the "comfort women" issue at UNCHR Sub-
Commission Working Group on Contemporary Forms of Slavery.

The Working Group then addressed a request to the secretary general
that he submit information on the "comfort women" to Theo van Boven, a
Dutch professor of law and a UN-appointed Special Rapporteur on the right
to restitution, compensation, and rehabilitation for victims of gross viola-

tions of human rights and fundamental freedoms. The Sub-Commission, in its resolution 1992/2, endorsed this request—paragraph 18.[2] This was the first action the UN took regarding the violations of human rights of the former "comfort women."[3] In August 1992, Hwang Kum-ju (a.k.a. Hwang Keum Ju), a former "comfort woman" from Korea, testified in Geneva to the UNCHR Sub-Commission for the Prevention of Discrimination and the Protection of Minorities. Thus began the belated deliberation by the United Nations of the Japanese military "comfort women" system as a crime against humanity that violated the human rights of Asian women and the international agreement prohibiting forced labor that Japan signed in 1932.

Subsequently, investigations into the problem by the Special Rapporteurs assigned by the UNCHR have confirmed an unprecedented involvement of the state in provisioning sex to the troops and in exploiting the sexuality of young females recruited mostly from colonial and occupied territories in the process. In February 1996, based on the reports submitted by the Special Rapporteur on violence against women, Ms. Radhika Coomaraswamy,[4] the United Nations pronounced its conclusive condemnation of Japan for forcing tens of thousands of women into sexual slavery for its troops before and during World War II. The 1998 report on Wartime Slavery submitted by another Special Rapporteur, Gay J. McDougall, defined the "comfort stations" as the "rape centers" and recommended concrete measures to resolve the wartime "comfort women" issue, including state compensation to the individual survivors.[5]

Yet, in an effort to deny state responsibility, some Japanese—including veteran politicians and cabinet ministers—have intermittently asserted that the "comfort women" were licensed prostitutes engaged in commercial transaction. In response, the Korean media have routinely labeled such Japanese assertions as "absurd remarks" (mangŏn). A prominent exercise in the Japan–Korea political ping-pong on the "comfort women" issue took place on the eve of the summit meeting between the Japanese prime minister, Hashimoto Ryutaro, and the Korean president, Kim Yong Sam, in January 1997, when the chief secretary of the Cabinet, Kajiyama Seiroku, mentioned the need to consider the social background of licensed prostitution in prewar Japan in understanding the "comfort women" issue.

In contrast to the portrayal of the "comfort women" as "public prostitutes" by many conservative Japanese, human rights activists and feminist organizations in Japan, Korea, and elsewhere have, since the June

1993 UN Human Rights Conference in Vienna, consistently represented the "comfort women" as "sex slaves" conscripted by the Japanese military and the government during World War II.

So, who were the "comfort women"? Were they prostitutes engaged in "business," selling their sexual services to earn money? Or were they wartime victims of state and military power, who were forcibly recruited and were subjected to the daily routine of sexual slavery and gendered violence? What is the truth about the Japanese institution of military "comfort women"? Why was the case not dealt with at the end of World War II? These are some basic questions that must be addressed for a fair resolution of the "comfort women" redress movement. In this chapter, I suggest that the categorical representations of "comfort women" as either prostitutes or sex slaves are only partial truths, deriving from the political interests and the ethical stances of the opposing camps—namely, the Japanese state denying its legal responsibility for the survivors and the human rights activists and the nongovernmental organizations in Japan, Korea, and elsewhere demanding Japan's formal apology and compensation to the survivors.

As a historical reality, the issue is complex, and there is more than one side to the identity of the "comfort women," as reflected in the variety of the names used to refer to them. This chapter focuses on the perspectives of the three principal groups—namely, the state, the troops, and the activists—as the main participatory or contesting social entities in the "comfort women" issue. As the provisioning agency, as the consumers, and as the contestants, respectively, the state, the troops, and the activists all have exercised the power to name and thereby to represent categorically the innumerable "comfort women," while most of the so-called "comfort women" will remain forever nameless and voiceless.

An important implication of the multiple symbolic representations of the "comfort women"—as reflected in the various terms used to refer to them, such as *ianfu*, the "*p*," and sex slaves—is the powerful role of the ideologies in defining the identity of the "comfort women." I refer to the ideological perspectives of the three principals in the "comfort women" controversy as "patriarchal fascism," "masculinist sexism," and "feminist humanitarianism." These abstract concepts combine to provide the basic framework for us to understand the multiple, partial, and competing representations of the historical institution of the "comfort women" and the politics of the transnational redress movement. The contending representations of the "comfort women" as prostitutes versus sex slaves also underline the multiplicity and variability of "the truth" of controversial historical institutions such as the "comfort system."

This chapter draws on an ongoing project on the "comfort women" issue. A major objective of this research project on the "comfort women" is to present a balanced picture of the complex issue. As an anthropologist, I am committed to cultural relativism as a heuristic tool in order to understand human behaviors from the insider's perspectives and, at the same time, as a woman, I support the international feminist movement to engender the concept of women's rights as human rights, so as to help improve women's security in war and peace.

The Politics of Representing the Military "Comfort Women"

An English translation of Japanese officialese *jugun ianfu* (military "comfort women"), the term "comfort women" categorically refers to women of various ethnic and national backgrounds and social circumstances who became sexual laborers for the Japanese troops before and during World War II. The issues involved in the "comfort women" case are complex, running the gamut from the problem of "militarized prostitution" to that of sexual slavery based on gender, age, class, and ethnicity. The coerced sexual labor—that is, sexual slavery—was inflicted primarily on lower-class young females of colonial Korea by Imperial Japan during the Pacific War,[6] but not every former "comfort woman" had been forcibly drafted. In addition, while women from colonized Korea constituted the overwhelming majority, Japanese women and women of other occupied territories (such as Taiwan, the Philippines, Indonesia, Burma, and Thailand) were also used as "comfort women" during the fifteen-year war of aggression Imperial Japan pursued, starting from the Manchurian invasion in 1931 to Japan's unconditional surrender in 1945. There is no way to determine precisely how many women were forced to serve as military "comfort women." The estimates range between fifty thousand and two hundred thousand.[7] Some believe that over 80 percent of them were Korean.[8]

As indicated above, a major source of disagreement that has put the Japanese government and the feminist human rights activists at loggerheads in the precedent-setting international debate on women's human rights is the interpretation of the institution of the "comfort women." Therefore, it is important to understand the symbolisms involved in the politics of representing the military "comfort women," by analyzing the various terms that the three disparate interest groups have used to refer to these women. And in the process, we will consider the sociohistorical, cultural, and political contexts in which the hegemony of the patriarchal orthodox heterosexuality and the underlying subtexts of a sexual double standard for males and females have been enshrined for centuries, and against which the revolutionary concept of women's human rights has been launched in the transnational feminist alliance for more egalitarian gender power relations worldwide.

Patriarchal Fascism and the Provision of the "Imperial Gifts"

Fascism, according to *Webster's Dictionary*, is defined as a political philosophy, movement, or regime that exalts nation and often race above the individual and that stands for a centralized autocratic government headed by a dictatorial leader, severe economic and social regimentation, and forcible suppression of opposition. I use the concept of "patriarchal fascism" to add the dimension of the underlying ideology of male superiority to the ideological perspectives of the fascist regime of wartime Japan. Imperial Japan, which was rooted in the Confucian patriarchal tradition, began actively to promote ultranationalism by molding the indigenous folk-belief system of Shinto as the national religion and coaxing absolute loyalty of its subjects to the emperor as a living god.[9] The emperor system and the elevation of Shinto as the national religion served as the unquestionable ideological sources of popular support for the expansionist militarism and legitimacy for the mobilization of the populace for wartime fascist projects.

When Japan began an active program of assimilation policy for colonized Koreans in 1937, for instance, the agenda included reciting the "Pledge of the Imperial Subjects," hoisting the Japanese national flag, worshipping the emperor, and attending Shinto ceremonies. Further assimilation policies followed, requiring the changing of Korean names into Japanese ones and creating a new national identity for the colonized Koreans. In 1939, the Japanese government enforced the all-out systematic mobilization of Koreans of both sexes for war efforts. They sent Korean laborers to Japan, Sakhalin, and many other parts of Asia.[10] As the Sino–Japanese War escalated into the Pacific War in 1941, the drafting of Korean men and women as laborers and "comfort women" became more organized and compulsory.

There is no denying that the fact Korea was under Japanese colonial rule (1910–1945) facilitated the conscription of the great majority of "comfort women" from Korea. However, the social fact that Korean sexual mores strictly prescribed young females to maintain their virginity until marriage made colonial Korea a desirable pool for Imperial Japan to mobilize young females as "comfort women." The Japanese rationale for the "comfort system" was to enhance the morale of the military engaged in the Sino–Japanese War by providing amenities for recreational activities. One may argue, from the perspectives of the fascist state of Imperial Japan, that the system of "comfort women" was an institutionalization of paternalistic *omoiyari* (consideration) to reward the emperor's warriors with a regulated liberation from their battlefield duties, so that they may enjoy brief moments of rest and recuperation.

The establishment of military "comfort stations" (*ianjo*, where the Japanese troops could engage in recreational sex under the supervisory control of the state) came into being by early 1932, in China at least, in order to take care of the soldiers stationed in Shanghai after the Manchurian Incident started the Sino–Japanese War in the previous year.[11] The authorities believed such facilities for the regularized provision of recreational sex would help prevent soldiers from committing random acts of sexual violence toward women of occupied territories, which became a real concern after the infamous Nanking (a.k.a. Nanjing) Massacre in 1937. Besides its reputation, the military authorities were also concerned with the health of the troops, which prompted their close supervision of the hygienic conditions in the "comfort stations" in order to help keep sexually transmitted diseases under control.

In 1938, when Aso Tetsuo, an army doctor of the Shanghai Expeditionary Force, conducted a physical examination of Korean and Japanese women to be dispatched to an army "comfort station," he found that many of these Japanese women were older and had the problem of spreading venereal diseases because of their prior occupational history as prostitutes. In contrast, the Korean women he examined were young and had been virgins before their mobilization, and thus free from venereal disease. He then suggested that unmarried Korean women would be more appropriate than Japanese prostitutes as "gifts for the Imperial warriors."[12] One may note here that in the psychology of gift-giving, the gift receivers are obligated to return the favor of the gift, which, in this case, means that the soldiers become obligated to return the imperial favor by doing their best to win the war.

Between 1932 and 1945, the "comfort stations" existed in close physical proximity to the Japanese troops not only in Japan, Korea, and China, but across the expanding Japanese Empire—in the Philippines, Indonesia, Singapore, Burma, and the various islands in the Pacific.[13] Gradually, the "comfort women" became essential supplies for the military, in order to help keep their morale high. In fact, when the "comfort women" were transported on the military ships, they were simply listed as "military supplies" with no records of their personal identities.

The patriarchal fascism of wartime Japan, which helped spawn the systematic exploitation of non-Japanese women's sexuality for their troops, is well-illustrated in the manner in which the army maintained and supervised the military "comfort stations" in various places at the front. The "regulations on the soldiers' club," for instance, stipulated, among other things, that designated army doctors make a regular physical examination of service women and report the results, and that the soldiers and civil employees of the army be prohibited from using the local entertaining places. In addition, supplementary provisions of the regulations stipulated that military "comfort women" be regarded as common properties of the soldiers.[14] Korean "comfort women," for their part, as imperial subjects were instructed to exhort their Japanese visitors to devote themselves to the country selflessly. However, even though these Korean women were engaged in the same "patriotic" service to Imperial Japan, ethnicity was a source of further social discrimination against them. For instance, in Okinawa, Korean "comfort women" were used by enlisted men, while Okinawans were reserved for officers. Furthermore, Okinawan women as Japanese nationals were remunerated for their "services," while Korean women as colonial subjects were unpaid for the same sexual services. Although the local people in Okinawa were cruelly mistreated by mainland soldiers, Okinawans themselves in turn were contemptuous of Koreans for being colonial subjects.[15]

With regard to Japan's mobilization of young females to support the war efforts, the draft of Korean women was made legally possible by 1942. However, their recruitment was nominally carried out on the basis of "voluntary" participation into *Teishintai* (*Chŏngsindae* in Korean), the "Volunteer" Labor Corps.[16] Remarkably, *Teishintai* literally means the "Voluntarily submitting-body" (*teishin*) Corps (*-tai*). From the patriarchal fascist state perspective, Korean women, as colonial subjects of Imperial Japan, were performing their patriotic, gendered labor by letting their young sexually inexperienced bodies free of venereal dis-

eases be available as the "imperial gifts" to the soldiers, thereby help-
ing them satisfy their "sexual needs." However, the testimonies given
by Korean survivors indicate that many of them were deceived by the
enterprising middlemen—both Korean and Japanese—to believe that
they were going to work at a factory or hospital. Others stated that
they were forcibly taken by the police and/or the military into the "comfort stations."[17]

Once at the "comfort station," non-Japanese "comfort women" were
either given a Japanese first name by the management or commanded to
adopt one. Jan Ruff-O'Herne, a white Dutch survivor, states that her
first name was changed to a Japanese name of a flower.[18] The forced
personal name change is another expression of the patriarchal fascism
of the Japanese state and the military that put the psycholinguistic comfort of their soldiers over the integrity of the personhood of the non-
Japanese women. One may suggest that the name change was a symbolic
wrapping of non-Japanese "comfort women" with a culturally appropriate label suitable as an imperial gift to the troops.

In addition to the term *ianfu*, the state and the military of wartime
Japan seem to have used some other terms to refer to the "comfort
women," such as "waitress" (*shakufu*) and "special" (*tokushu*) *ianfu*.[19]
In fact, the Japanese officialese, *jugun ianfu*, seems to have originated
with Senda Kako, a journalist who published a book titled *Jugun Ianfu*.
The phrase is translated into English as "military comfort women." Yet
the term *jugun* (*chonggun* in Korean) has the connotation of "following" (*ju* in Japanese, *chong* in Korean) the military (*gun*) due to the
nature of one's occupation—such as nurse, journalist, or photographer—
and thus gives the mistaken impression of the "comfort women" as voluntary camp followers. In reality, some "comfort women" who served
frontline soldiers in remote battlefields were indeed forced to follow the
move of the military units, but those who labored in settled and/or urban
areas such as Shanghai had no need to follow the troops.

It should further be noted that the Chinese character for *ju* in *jugun*
also connotes "obedience." Thus, from the patriarchal fascist perspective, *jugun ianfu* in conjunction with *Teishintai* (the "Volunteer" Labor
Corps), in effect, signified metalinguistically an additional dimension
of obedience (to the nation-state), to be appended to the traditional Confucian edict of Triple Obedience for the female—that is, obedience to
the father as a daughter, obedience to the husband as a wife, and obedience to the son as an old widow.

Notably, the South Korean official term for the "comfort women," as used in the Government Interim Report of July 1992, is *ilcheha kundae wianbu* ("military 'comfort women' under Imperial Japan"). Although both *kundae wianbu* and *chonggun wianbu* are translated as "military comfort women" in English, *kundae* simply refers to the military without the connotation of following the military. Also, since the word *wianbu* has been used by the media in contemporary Korea to refer to sex workers—especially those working in the U.S. military camp towns in Korea—as well, the South Korean official phrase *ilcheha kundae wianbu* specifies the "comfort women" of Imperial Japan.

Masculinist Sexism and the Consumption of the "P"

While the Japanese officials may have coined the phrase "comfort women" to refer to sex laborers euphemistically, the soldiers themselves used crude terms that reflected their masculinist sexism toward the females with whom they had sex. (I use the term "masculinist" to refer to those men and women who believe that men's sexual needs are biological and consequently concede to men their "natural" right to recreational sex with females.) The graphically objectifying phrase "public toilet," and a jargon term "*p*" that the soldiers used to refer to "comfort women," symbolically revealed their dehumanization and objectification of women as sex objects.

The use of the phrase "public toilet" (*kyodo benjo*) to refer to "comfort women" originates with Dr. Aso Tetsuo,[20] who not only conducted physical examinations of the "comfort women" (as mentioned above), but also drafted the rules and regulations for the "comfort stations." Aso wrote, among other things, that "the special military comfort station should not become a place of hedonistic pleasure because it ought to be a hygienic public toilet."[21] The doctor's conception of the "comfort station" as a public toilet epitomizes a phallocentric essentialist perspective on male sexuality. For him and other masculinists, the "comfort women" were the receptacles of their sexual energy. What should be noted here is that this particular expression of masculinist sexism toward females presumes upon male superiority and privilege and that it was not limited to the wartime military. Up until the 1970s, even male college students in Japan used the word "toilet" to refer to the females with whom they had recreational sex.[22]

The "*p*" is a Chinese term meaning goods or articles, which, as a jargon, stood for female genitals.[23] The Chinese jargon phrase, *p-mai* (*p*-purchase), underlined the objectification and commodification of the sexuality of "comfort women." Conscious of ethnic differences among "comfort women," the soldiers would also identify the ethnicity of the "comfort women" by referring to them, for example, as a "Korean *p*" or a "Chinese *p*."[24] In the case of Korean "comfort women," the Japanese soldiers had two versions of the phrase, the "'*Sen p*" and the "*Chosen p.*" The '*Sen* was a derogatory term for *Chosen* (Korea).

According to a Japanese former soldier and a medical doctor whom I interviewed in Tokyo, the great majority of the soldiers felt no compunction in regarding the non-Japanese "comfort women" as sex objects and in exercising violence against them to release their tension. The elderly doctor stated during our interview in June 1997 that only those very few who developed close, friendly relations with non-Japanese "comfort women" would treat them with respect and compassion as fellow human beings. And the testimonies of the survivors amply support his statement about both the prevalence of abuse and the existence of intimate relationships of affectionate care.[25]

Since Japan had a state-regulated system of licensed prostitution until 1957, one could surmise why both the state and the society in general must have perceived the system of "comfort women" as nothing more than a special extension for the troops of the commercial service available to other Japanese men, so that the soldiers could enact their masculinist sexual rights. In the traditional masculinist sexual mores of Japan and Korea, having recreational sex outside matrimony was one of the unchallenged prerogatives of the husband. The Japanese Criminal Code of 1908, for example, punished wives for committing adultery, but philandering husbands were not penalized unless their partner was someone else's wife.[26] In contrast, the wife was expected to be chaste, even after the death of her husband. Despite much improvement in women's status through legal reforms enacted throughout the twentieth century, the asymmetrical power relationship between the two sexes still prevails in contemporary Korea and Japan (as it does elsewhere).

In this patriarchal social context, the unequal subtexts of gendered lives are poignantly underlined in the patterns of postwar personal lives of many former "comfort women" in comparison with those of former soldiers. The survivors tried their best to conceal their wartime lives as "comfort women" from their families and friends. Many of them suffered from low self-esteem, abiding psychological trauma over the loss of their virginity, and bodily pains from physical injuries and/or sexual abuses. And many of the survivors have been unable to lead a normal family life.

One of my informants said that she had to leave her home when her mother, without knowing about the daughter's past, tried to arrange a marriage for her. She has never married. Now, consider the case of Kim Hak-sun (a.k.a. Kim Hak Soon), whose 1991 public testimony as a former "comfort woman" provided a turning point in the Korean women's movement for redress. She was married to a Korean man who helped her escape from a "comfort station" in China. However, she had to suffer the hurt and indignity of being debased by her own husband who, when drunk, would abuse her in front of her son by calling her names for having been a "dirty" bitch who prostituted for the soldiers. Since her husband's accidental death in the 1950s, she has remained single. In contrast, the former soldiers and officers who had sex with "comfort women" had no problem reintegrating into their families and/or marital lives after the war ended. Some even wrote about their sexual experiences with women of varied ethnic backgrounds in their memoirs on wartime experiences.

Feminist Humanitarianism and the Redress for Military Sex Slaves

In the context of the masculinist sexual cultures under the patriarchal states of Japan, Korea, and many other countries, it is not surprising that the official silence over the "comfort women" issue had been maintained for more than four decades after the war ended in 1945. In Korea, perhaps the historical fact that an indigenous institution of professional female entertainers (*kisaeng*) existed in dynastic Korea may have helped many Koreans to accept the system of "comfort women" as a fact of life. It is interesting to note that one of the arguments against abolishing the institution of *kisaeng* was that they were necessary to "entertain" the soldiers stationed in the northern borderline of the Choson Dynasty (1392–1910).[27]

In 1990s Korea, however, the feminist movement for redress, backed by the concept of women's rights as human rights, has redefined the issue of "comfort women" as that of military sexual slavery endorsed by the state and the military of Imperial Japan. The idea that human rights include a woman's right to her bodily integrity was a revolutionary cornerstone of the feminist humanitarianism of the late twentieth century. In comparison to the Geneva Conventions, which characterize rape as a crime against the honor and dignity of women, feminists have argued that rape is a crime of violence against women's bodies, autonomy, and integrity, comparable to other cruel and inhuman treatment.[28] From the perspectives of feminist humanitarianism, sexual violence against women is a violation of human rights, and rape by the military in wartime, a war crime.

In Korea, Yun Chŏng-ok (a.k.a. Yun Chung Ok) was the first academic to raise the "comfort women" issue publicly, at an international conference dealing with sex tourism in 1988. The so-called *kisaeng* tours became enormously popular among predominantly Japanese male visitors to Korea from the late 1960s onward. The commercially organized *kisaeng* tours, in fact, became a source of easy money for young Korean females and of valuable foreign currency for their nation. At any rate, Yun's paper helped the conference participants confront Japan's wartime legacy of exploiting primarily non-Japanese female sexuality through the "comfort women" system. For many participants, meeting with Professor Yun was their "first encounter" with the "comfort women" issue.[29] As a way of dealing with the Japanese men's exploitation of Korean female sexuality, leaders of women's organizations in Korea and Japan demanded of their governments that the issues of the forced labor of the "comfort women" as members of the "Volunteer" Labor Corps be investigated and that the victims be compensated. The efforts of women's leaders languished, however, mired by the bureaucratic walls of evasion and the masculinist indifference of the masses in both countries until 1992, when the activists appealed to UNCHR.

It is worth noting here that Chŏngsindae Munje Taech'aek Hyŏpuihoe, the Korean name of the Korean Council (commonly referred to by its acronym, Chŏngdaehyop), uses the term *Chŏngsindae* (Volunteer Labor Corps), and not *wianbu* ("comfort women"). This particular naming of the organization reflects the generalized Korean perception to identify the members of Chŏngsindae as "comfort women," despite the fact that some members of Chŏngsindae performed only manual labor and no sexual labor. One might suggest that the Korean practice of using the term *Chŏngsindae* to refer to "comfort women" is a considerate euphemism to avoid the negative symbolism evoked by the word *wianbu*. One might also suggest that it is a political strategy to highlight the deceptive and/or coercive methods that had been used in the recruitment of "comfort women" in colonial Korea.

Initially, the English name of the Chŏngdaehyŏp was the Korean Council for Women Drafted for Sexual Service by Japan—as shown in Co-Representative Lee Hyo-Chae's letter of 4 March 1992 to the United Nations Human Rights Commissioner. It contained the phrase "sexual service," and not "sexual slavery." The paradigmatic shift in viewing the "comfort women" case as an instance of military sexual slavery came after the series of the 1992 UNCHR hearings mentioned earlier, and the 1993 UN World Conference on Human Rights in Vienna.

Slavery may be defined as an extreme form of the human relation of domination, and it can be conceived both as a personal relation and as an institutional process.[30] Sexual slavery may be defined as a relation of domination based on sex. Following Kathleen Barry,[31] female sexual slavery is present in a social condition of sexual exploitation and violence from which a woman or a girl cannot get out. Testimonies of the majority of the survivors reveal that they were forced into a condition of sexual slavery and could not escape. One must point out, however, the categorical definition of "comfort women" as sex slaves ignores the historical reality of commercial sex in which some "comfort women" participated.

While the feminist humanitarian representation of "comfort women" as military sex slaves has finally thrown light on their abject victimization, I should caution that the categorical representation of "comfort women" as sex slaves denies—however unintentionally—the remarkable human agency exercised by some of the "comfort women" against gendered oppression in their adverse social conditions. The life stories of some survivors clearly reveal their independent spirit and risk-taking actions in search of a better life, which unfortunately led them to the "comfort stations," but at the same time, which perhaps also contributed to their survival of the ordeal against many odds. If we adopt the Foucauldian conception of power as "a stream of energy flowing through every living organism and every human society, its formless flux harnessed in various patterns of behavior,"[32] it is not difficult to concede that not all "comfort women" were powerless victims. Instead of presenting the survivors only as helpless victims, we should also recognize the powerful human agency and their personal strength in overcoming the hardships of their life both during and after the war.

Prostitution and Female Sexual Slavery

At the core of the contestation over the representation of the military "comfort women" is the issue of state responsibility. On a deeper level, however, many of the central issues around sexual violence in warfare and its relationship to the cultural constructions of gender and human sexuality—more specifically heterosexuality—in both Korean and Japanese patriarchies, are being called into question. Indeed, the issues involved in the "comfort women" problem are complex, ranging from the masculinist sexual culture in patriarchal societies and the perennial question concerning the proper relationship between prostitution and the state to colonial exploitation, class inequality, and ethnic discrimination in the unprecedented abuse of power by the state in forcing tens of thousands of women, including premenarche teenage girls and young married women, into sexual slavery during the war.

Systematic provision by the military for the sexual needs of the soldiers is not unknown and may be understood as a paternalistic practice rooted in the masculinist view of female sexuality as a commodity, which is prevalent in the customs of patriarchal societies. Thus, it is not surprising to learn that the British military authorities, for example, officially regularized the provision of Indian women as prostitutes to serve British soldiers in Bombay from 1793 to 1905. The colonial administration in Indonesia also regulated prostitution for the Netherlands Indies Army from the mid-1890s to about 1913.[33] The Rest & Recuperation (R & R) program for the U.S. soldiers during the Vietnam War was a more recent example of the military institution looking after the physical needs of male soldiers.[34]

However, what is unprecedented about the system of "comfort women" for the Japanese military is not that it provided regulated prostitution for the soldiers, but that, during its more than a decade-long existence, it evolved into a system of female sexual slavery, using mostly colonial subjects drafted coercively by the state power and shipped even to the front lines in remote foreign lands. When the war ended, Japanese soldiers informed *Japanese* "comfort women" of Japan's defeat and fled with them. In contrast, Korean "comfort women" were either simply deserted or, in some extreme cases, they were killed by the retreating Japanese army that drove the women into trenches or caves and bombed, burned, or opened fire on the women, creating mass graves on the spot.[35] The massacre of Korean "comfort women" at the end of the war by the Japanese military may have reflected the military's fear of the revelation of their atrocities. One may also suggest that it was rooted in the generalized disdainful, ethnocentric attitude of the Japanese toward Korean "comfort women." As Japan's colonial subjects and "comfort women," they had been reduced to expendable military supplies, too cumbersome to be taken along at the end of the war.

In short, the "comfort system" evolved into something qualitatively different from the officially regulated prostitution, as mentioned above in the cases of the British and Dutch military. Prostitution, by definition, includes the payment for sexual union,[36] while slavery carries the notion of the social outcast, of property, and of compulsory labor.[37] The majority of Korean survivors testified that they were *not* paid for their sexual services to the Japanese soldiers. Testimonies of the Chinese, Dutch, and Filipina survivors prove that in addition to colonial Koreans and Taiwanese, many of the women in occupied territories were also forced into compulsory sexual labor, were regarded as the common property of the soldiers, and were despised as sex objects. For many "comfort women" who suffered gross violations of human rights, their lives as "comfort women" can only be described as sexual slavery.

Conclusion

The three basic ideologies I have discussed above reflect, in essence, the statist, masculinist, and feminist positions in the conceptualization of the institution of the military "comfort women" and the representation of the "comfort women." The statist perspective of Imperial Japan, which was rooted in patriarchal fascism, conceived of the "comfort system" as a systematic provision of "imperial gifts" to the troops to enhance their morale. The masculinist perspective of the troops, which was derived from their patriarchal sexist culture, regarded the "comfort women" as sex objects to be purchased for men's recreational activity. The feminist perspective of the activists is backed by the concept of women's rights as human rights and conceives of the "comfort system" as military sexual slavery enforced by state power, resulting in gross violations of women's human rights. These different conceptions of the "comfort system" are directly reflected in the symbolic representations of the women who labored as sex workers for the military as the "comfort women," the "*p*," and the "sex slaves."

The boundaries of these perspectives, however, are permeable. The patriarchal fascism of Imperial Japan, for example, encompassed masculinist sexism. That is, both the wartime and contemporary statist perspectives, as well as the generalized masculinist perspectives of the military and civilians, all share a common understanding of the ultimate function of the "comfort system" as recreational sexual amenities for the troops. Further, the masculinist representation of the "comfort women" as prostitutes does not necessarily preclude humanitarian recognition and/or sympathy toward the slaverylike conditions in which many of these women were placed. Feminist humanitarianism, however, rejects acknowledging either the sociohistorical, sexual cultural contexts of the "comfort system" or the varying situations and life experiences of individual "comfort women." In the politics of the redress movement and the compensation issue, fuzzy boundaries between ideologically based, multiple symbolic representations have solidified into dichotomous monoliths of prostitutes versus sex slaves to strengthen the positions of the particular interest groups.

In Japan, it was the feminist humanitarian perspective that dominated the activist groups until the latest history textbook controversy erupted in 1996. Now the conservative nationalist forces are countering the feminist humanitarian activist groups under masculinist rhetoric, by asserting that wartime "comfort women" were nothing more than licensed prostitutes and that the mention of the "comfort women" issue in history textbooks for junior high school students should be eliminated. Some of them are members of the Society for Making New Textbooks that will teach the young Japanese from a "liberalist" perspective, so that they may be proud of their national identity.[38]

In Korea, it was the feminist humanitarian perspective that helped break the long silence about the "comfort women" issue. Their persistent activism has changed the nature of the "comfort women" issue from a bilateral dispute to a universal human rights issue. Their dealings with the Japanese government and dissenting voices among the survivors, however, appear to have been swayed by self-righteous nationalism, rather than pragmatic humanitarianism.[39] Despite their spectacular success in internationalizing the issue, their political power and social influence within Korea is limited, as judged by the amount of funds the group could raise in Korea.[40] Out of national pride, some objected to demanding monetary compensation from Japan over the "comfort women" issue, and the silent majority appears to be steeped in the masculinist sexual culture.

The resolution of the redress movement appears to hinge much on the definition of the "comfort women" as either prostitutes or sex slaves, because of the importance of its symbolism for Japan's national identity and for the social meaning of the sufferings endured by the survivors. I note here that the subtitle of George Hicks's book, *The Comfort Women*, has two versions: The Australian edition contains the phrase "sex slaves," while the American edition contains the phrase "enforced prostitution." As I indicated in my review of the book,[41] the different subtitles might reflect the author's shifting or ambivalent positions in his definition of the "comfort women" (although they might simply indicate the publishers' marketing strategies). The issues raised by the "comfort women" movement, such as sexual exploitation and violence against women in wartime, will continue to haunt humanity as long as nations cling to ethnocentric nationalism, and as long as patriarchal societies continue to maintain a masculinist sexual culture in gender relations. We need to go beyond national and gendered boundaries to achieve the goals of feminist humanitarianism.

Notes

1. Etsuro Totsuka, "Chonggun Wianbu, Kangje Yŏnhaeng Munje wa U.N.," in *Chŏngsindae Charyŏjip IV* (Seoul: Chŏngdaehyŏp, 1993), pp. 69–76.
2. U.N. Doc.E/CN.4/Sub.2/1993/8, p. 12.
3. Totsuka, "Chonggun," p. 71.
4. U.N. Doc.E/CN.4/1995/41, paras. 286–292; E/CN.4/1996/53/Add.1.
5. U.N. Doc.E/CN.4/Sub.2/1998/L.26.
6. Since many Asians, including Koreans and Japanese, refer to the Second World War fought in the Asian and Pacific theaters as the Pacific War, I follow the common usage in this chapter.
7. Yoshiaki Yoshimi, *Jugunianfu* (Military "comfort women") (Tokyo: Iwanami Shoten, 1995).
8. Il Myon Kim, *Tenno no Guntai to Chosenjin Ianfu* (The emperor's forces and Korean "comfort women") (Tokyo: San'ichi Shobo, 1976).
9. Sheldon Garon, *Molding Japanese Minds: The State in Everyday Life* (Princeton, NJ: Princeton University Press, 1997).
10. The existence of sizable Korean communities in China, the former Soviet Union, and Japan is a vivid legacy of the Japanese colonial rule.
11. Yoshiaki Yoshimi, *Jugun Ianfu Shiryoshu* (Collection of reference materials on military "comfort women") (Tokyo: Otsuki Shoten, n. d.).
12. Tetsuo Aso, *Shanghai yori Shanghai e* (From Shanghai to Shanghai) (Fukuoka: Sekifusha, 1993).
13. Yoshiaki Yoshimi, "Documenting the Truth: The Japanese Government and the 'Comfort Women' Issue" (paper presented at the annual meeting of the Association for Asian Studies, Boston, MA, March 1994).
14. Aso, *Shanghai yori Shanghai e*.
15. Chizuko Ueno, "Japan's Enduring Shame," in *Asahi Shimbun*. (Reported in *Korea Times*, Los Angeles edition, 17 March 1993.)
16. This is why the present-day Japanese government persistently denied until

1993 any coercion in the recruitment of Korean women into the Teishintai. The recruited women included professional sex workers, women who were deceptively coaxed by enterprising middlemen and sold to military brothels, and women and young girls who were forcibly drafted into the Chŏngsindae by the agents of the state to be sent to "comfort stations."

17. Chŏngsindae Yŏn'guhoe and Chŏngdaehyŏp, eds., *Kangje-ro Kkŭllyŏgan Chosŏnin Kunwianpudŭl* (Forcibly recruited Korean military "comfort women") (Seoul: Hanul, 1993), p. 17.

18. Jan Ruff-O'Herne, *50 Years of Silence* (Sydney, Australia: ETT Imprint, 1994).

19. Yoshiaki Yoshimi and Hirohumi Hayashi, *Kyodo Kenkyu Nihongun Ianfu* (Japanese military "comfort women") (Tokyo: Otsuki Shoten, 1995), p. iv.

20. Rumiko Nishino, *Jugun Ianfu: Moto Heishitachi no Shogen* (Military "comfort women": Testimony of former soldiers) (Tokyo: Akashi Shoten, 1992).

21. Aso, *Shanghai yori Shanghai e*, p. 222 (my translation).

22. Chizuko Ueno, private communication, 31 March 1995.

23. Nishino, *Jugun Ianfu*, p. 46.

24. Nishino, *Jugan Ianfu*, passim.

25. See, for example, Keith Howard, ed., *True Stories of the Korean Comfort Women* (London: Cassell, 1995).

26. Sheldon Garon, "The World's Oldest Debate? Prostitution and the State in Imperial Japan, 1900–1945," *American Historical Review* 98, 3 (1993) : 722.

27. Sa-hun Chang, "Women Entertainers of the Yi Dynasty," in *Women of the Yi Dynasty*, ed. Park Young-hai. (Seoul: Research Center for Asian Women, Sookmyung Women's University, 1986), p. 261.

28. See Rhonda Copelon, "Gendered War Crimes: Reconceptualizing Rape in Time of War," in *Women's Rights, Human Rights: International Feminist Perspectives*, ed. Julie Peters and Andrea Wolper (New York: Routledge, 1995), pp. 197–215. I owe this reference to Margaret D. Stetz.

29. JAPA (Japan Anti-Prostitution Association), *Against Prostitution and Sexual Exploitation in Japan* (Tokyo: JAPA, 1995).

30. JAPA, 1995.

31. Orlando Patterson, *Slavery and Social Death: A Comparative Study* (Cambridge, MA: Harvard University Press, 1982).

32. James Miller, *The Passion of Michel Foucault* (New York: Simon & Schuster, 1993), p. 15.

33. Thanh-Dam Truong, *Sex, Money and Morality: Prostitution and Tourism in Southeast Asia* (London: Zed Books, 1990), p. 80.

34. Cynthia Enloe, *Bananas, Beaches & Bases: Making Feminist Sense of International Politics* (Berkeley: University of California Press, 1990); Cynthia Enloe, *The Morning After: Sexual Politics at the End of the Cold War* (Berkeley: University of California Press, 1993); Sandra P. Sturdevant and Brenda Stoltzfus, *Let the Good Times Roll: Prostitution and the U.S. Military in Asia* (New York: The New Press, 1992).

35. Chung-Ok Yun, "Jungshindae—Korean Military 'Comfort Women.'" Unpublished ms., n.d.

36. Truong, *Sex, Money and Morality*, p. 11.

37. James L. Watson, ed., *Asian and African Systems of Slavery* (Oxford: Blackwell, 1980).

38. Yoshifumi Tawara, *"Ianfu" Mondai to Kyokashokogeki* ("Comfort women" issue and textbook attack) (Tokyo: Kobunken, 1997).

39. See Chunghee Sarah Soh, "Human Rights and the 'Comfort Women,'" *Peace Review* 12, 1 (2000): 123–29; for an expanded and more comprehensive discussion of related subjects, also see Chunghee Sara Soh, "From Imperial Gifts to Sex Slaves: Theorizing Symbolic Representations of the 'Comfort Women,'" *Social Science Japan Journal* 3, 1 (2000): 59–76.

40. See Chunghee Sarah Soh, "Korean 'Comfort Women': Movement for Redress," *Asian Survey* 36, 12 (1997):1227–1240.

41. Chunghee Sarah Soh, review of *The Comfort Women: Japan's Brutal Regime of Enforced Prostitution in the Second World War*, by George Hicks, *Korea Journal* 37, 2 (1997):136–141.

Part II

Academic and Activist Responses

Chapter 5

Wartime Sexual Violence against Women

A Feminist Response

Margaret D. Stetz

There has always been sexual violence directed against women during war. Sometimes the acts of aggression and domination have been individual, and sometimes collective. Sometimes they have been spontaneous, but other times, they have been organized and officially sanctioned, especially when dealing with the procurement of women for sexual use by combatants.

To acknowledge this historical record will take us through many cultures and settings. It will lead us back to what George Hicks has identified as a prototype for the "comfort system" in the Roman Empire, when "Slavery ensured a regular supply of captive females for the military brothels which were attached to every Roman garrison or campaigning army."[1] With many examples along the way, especially from the British Empire's nineteenth-century expansion,[2] it will carry us to the turn of the twentieth century, to Elizabeth Salas's research on the Mexican Revolution; in that conflict, revolutionary forces and federal soldiers alike kidnapped and raped women, called them prostitutes, and compelled them to perform both sexual service and housekeeping at the front lines.[3] It will bring us to the early 1970s and to Susan Brownmiller's investigations into the abduction and gang rapes of women, both in Bangladesh, by Pakistani soldiers, and in Vietnam, by American soldiers.[4] It will, of course, send us to the testimony of the former inmates of the Bosnian rape camps collected by Alexandra Stiglmayer.[5] And it will force us to read the headlines of so late a date as 23 September 1996, when the *New York Times* surveyed the plight of thousands of women who, during the

Rwandan civil war, were "raped by individuals, gang-raped, raped with sharpened stakes and gun barrels and held in sexual slavery, sometimes alone, and sometimes in groups."[6] It will even lead us to the very threshold of the twenty-first century with the abductions and rapes by Serbian soldiers and police of ethnic Albanian women fleeing Kosovo in the spring of 1999.

The chronological record of wartime rape is long. So, too, is the history of how systematic sexual violence by invading or occupying military forces has been disguised as "prostitution," to mitigate atrocities by dismissing them as ordinary commerce. But only recently have there been feminist movements, activists, or scholars to expose these abuses and address these concerns. In the context of the subject of Asian "comfort women"—the question of some two hundred thousand women, roughly 80 percent of whom were Korean, forced to provide sexual service to the Japanese military before and during World War II—I want to ask, what difference has the presence of feminist analysis made, especially in Asia and the West, over the past twenty-five years? What stories have become visible because of it, and what changes in thought and action may now result? If, as many feminists have argued, rape is a "weapon" of war,[7] in what ways does feminism itself serve as a counter weapon?

I would like to propose that shared Asian and Western feminist perspectives not only have made it possible to confront the subject of wartime rape in new ways, but also to confront it at all. Through the concerted efforts of feminist academics and activists, rape has become a subject that can be spoken about, and the victims of rape themselves have become speaking subjects on the international stage. Because of feminist-initiated research, not only does the world know more about the so-called "comfort system" of World War II, but it also recognizes that this system has appeared in many forms, whenever and wherever military imperialism has combined with masculine privilege. Most recently, feminist pressure worldwide has resulted in a changed legal concept of rape as a war crime—a development that, for the first time ever, holds out hope for the prosecution and punishment by international tribunals of those who commit sexual violence, or who order it to occur.

When I speak of the work of feminists, of course, I am not referring to women alone, but to both female and male thinkers who put the critical examination of gender and its relationship to power at the center of their analyses. And by gender, I mean the dynamic through which human beings are constructed as masculine or feminine subjects within a given cultural and historical framework, then made to occupy unequal social roles.

Perhaps the chief service that feminist analysis has performed is in distinguishing what is customary and familiar from that which is biologically ordained and thus inevitable. In other words, feminism has made it possible to say that, although there has always been sexual violence against women during war, there is nothing normal or justifiable about it. As Ruth Seifert writes, "The most popular and effective myth is that rape has to do with an uncontrollable male drive that, insofar as it is not restrained by culture, has to run its course in a manner that is unfortunate, to be sure, but also unavoidable."[8] To counter such a myth, academic feminists have produced research demonstrating that "rape is not an aggressive manifestation of sexuality, but rather a sexual manifestation of aggression" and that such assaults, whether spontaneous or systematic, "are acts of extreme violence implemented by sexual means."[9]

When sexual violence against women is part of warfare, moreover, feminists have urged the world to look beyond individual perpetrators, to the culture, laws, military systems, and governments that license and encourage it. In the view, for instance, of Larry May and Robert Strikwerda, rape

> is something that men, as a group, are collectively responsible for, in a way which parallels the collective responsibility of a society for crimes against humanity perpetrated by some members of their society. Rape is indeed a crime against humanity, not merely a crime against a particular woman. . . . [And] men receive strong encouragement to rape from the way they are socialized as men.[10]

To understand that rape is not an inevitable "release" for male sexuality and that governments themselves acknowledge this, we have an interesting example before us. For a period of six months in 1996, two nations put male and female personnel together into a prolonged situation of unimaginable physical danger, stress, fear, loneliness, and absolute isolation—that is, aboard the space station *Mir*. Yet neither Russia nor the United States expected astronaut Shannon Lucid to be raped, nor was she. She was not raped because it had been made clear that rape was not being anticipated, permitted, or condoned, regardless of the extreme conditions and absence of other outlets, and that rape would have gone against the two nation's political interests. Therefore, when governments argue that men "need" sex with women, and that if women are not provided, rape is the unavoidable result, feminist analysis enables us to see that the argument conceals another agenda—that the government in question must, in fact, view a situation in which women are being violated, dominated, humiliated, and treated as chattel as serving its political interests. When it is not in the political interests of a government or of its military arm, then rape stops.

But feminists have not only provided new methods of looking at these questions; they have also demanded new sorts of listening. Around the globe, they have focused on the silencing of women, emphasized the importance of attending to women's speech, and uncovered its political implications. Through great struggle, they have created a climate in which it has been possible for surviving former "comfort women" to break their silence and politically impossible for governments to pretend not to hear them. In 1985, when Joan Ringelheim interviewed Jewish female concentration camp survivors who described being raped both by the SS and by male prisoners, such women still feared that their abuse represented a trivial, or merely personal misfortune. One survivor told Ringelheim "that it 'was not important . . . except to me.' She meant that it had no significance within the larger picture of the Holocaust."[11] Today, thanks to Asian and Western feminist agitation, no historian, government, or international tribunal can afford to treat the story of any individual "comfort woman" as lacking "significance within the larger picture."

In defiance of cultural norms, feminists have heeded and acted on the oral testimony of rape victims, a group often discredited by antifeminists. This has been a crucial development in making the plight of the "comfort women" known. As George Hicks noted in 1994, "The central evidence that coercion and deception were used by the Japanese military to recruit women for the comfort system comes, as this book has shown, from the women themselves. At the time of writing, there are no official documents to back up such evidence."[12] Feminists have asserted, too, that a woman's past sexual history does not invalidate a charge of rape—an important point for the testimony of some women (including some Japanese women) who worked in the sex trade, before being used in the "comfort system." Even prostitutes are raped, and when they are, the crimes against them, too, must be prosecuted.

Recently, prosecutions have become more likely, thanks to feminists such as Rhonda Copelon, who repeatedly criticized the old definitions of the Geneva Conventions, under which wartime rapes were "categorized as crimes against honor, not as crimes of violence comparable to murder, mutilation, cruel and inhuman treatment and torture," and thus not deserving separate legal redress.[13] After a long struggle, feminist activism has succeeded in altering this way of thinking. The *New York Times* and other newspapers reported on 28 June 1996 that the UN's International Criminal Tribunal of the Hague broke precedent and, for the first time in any such court, indicted eight Bosnian Serb military and police officials for rape, treating it separately as a war crime in and of itself. On 9 March 1998, this development brought concrete results; Dragoljub Kunarac pleaded guilty to the charge of rape as a crime against humanity (although he later reversed his plea)—the very first such conviction by an international court, but surely the first of many in the future. More recently, in August 1999, a paramilitary leader named Radomir Kovac, a Bosnian Serb, was indicted by the International Criminal Tribunal for the Former Yugoslavia on charges of having run a military "brothel" in Foca, where Muslim women were imprisoned and repeatedly raped by Serbian soldiers, much as women were in Asian "comfort stations" during World War II. The interviewing of ethnic Albanian women by human rights workers in the Balkans, immediately following the war in Kosovo in the spring of 1999, will doubtless soon lead to the indictments of Serbian officials for that round of wartime rapes, too.

Feminist attention to the testimony of rape victims has also produced a new understanding of the physical and mental effects of rape—of why it must be seen as a weapon of destruction and suffering, both in wartime and in what we may choose to call peacetime. (And, of course, feminists have remarked upon the likeness between peace and war, if we consider the role that sexual violence or its imminence plays in women's daily lives around the world.) Moreover, feminist psychologists such as Laura S. Brown and Patricia A. Resick have been responsible for implementing new forms of therapy to treat the trauma of women recovering from war atrocities.[14]

Through feminist efforts, the stories of women raped during war are being broadcast globally, and are becoming the stuff of international legal action and of historical narratives, forcing the rewriting of war to highlight crimes based on gender. Susan Brownmiller warns of what happens when such feminist pressure is not exerted: "The plight of raped women as casualties of war is given credence only at the emotional moment when the side in danger of annihilation cries out for world attention. When the military histories are written . . . the stories are glossed over, discounted as exaggerations, deemed not serious enough for inclusion in scholarly works."[15]

But new sorts of histories are appearing, and Japanese feminists, in particular, deserve credit for bringing the gendered crimes of militarism, along with the plight of Asian "comfort women" of World War II, into the official Japanese story. I would single out, from among many, Tomiyama Taeko, the artist who has used both visual and verbal means to record the horrors of an imperialist past, and also Takazato Suzuyo, city councillor in Okinawa, who in the 1990s led investigations not only into the use of "comfort women" on Okinawa by Japanese soldiers, but also by American forces, after the island's invasion and capture. Matsui Yayori, a retired journalist who now heads a major Asian feminist organization, has been instrumental, as well, in leading protests against the censorship of Japanese war crimes in textbooks and in recording and disseminating interviews with the surviving former sex slaves of the Japanese military. Japanese feminists' determined resistance to further efforts at silencing has been unceasing, as has been their readiness to work together with Asian and Western women alike in networks of support. During December 2000, for instance, in her role as chairperson of the Violence against Women in War Network–Japan, Matsui Yayori helped to organize and to host the Women's International War Crimes Tribunal on Japan's Military Sexual Slavery, which was intended to bring representatives from women's groups from around the globe to Tokyo with the express purpose of documenting fully the crimes of the past, identifying the perpetrators, seeking their punishment, and making the Japanese government at last accept its legal responsibility toward the former "comfort women." In raising both domestic and international awareness, Miki Mutsuko—widow of Japan's former prime minister, Miki Takeo—has also been an important ally. Her championing of the cause of the survivors of military sex slavery has led her to denounce (perhaps most publicly at "The 'Comfort Women' of World War II: Legacy and Lessons," the conference on "comfort women" held at Georgetown University from 30 September to 4 October 1996) the Japanese government's efforts to avoid paying reparations by creating a so-called private fund for compensation.

Throughout Asia, academic and nonacademic feminists alike have united both within and across national boundaries to build coalitions around these issues. No clearer example of successful action and coalition-formation exists than in the Philippines. The Task Force on Filipino Comfort Women began in 1992 largely thanks to the initiatives of

Filipina feminist leaders such as Nelia Sancho and Indai Sajor. Soliciting the stories and participation of victims of the "comfort system," Sancho and Sajor brought to the fore "comfort women" such as Maria Rosa Henson (1928–1996), a remarkable woman who had survived not only a year of sexual slavery by the Japanese imperial forces, but postwar Philippine revolutionary struggles and government crackdowns that had resulted in the murder of members of her family. Until Henson's death, Filipina feminists worked with her in a variety of capacities, including the filing of a lawsuit in a Tokyo district court for financial redress from the Japanese government. Along with other members of the task force, moreover, Sancho and Sajor helped to record, preserve, and circulate Henson's important testimonial, which has recently been issued in English as *Comfort Woman: A Filipina's Story of Prostitution and Slavery under the Japanese Military* and which has given to the history of this subject a personal voice and a new immediacy for readers everywhere.[16]

Feminists have been linking internationally over the issue of sexual victimization. But even now, there are conservative movements in the United States that wish to frighten American feminists out of such alliances by demonizing the examination of oppression—demonizing even the use of that word—and by deriding the term "victim," along with any correlative analysis of what victimhood means or of the forces that produce this status.

Contrary to what their detractors have said, feminists know quite well that "woman" and "victim" are not identical and interchangeable terms. Victimhood is not the defining status of women, either as a class or as individuals. But ignoring the concept of victimization and failing to embrace the cause of those who have been victimized would be moral cowardice. American feminists must stand up to the new effort at silencing by certain antifeminist, right-wing forces and stand with their Asian counterparts. They must stand with the feminist scholars who have awakened the world to the plight of victims of wartime sexual violence, and they must stand with the survivors themselves.

The world has learned the stories of "comfort women" through the pioneering work of feminist academics such as Professor Yun Chung Ok of South Korea. She, in turn, has inspired a further generation of activist professors in South Korea, such as Professor Shin Heisoo of Hanil Presbyterian University, a prominent member of the organization called the Korean Council for the Women Drafted for Military Sexual

Slavery by Japan, as well as faculty at institutions of higher education in the Philippines, Australia, and elsewhere throughout the Pacific region. In Japan, the government has had to confront the subject of past war crimes, due to pressure not only from opposition politicians and journalists (and from important public figures such as Miki Mutsuko, who has used her access to political inner circles and to the media alike to great effect), but also from academics such as Professor Emerita Tsurumi Kazuko, who spoke out on NHK-TV, on the fiftieth anniversary of the end of World War II, about the need to uncover all the buried history and to take responsibility for it. These examples should encourage Western feminist academics to involve themselves in the world outside the academy—to appreciate the deep and essential connections between the history we unearth as scholars and the situation of women today, which our research can influence and change.

Yet there are growing numbers of organizations in the United States that are trying to sever this connection between scholarship and women's lives around the globe, insisting that universities must confine themselves to the study of classical texts, the works of Western thinkers, and the histories of great men. Using threats to cut off funding, these rightwing groups hope to discourage American academics from engaging in research or teaching that could be read as "political" and to send us back to the ivory tower. I would remind everyone that a tower made of ivory grows sinister, if we consider what ivory is, where it comes from, and how it is procured. It is all white; it is constructed out of the takings of imperial conquest and despoilation; it represents the valuing of the dead object over the living subject.

At the moment, former "comfort women" are still living subjects. For almost twenty years, they have been telling their stories again and again, and governments have begun to respond. Progress continues to occur in the quest for official apologies and reparations, although it will not come fast enough to benefit many of the survivors, who are now both old and ill. When the last witnesses are gone, historians must repeat their stories everywhere, and a new generation must listen. But it has been and will be the special responsibility of feminist scholars, both in Asia and the West, not merely to attend to these stories, but to study and teach them. For it is up to us, using the methods and philosophy developed through our scholarship, to elucidate and transmit the lessons of this legacy—a legacy that has also begun to inform the worlds of the visual arts, literature, theater, film, and video on both sides of the Pacific.

In her book *Rape Warfare*, Beverly Allen, a professor of women's studies, calls on her readers: "[Our] task ... is to aid the survivors, judge the perpetrators, and do anything else that will guard against such atrocity in the future. Thus shall we move toward new formulations of community and justice and peace."[17] But only if we move together can such a possibility be realized. Let that be our commitment, as feminists and as academics, and let that be our goal.

Notes

1. George Hicks, *The Comfort Women: Japan's Brutal Regime of Enforced Prostitution in the Second World War* (London and New York: W. W. Norton, 1994), p. 29.
2. Luise White, *The Comforts of Home: Prostitution in Colonial Nairobi* (Chicago: University of Chicago Press, 1990), p. 3.
3. Elizabeth Salas, *Soldaderas in the Mexican Military: Myth and History* (Austin: University of Texas Press, 1990), pp. 39–40.
4. Susan Brownmiller, "Making Female Bodies the Battlefield," in *Mass Rape: The War against Women in Bosnia-Herzegovina*, ed. Alexander Stiglmayer (Lincoln: University of Nebraska Press, 1994), pp. 180–182.
5. Alexandra Stiglmayer, "The Rapes in Bosnia-Herzegovina," in *Mass Rape: The War against Women in Bosnia-Herzegovina*, ed. Alexandra Stiglmayer (Lincoln: University of Nebraska Press, 1994), pp. 82–169.
6. James C. McKinley Jr., "Legacy of Rwanda Violence: The Thousands Born of Rape," *New York Times*, 23 Sept. 1996, sec. A, p. 3.
7. Melinda Lorenson, "No Woman Was Spared," *Ms.* (May/June 1996): 25.
8. Ruth Seifert, "War and Rape: A Preliminary Analysis," in *Mass Rape: The War against Women in Bosnia-Herzegovina*, ed. Alexandra Stiglmayer (Lincoln: University of Nebraska Press, 1994), p. 55.
9. Seifert, "War and Rape," p. 55.
10. Larry May and Robert Strikwerda, "Men in Groups: Collective Responsibility for Rape," in *Special Issue: Feminism and Peace*, ed. Karen J. Warren and Duane L. Cady, *Hypatia* 9 (spring 1994): 135–137.
11. Joan Ringelheim, "Women and the Holocaust: A Reconsideration of Research," in *SIGNS: Journal of Women in Culture and Society* 10 (summer 1985): 745.
12. Hicks, *Comfort Women*, p. 270.
13. Rhonda Copelon, "Gendered War Crimes: Reconceptualizing Rape in Time of War," in *Women's Rights, Human Rights: International Feminist Perspectives*, ed. Julie Peters and Andrea Wolper (New York: Routledge, 1995), p. 200.
14. See Laura S. Brown, "From Alienation to Connection: Feminist Therapy with Post-Traumatic Stress Disorder," pp. 13–26, and Patricia A. Resick, "Post-Traumatic Stress Disorder in a Vietnam Nurse: Behavioral Analysis of a Case Study," pp. 55–65, in *Another Silenced Trauma: Twelve Feminist Therapists and Activists Respond to One Woman's Recovery from War*, ed. Esther D. Rothblum and Ellen Cole (New York: Harrington Park Press, 1986).

15. Brownmiller, "Making Female Bodies the Battlefield," p. 182.

16. See Maria Rosa Henson, *Comfort Woman: A Filipina's Story of Prostitution and Slavery under the Japanese Military* (Lanham, MD: Rowman & Littlefield, 1999).

17. Beverly Allen, *Rape Warfare: The Hidden Genocide in Bosnia-Herzegovina and Croatia* (Minneapolis: University of Minnesota Press, 1996), p. 144.

Chapter 6

"Such an Unthinkable Thing"

Asian American Transnational Feminism and the "'Comfort Women' of World War II" Conference

Pamela Thoma

> Her words, coiled tightly in my script, tied her spirit to her body and bound her to this life. When they burned, they would travel with her across the waters, free.[1]

"The 'Comfort Women' of World War II: Legacy and Lessons" conference, held in 1996, is part of an Asian American feminism that both resists and constructs postmodernity.[2] Bringing together activists, academics, and cultural workers to analyze and discuss the structural causes of Japanese military sexual slavery, the conference not only illuminated the pervasive presence of multinational capitalism and how nation-states are implicated in it, but also responded to and intervened in multinational operations that attempt to control women, particularly in militarized and colonizing situations.[3] Though it explicitly participated in transnational feminist activism, the conference was more specifically indebted to Asian American transnational feminism.[4] In contrast to other women of color feminisms in the United States, Asian American feminisms, whether locally, nationally, or internationally organized, have often gone unrecognized and have been undertheorized by activists and scholars in the fields of Asian American studies and feminist studies alike.[5]

Although there are sometimes conscious and complex reasons for this paucity, which I will briefly address below, the conference offers an opportunity to recognize and analyze Asian American transnational feminist cultural production and its contribution to shaping postmodernity. By providing a forum for the presentation of Asian American cultural texts, the conference presents the politics of this feminism, but also constitutes an autobiographical text of Asian American transnational feminism. As an autobiography of the coalition politics of Asian American transnational feminism, the conference creates as well as critiques postmodernity by producing a text that establishes an alternative community to modernist nationalisms.[6]

Transnational Feminisms

Transnational feminisms are broadly defined as those various comparative forms of feminist practice and movement that oppose particular and global versions of economic and cultural hegemony and seek social change for women in different locations.[7] They are indebted to postmodernisms in their critique of modern nationalist, capitalist, and patriarchal projects, and to postcolonial studies in their critique of Western cultural imperialism and their emphasis on the contributions of postcolonial culture in the formation of a heterogeneous postmodernity. More specifically, transnational feminisms incorporate feminist and postmodern concepts of multiple subjectivity, which recognize the complex relationship between subjectivity and space, to investigate collaboratively the limitations of nationalist communities and to elaborate alternative communities. I consider the various practices and products of transnational feminism forms of resistance that specifically address the hegemonic policies of nation-states that promote and protect multinational capital for the growth of their economies. Or, as Inderpal Grewal and Caren Kaplan write in the introduction to their important volume *Scattered Hegemonies: Postmodernity and Transnational Feminist Practices*, transnational feminisms "articulate the relationship of gender to scattered hegemonies such as global economic structures, patriarchal nationalisms, 'authentic' forms of tradition, local structures of domination, and legal-juridical oppression on multiple levels" (p. 17). The collaborative nature of transnational feminisms works "to compare multiple, overlapping and discrete oppressions rather than to construct a theory of hegemonic oppression under a unified category of gender," which the authors contrast to the failed notion of "global feminism." Global feminism, as many critics have pointed out, "has elided the diversity of women's agency in favor of a universalized Western model of women's liberation that celebrates individuality and modernity."[8] Elsewhere, Kaplan writes that transnational feminism is "an anti-racist and anti-imperialist feminism":

[It] must articulate differences in power and location as accurately as possible. It must also find intersections and common ground; but they will not be utopian or necessarily comfortable alliances. New terms are needed to express the possibilities for links and affiliations, as well as differences among women who inhabit different locations.
      Transnational feminist activism is one possibility. I would argue that this mode of affiliation occurs in many academic and nonacademic contexts and that its histories and present existence often remain to be read.[9]

Transnational feminisms are recognizable by their coalitional, antinationalist, antiexploitative politics rather than by their association with a particular group of feminists defined by class, race, ethnicity, nationality, or some other monolithic category. At the same time, transnational feminist activism may be included on the agendas of groups or individuals who primarily identify themselves in ways other than as transnational feminists.

Asian American women participating in various organizations and alliances and producing cultural texts often demonstrate transnational feminist politics, but their work is frequently not recognized as either transnational or feminist, because (a) scholars simply overlook Asian American discourse, (b) some Asian American women do not want to identify with hegemonic feminism, and, perhaps most significantly, (c) there has been strong pressure to unify Asian American discourse. While the Asian American movement, combined with the other social protest movements of the 1960s and early 1970s, led to more public awareness of Asian Americans, the population of Asian Americans relative to other ethnic minorities often leads to their absence in research and scholarship, and hegemonic feminist studies are not an exception to this pattern of neglect and omission. It is also important to recognize that an insidious racial hierarchy persists, even in some of the most racially conscious feminist research; studies of African American women are sometimes mistakenly taken or presented as studies of all women of color or the "real" women of color in the United States, and Asian American women are considered "too close" to whites to be "authentic" female subjects of color. The disregard of Asian American contributions to transnational feminisms also comes, quite understandably, from within Asian American discourse.[10] As the editors of *Scattered Hegemonies* point out, "Many women who participate in decolonizing efforts both within and outside the United States have rejected the term 'feminism' in favor of 'womanist' or have defined their feminism through class or

race or ethnic, religious, or regional struggles."[11] Yet, advances in feminist theorizing have clarified gender oppression as one of several oppressions that can combine in various ways, and these advances have
been useful in understanding the different experiences of women.

Beyond resistance to or skepticism about hegemonic feminism, there
has been and is pressure to create and maintain a decidedly Asian American culture.[12] And while Asian American feminists certainly critiqued
in the Asian American movement the limitations of a cultural nationalism, which posited an American-born male of East Asian ancestry as its
authentic subject and creator of cultural tradition, they were often accused of disloyalty for doing so, and a newer incarnation of this tension
remains in Asian American discourse.[13] A possible example of how the
internal pressures to choose between ethnic and feminist alliances in
Asian American discourse are still negotiated is evident in two versions
of a recent essay entitled "Work, Immigration, Gender: Asian 'American' Women" by Lisa Lowe, who describes several narratives by Asian
American women as part of a linkage that is "crucial to Asian American
feminist and women of color politics" in the 1997 version appearing in
Making More Waves: New Writing by Asian American Women.[14] However, in the fuller 1996 version appearing in her influential book *Immigrant Acts: On Asian American Cultural Politics*, she refers to the
narratives under discussion as "Asian American cultural production."[15]
In both essays, Lowe analyzes these texts as "linked to an emergent
political formation, organizing across race, class, and national boundaries, that included other racialized and immigrant groups as well as
women working in, and immigrating from, the neocolonized world" and
as "belonging to a new mode of cultural practice that corresponds to the
new social formation of globalized capitalism."[16] But while Lowe cites
Grewal, Kaplan, Mohanty, and others who have identified such cultural
production as feminist, and while all of the texts Lowe discusses are
texts produced by women, she does not clearly designate the
transnationalism of Asian American women "feminist" in the version
appearing in her book. It is clear that Lowe wants to signify a new political collectivity, citing the "reconceptualization of the oppositional
narratives of nationalism, Marxism, and feminism," under globaliza-
tion, and it is also clear that Lowe does not want to reinstall a liberal
feminist narrative of emancipation (p. 165). But feminism has arguably
come a long way in recent years, and as Lowe acknowledges, U.S. feminists of color have developed "'situated' non-totalizing perspectives on

conjoined dominations, as well as the emergence of policitized critiques of those conjunctions."

I argue that in numerous types of cultural texts and practices produced by Asian American women, and in particular those presented and created at the "'Comfort Women' of World War II: Legacy and Lessons" conference, lie the opportunity to read and to understand collaborative and decidedly feminist practices useful in affecting the world-system of postmodernity. To not read them as transnational feminist texts is possibly to miss or misread their significant messages about alternative communities. Asian American feminists have a history of international activism that includes involvement in the antiwar movement and the ongoing relationship of established communities of Asian American women with Asian and Asian immigrant women who obviously have close connections to other nations and their political and social issues.[17] Recent activism and cultural production evidence, moreover, the transnationalism of contemporary Asian American feminism, and the "'Comfort Women' of World War II" conference is one of a rich array of such works.[18]

Autobiography and Transnational Feminist Cultural Production

"The 'Comfort Women' of World War II" conference is a text of Asian American transnational feminism. It involved the efforts of numerous differently affiliated women, it critiqued the imperialist and nationalist politics of the Japanese government that administered military sexual slavery as well as the multinational economics of governments that have instituted similar systems or refused to acknowledge the role of nation-states in the sexual assault of women, and it participated in creating a community or coalition of feminists who want to abolish such abuses of women in different locations. Providing a history of the coalition politics of Asian American transnational feminism around the "comfort women" issue, the conference is, more specifically, a cultural autobiography. It details the ways at least one transnational feminism operates, and an analysis of the autobiography of the "'Comfort Women' of World War II" conference is revealing. It should first be placed, however, in the context of a range of transnational feminist autobiographical texts to appreciate fully the various ways different women contribute to critiquing and constructing postmodernity. In her essay "Resisting Autobiography: Out-Law Genres and Transnational Feminist Subjects," Caren Kaplan considers certain forms of autobiography "out-law" genres, and begins the work of understanding the contributions of feminists in various locations whose writing challenges modernist concepts of individual subjectivity, patriarchal nationalism, and multinational capitalism. Though her discussion does not include texts written by Asian American women, they certainly have participated in transnational feminist production, and a review of the characteristics and functions of outlaw genres that Kaplan highlights can help us consider the participation of Asian American women in this mode of cultural production.[19]

While not foreclosing the possibility of additional forms, the types of outlaw genres Kaplan identifies include prison memoir, testimonial literature, ethnographic writing, "biomythography," "cultural autobiography," and "regulative psychobiography." Rather than privilege personal explorations of individuals, these alternative versions of autobiography challenge the power relations of the literary production site and marketplace, the specific social and historical context of the autobiographical subject, and the global world-system of transnational economic production with its gendered international division of labor. More specifically, at the level of literary production, outlaw genres destabilize the conventions of genres by deconstructing the individual bourgeois author, by questioning the authority of written expression, and by reasserting the interpretive or critical role of the autobiographical subject and text. The iconoclastic features of outlaw genres include resistance to imperializing Western feminist autobiography. For example, as outlaw genres engage the "discourse of situation or the politics of location instead of the discourse of individual authorship," they critique a simple identity politics based on gender and explore coalition politics, or what some observers call the politics of difference, to realign the concepts of self and community. Further, outlaw genres rigorously provide materialist analyses of asymmetrical local and transnational labor conditions. As "a global project that employs the efforts of many people, rather than the act of a single hand lifting pen to paper or an individual pressing the keys on a keyboard"—one that challenges "the hierarchal structures of patriarchy, capitalism and colonial discourse"—outlaw genres are forms of transnational feminist cultural production.[20]

The implications of outlaw genres as forms of transnational feminist cultural production are potentially revolutionary: They can reveal the socially constructed and therefore mutable modernist concepts of nationalism and individualism; they can help us imagine and construct alternative communities for a changing world; and they can release "the representation and expression of women from different parts of the world" from hegemonic representational traditions. Yet these potentialities will not obtain until or unless the critic truly collaborates *in* the process of producing a text, instead of appropriating the process. To participate in the revolution of transnational feminist cultural production, the critic must reveal her relation to the author, extend the process of collaboration to the reception of texts, shift "the subject of autobiography from the individual to a more unstable collective unity," and learn to read the differences between outlaw genres to reveal "possible strategic similarities."[21] In other words, to participate in and understand transnational feminist cultural production, the Western feminist critic must be politicized and read in an oppositional mode, considering texts that are usually overlooked. As a privileged feminist critic located in an elite academic institution in the United States, I engage the "'Comfort Women' of World War II" conference as an autobiographical outlaw genre to include texts that are often disregarded—Asian American texts by women—in the process of understanding a new transnational feminist cultural production, activism, and politics.

The "Comfort Women" Conference as Cultural Autobiography

Extending the process of collaboration, shifting the subject of autobiography, and reading the differences between outlaw genres in order to locate similar strategies for collaborative social change and to understand ways to construct alternative communities within postmodernity, I analyze in this section the "'Comfort Women' of World War II" conference as a cultural autobiography of Asian American transnational feminism. I will compare and contrast the larger text of the conference with the more personal form of cultural autobiography that I recognize in Christine Choy's film *In the Name of the Emperor* (1995). But first I examine two individual texts from the conference that are not only recognizable elements of the larger transnational feminist cultural text of the conference, but that are also discrete hybrid autobiographical texts or outlaw genres themselves. I consider Kim Yoon-shim's "Testimony" in the second session of the conference a testimonial narrative and Choy's film a cognate testimonial and cultural autobiography.[22]

The session in which Kim Yoon-shim's "Testimony" was scheduled was entitled "Roundtable Discussion: Testimony from the Frontline," though it was not precisely a discussion, since it soon became clear that, while collaborative, the testimonial situation demands a listener, as well as a speaking subject. The session began with a short video produced by the Washington Coalition for Comfort Women Issues, Inc. (WCCW), and a few introductory comments from Dongwoo Lee Hahm, the president of WCCW, but the focus of the session was Kim Yoon-shim's testimonial (see the transcript elsewhere in this volume). It was apparent from the moment she began that retelling her story was psychologically difficult and painful. Kim Yoon-shim's testimony, uttered slowly and punctuated with sobbing pauses, recalled the circumstances of her abduction from her village by Japanese soldiers, the journey that led to her enslavement in China, the conditions of the two "comfort stations" Kim Yoon-shim survived, her eventual escape and return to Korea, and the difficult life—what she called a "hidden life"—that she lived after the war. In startling detail but with few words and nearly no adjectives, Kim Yoon-shim relayed her thoughts as a fourteen-year-old girl, the specific physical trauma and health problems she endured, and, most vividly, the strength and dignity of her life. Her testimonial was a courageous act of "bearing witness," and the audience took on the role of listener without responding in a discussion. Although one could understand the reticence of the audience as a lack of participation or as a failure to connect with Kim Yoon-shim, I understand it as part of a recognition that listening is a necessary and participatory aspect of testimonial narrative.[23]

Reviewing contemporary definitions, one may consider Kim Yoon-shim's "Testimony" part of the category of testimonial narrative somewhat provisionally, but a look at recent analyses of the form reveals that the provisional aspects of Kim Yoon-shim's text are what enable its full participation in the form's "extraliterary" and "antiliterary" project of avoiding appropriation by the literary marketplace, and are what thoroughly establish Kim Yoon-shim's "Testimony" as a transnational feminist text. As John Beverley describes testimonial, it is "a literature of personal witness and involvement," and testimonial narrative is usually thought of as a written text that is "elicited or transcribed and edited by another person." Although Kim Yoon-shim's life story did not follow this written convention at the point she gave it at the conference, I read it as testimonial primarily because of the characteristic first-person oral account that initiates the genre.[24] In addition, Norma Field advises that "[w]e need to be prepared to extend our imagination to fragmentary testimonies, to barely distinguishable testimonies," and even "to testimonies that never reach us because their utterers perished first and because their locus, in terms of political geography, didn't matter enough." Kim Yoon-shim's narrative is a moving personal account of the horrific events and courageous struggle of her life, but the orality of the text does not render it any less a testimonial.

The oral status of Kim Yoon-shim's narrative is, in fact, the very element that makes it radically transnational and feminist. Testimonial narrative involves collaborative work across cultural divides where the politics of production and reception can impinge on the relationship between the narrator and the recorder or editor and between the narrator and the audience—that is, between women in different locations.[25] But the collaborative process of Kim Yoon-shim's testimonial included steps to guard against the appropriation of the text by elite feminists. The organizers of the conference (the "editors") presented the original moment of testimony and immediate interpretation to a diverse audience open to the public without charge, rather than producing a translated and transcribed (read "carefully edited") version of it for a paying audience or readership.[26] This refusal to commodify the testimonial text stands in contrast to the sensationalist journalists who have gone to great lengths to search out and pay former "comfort women" for their stories. The "democratic and egalitarian" aspect of the production of testimonial, according to both Beverley and Kaplan, in which "any life so narrated can have a kind of representational value," is extended to its reception, so that the voice of the speaker is no longer disembodied and commodified, although I acknowledge that academic conferences and essays such as my own participate in the extraction of another kind of value or commodification. Furthermore, through seating the interpreter next to Kim Yoon-shim and making the relations in testimonial visible to a plurality of "listeners" in the audience, the conference organizers avoided "the documentary 'truth-value' of the category of 'oral history' by highlighting the relationship between the 'editor' or 'facilitator' and 'subject' or 'speaker.'" The drawback of this compromise was that Kim Yoon-shim's testimonial was in clear danger of becoming a spectacle and even risked fetishization, since local and university media attempted to record the testimonial as an "event."[27] Despite the pitfalls, however, the decision to open up Kim Yoon-shim's testimonial to more "editors" who are also an audience of "readers" without obfuscating the mediation and translation and without directly commodifying the text resists both the alienating and exploitative forces of multinational capitalism and the subordinating and hierarchical forces of patriarchy that transnational feminist practices struggle against.[28]

Kim Yoon-shim's narrative additionally shares with testimonial a connection to a specific collectivity that has been or is oppressed and is attempting to build support for its struggle.[29] Though it is, as Kim Yoon-shim aptly said, "such an unthinkable thing," her personal story speaks to the similar stories of the one hundred to two hundred thousand women forced into sexual slavery by the Japanese military, and supports their demand for accountability. Before beginning the narrative account, Kim Yoon-shim clarified the purpose of her testimony, stating that the former "comfort women's" "stories are all the same, though they looked different"; that "their painful stories are not for sale" (money was not the goal); and that the "number of women is small and getting smaller, we must act now before it is too late." These prefatory statements indicate that her testimony is primarily concerned with the "collective situation in which the narrator lives," and that she "speaks for, or in the name of, a community or group."[30] Kim Yoon-shim's testimonial, combined with the other texts composing the conference, made it evident that she speaks for the former "comfort women" and a decentered coalition of transnational feminists (Korean, Japanese, Filipina, Asian American, and so on) who want the Japanese to take both moral and legal responsibility for the military sexual slavery they officially instituted and operated.

The collective voice of the testimonial is complicated, however, by the fact that the conference devoted much of its attention to Korean women without thoroughly acknowledging its partial focus.[31] Some elements of the conference emphasized that women of other nations were abducted and assaulted by the Japanese system, most notably Yuki Tanaka's presentation and Choy's film *In the Name of the Emperor*. Because the conference was co-sponsored by the Korean-oriented WCCW, and the Korea Society, though not other national societies, and the fact that Korean studies is the specialty of one of the conference organizers, the emphasis was on Korean women, and that resulted in the elision of the heterogeneity of the collectivity of "comfort women." Though the result was obviously not intended by the organizers of the conference and surely has more to do with the reception of testimonial than with Kim Yoon-shim as a testifying subject, the absence of Filipinas and Filipina Americans in particular, because they also have been very politically active in exposing the "comfort women" system, somewhat weakened the collaborative and transnational message of the conference.[32] As Robert Carr points out, the testifying subject is often taken as a representative:

> Although it has become standard operating procedure to assume an easy metonymic relation between the subject of testimonial and the ethnic group from which she or he comes, such closure on difference within the group celebrates the elite reader's ignorance as the group is conversely constituted as infinite duplicates of the 'original' subject presented in . . . the testimonial.[33]

While Carr is here discussing the ethnicity of the testifying subject standing for the ethnicity of an entire group, when the reader does not carefully regard the testifying subject's positionality, the same kind of misreading can happen in terms of other aspects of identity, including nationality and class status. Recognizing the diversity of women who were assaulted in the "comfort women" system is crucial to understanding how nationalism, patriarchy, and capitalism combine in militarized sexual slavery, but the range of women involved in the system was not underscored in the conference. There are probably several ways this homogenizing effect could have been avoided, the most obvious but surely the most difficult of which would have been to include additional testifying subjects, creating a polyphonic testimonial, similar to Sistren and Ford-Smith's *Lionheart Gal: Life Stories of Jamaican Women*.[34] Other more feasible measures might have been to include an activist from the Filipina branch of the movement, such as Indai Sajor, Nelia Sancho, Ninotchka Rosca, or Sheila Coronel, in one of the sessions, or even further to narrow the title of the conference, so as to safeguard against suggesting representativeness.[35]

As testimonial that is presented acoustically to a large and diverse group of listeners in a public forum, Kim Yoon-shim's "Testimony" constitutes an indeterminate and modified form that foregrounds its accessibility and its difference from the cultural and aestheticized forms of bourgeois literary discourse. In an analysis of the representations of Japanese military sexual slavery in Japanese and Korean nationalized school textbooks, Hyun Sook Kim writes that we should read the testimonies of former "comfort women" as countermemory to official written history: "the women are challenging us to question the received 'truths' about imperialism, colonialism, nationalism, and gender oppression and patriarchy and to revise the narratives of national history through which we have come to understand our collective present."[36] Beverley (page 97) states that testimonial literature typically begins as a first-person oral narrative, is then transcribed and often requires a stage of translation, operations that challenge the authority accorded the written word and the primacy of the individual author. These challenges are extended and expanded by Kim Yoon-shim's testimonial and indicate the extent to which the conference, as well as individual presentations, are part of a feminism that concentrates on resisting multinational capitalism and creating transnational communities.

Choy's film, *In the Name of the Emperor* (1995), is another component of the transnational feminist cultural text of the conference, but it is also a discrete hybrid autobiographical text that more specifically delineates an Asian American feminism, because the film is a cognate testimonial and cultural autobiography. *In the Name of the Emperor* is a fifty-two-minute documentary film exploring the Japanese rape of thousands of women in Nanjing, China, in 1937 and its connection to the systemization of military sexual slavery by the Japanese.[37] Choy explained in her discussion following the screening that she originally intended to focus the film on Nanjing and its residents. However, once Choy arrived in China to begin her project, she was not allowed to travel to Nanjing and was prohibited from filming and interviewing even in Shanghai, where sexual slavery by the Japanese began as early as 1932. While the film contains footage of the rape of Nanjing, most of the documentary records interviews with Japanese veterans of the war and citizens on the streets of contemporary Japan. Choy calls her decision to interview Japanese an "aesthetic of emergency," but the interviews of the veterans, which operate more like confessions, present compelling dimensions of the testimonial genre. Additionally, Choy understands the film in terms of her own participation and sees it as a "living witness statement of a survivor," which again suggests that it is a type of testimonial narrative.

Choy's testimonial and the veterans' testimonials appear in *In the Name of the Emperor* and, through the layers of testimonial, variations of the form are visible. As mentioned above, the testimonial may include confession, and although I am not suggesting a similarity between the community of former "comfort women" as an oppressed group that seeks accountability and the community of Japanese veterans who committed war crimes, Choy's film seems to allow space for both groups.

Or, as Field has recently theorized, any meaningful apology to former "comfort women" would include remorse and testimony, and "testimony involves both victims and apologizers. It entails reciprocity." The confessional polyphonic testimony of the veterans also emphasizes comments Beverley makes about testimonial, including his point that "*testimonio* can come from the political right . . . [if it] signifies the need for a general social change."[38] Several of the veterans interviewed directly state or imply their desire to prevent the atrocities from happening in the future, and the interviews provide a model for legal testimony that the crimes were committed and that the Japanese military had a sexual slavery system.

The confession of veterans has played a significant role, in fact, in the struggle to elicit and verify the claims of former "comfort women," since governments and the international community (including the United Nations, until very recently) have been reluctant to admit to the system and take responsibility, and because individuals understandably fear the stigmatization and pain they face in coming forward.[39] Another aspect of the film that makes use of an interesting though problematic feature of much testimonial literature is that the viewer, similar to the reader of testimonial, is in the position of a jury member in a courtroom. Watching *In the Name of the Emperor*, we are not only given the responsibility of determining the sincerity of the veterans and confronted with the question of the individual accountability of soldiers in committing crimes that were based on orders from superiors or institutionalized military practices, but we are asked to consider the place of sexual violence in military aggression.[40] As in several of her previous films, Choy's text engages the viewers' "sense of ethics and justice," and the texts are constructed as testimonials, even if the testifying subjects are not speaking as part of an oppressed community.[41] While transnational feminists may agree that this construction of the viewer/reader as the arbiter of justice for testimonial is problematic, given the usual dynamic of the First World viewer/reader of the subaltern or Third World woman's testimony, in the case of *In the Name of the Emperor* some may think the gender and status of the polyphonic testifying subject as former colonial ruler make the politics of "crossing the divide" less complicated for elite female readers. But the politics of this arrangement are undoubtedly fraught, since they apparently maintain the Otherized position of the subaltern female subject, who does not speak and may not be heard in the film.[42]

But when we consider the film Choy's testimonial, or a "statement of a survivor," she is roughly analogous to the testifying, speaking subject in her role as director. Like the transcriber in traditional testimonial, the camera lens is a level of mediation through which Choy's first-person perspective is filtered, and the cinematographic visual organization of the film correlates to the written word, another level of mediation. In both the film and the printed testimonial, the final product also usually goes through an editorial process. Alluding to and partly confirming her role in the testimonial function of the film, Choy said she wanted to provide an "alternative, new historical view" of the rape of Nanjing, to redefine "global, especially Asian Pacific history," and to seek change from people. But here the testimonial crosses over into another outlaw genre of autobiography, because Choy was not a direct witness of the events she recounts. More exactly, *In the Name of the Emperor* is also Choy's cultural autobiography, since it is simultaneously an individual life story and a cultural history.[43] Choy declared the personal nature of the film when, after the screening, she identified herself as a Korean Chinese Russian American, and said, "all my films deal with my personal experience." She then linked her personal history and the social history explored in the film with several comments such as, "Internal conflict is created by external pressure." According to Kaplan's analysis of Bernice Johnson Reagon's notion of "cultural autobiography," it "works to construct both the 'safe' places and the border areas of coalition politics where diversity operates in crisis conditions to forge powerful temporary alliances."[44] Choy's original plan to return to one of her cultural "homes" in China and re-present the story of the Japanese attack of Nanjing is an effort to connect her personal life to a cultural community and history. Though Choy may not cherish this moment of her cultural community's history, similar to "bell hooks," she uses life writing to do the hard work of "sharing experiences," to preserve a cultural community, and to construct a cultural "home."[45]

The need to place her personal identity within a larger historical frame also seems to have influenced Choy's decision to interview Japanese veterans, which constitutes a "border area of coalition politics where diversity operates in crisis."[46] While she comments that "history comes from many points of view," we can only imagine how hard it must have been to interview the very men who brutalized those Choy sees as members of her community. But Choy must have felt an imperative to connect herself to that historical moment. As Reagon's now famous statement acknowledges, "You don't go into coalition because you just *like* it," but rather "the only reason you would consider trying to team up with some-body who could possibly kill you, is because that's the only way you can figure you can stay alive."[47] This description of coalition politics seems accurately to represent at least one of the reasons for the collabo-ration of Choy, a self-described Asian American who is culturally con-nected to and working on the "comfort women" case, and the Japanese veterans interviewed in her film. Another reason for this coalition cer-tainly includes the long-term change in international human rights transnational feminists are seeking, in working toward Japanese account-ability for the military sexual slavery in the Pacific War. Regardless of the reasons, when she says that we "have to collaborate with equality," Choy reiterates Reagon's reminder that in coalition, you have to allow people to "name themselves" and deal with them from that perspective. *In the Name of the Emperor* is a cultural autobiography in which Choy's personal history connects an "individual with [a] particular communit[y] at [a] given historical juncture."[48] The film is a personal cultural autobi-ography, but another form of cultural autobiography is collective and articulates the histories of coalitions.

So far I have argued that "The 'Comfort Women' of World War II" conference is part of an Asian American transnational feminism and that the types of cultural production deployed in at least two presenta-tions in the conference are Asian American transnational feminist auto-biographies: testimonial and cultural autobiography. Next, I would like to consider the conference as a whole a cultural autobiography of Asian American transnational feminism. Kaplan provides some guidance in beginning such an endeavor, for she encourages us to think about texts in alternative ways and to expand what we think of as "texts":

> An oppositional relationship to writing and to genres such as autobiogra-phy requires the difficult embrace of unfamiliar narrative strategies as well as the validating insertion of your own familiar modes of expression and your own systems of signification. The histories of coalitions—their dyna-mism and their difficulties—can be charted as cultural autobiographies of communities in crisis and resistance. The struggle *in* writing remains to be read and recognized by literary criticism. First, it is necessary to read the narratives of coalition politics as cultural autobiographies.[49]

Following this lead, possible narrative texts of coalition politics that can be read as cultural autobiography include those written personal histories that also tell the story of a movement or collaborative struggle:

Ché Guevara's *Reminiscences of the Cuban Revolutionary War* (1959), Mary Crow Dog's *Lakota Woman* (1990), and Audre Lorde's *Zami: A New Spelling of My Name* (1982); collections that demonstrate the collaboration of the coalition politics they narrate: Frank Chin, Jeffrey Paul Chan, Lawson Fusao Inada, and Shawn Hsu Wong's *Aiiieeeee!: An Anthology of Asian American Writers* (1974), Asian Women United of California's *Making Waves: An Anthology of Writings by and about Asian American Women* (1989), and Cherríe Moraga and Gloria Anzaldúa's *This Bridge Called My Back* (1983); film and video productions that visualize the histories of struggles or movements: Luis Puenzo's *The Official Story* (1986), Pratibha Parmar's *A Place of Rage* (1991) and *Warrior Marks* (1993); performative groups that enact and describe coalition politics: Luis Valdez's *Teatro Campesino*, Spiderwoman Theater, and Sweet Honey in the Rock; academic and political conferences that elaborate and/or elicit coalition politics: the 1982 "Scholar and the Feminist IX" conference at Barnard College, and the 1995 NGOs and Fourth World Conference for Women in Beijing; and even possibly legal proceedings such as the Anita Hill/ Clarence Thomas hearings, or the testimonies of South Africans documenting the crimes of Apartheid. While this is obviously not an exhaustive list, and these are not all examples of cultural autobiographies of transnational feminist coalition politics, they should give us some idea of the kinds of texts that can be read as autobiographies of collaborative struggle.[50]

To map the characteristics or to analyze the narrative strategies of the collective form of cultural autobiography, one can start by way of analogy to the personal form of cultural autobiography in which both a safe place of coalition politics is created and a border space or "contact zone" of coalition politics is explored.[51] Though these two features of cultural autobiography might seem to be contradictory, they echo Reagon's point that one has to have both a "home" and live and work in a world with others.[52] Coalition politics draws on the empowerment of identity politics, but demands that that empowerment be used to form alliances around differences. A safe place for Asian American transnational feminist political culture was consciously constructed by the organizers of the conference through creating a supportive environment for naming and articulating the sexualized nature of aggression under patriarchy generally, the sexual violence of war typically, and the racist, sexual enslavement of former "comfort women" specifically.[53] The conference was organized in an inclusive manner, and the supportive environment was described at the conference website:

> "The 'Comfort Women' of World War II: Historical Legacy and Lessons" will be an interdisciplinary event with wide appeal to faculty, students, and the public. It will use a variety of media and approaches to address an issue that is both historically significant and politically current and that is having a tremendous impact upon relations among Asian nations and within Asian-American communities. Its particular relevance, of course, will be to the lives of women, who are often the victims of sexual violence in war and whose experiences are rarely talked about. Although World War II has been the focus of much scholarly attention, perhaps no suffering from that war has been so invisible, at least until recently, as that of the women of Korea, China, Malaysia, Indonesia, the Philipines, [sic] and even Japan itself, who were forced into sexual slavery by the Japanese imperial army and who are still seeking official governmental compensation and apologies.
>
> "The 'Comfort Women' of World War II" will bring together scholars and activists from the DC area, New York, Australia, and Asia to consider this controversial subject in its many theoretical and pragmatic dimensions. Using historical, political, feminist, and legal perspectives, the participants will both illuminate the past and facilitate greater understanding in the future. Among the speakers will be Asian-American women makers of documentary films; representatives from human rights organizations, cultural societies, and advocacy groups; and faculty members from both Georgetown University and American University.[54]

Beyond deliberately structuring the conference as an inclusive space open to the public and involving activists, academics, legal and political professionals, and students, the organizers set up and/or promoted awareness of exhibits and screenings of works by Asian and Asian American women that deal with the "comfort women" issue in various ways. For example, WCCW's "Comfort Women" exhibit of photographs and documents, Tomiyama Taeko's artwork, and Miran Kim's paintings were displayed in the Intercultural Center of Georgetown University where the conference was held; a description of and information on Mona Higuchi's *Bamboo Echoes*, a multimedia installation "Dedicated to the 'Comfort Women'" at the Isabella Stewart Gardner Museum in Boston was distributed; and the films of WCCW, Nancy Tong and Christine Choy, Byun Young-ju, Diana Lee and Grace Lee, and Hye Jung Park and J.T. Takagi were all shown.[55] As the above discussion should illustrate, Kim Yoon-shim's testimony was central in creating a safe place, because her testimony named unequivocally the crimes of Japanese military sexual slavery and therefore modeled a discussion of sexual violence. The conference clearly created a safe place for the diverse collaborative efforts of Asian American transnational feminists involved in coalition politics.

In addition to the safe place that cultural autobiography constructs, it also mines the border area or contact zone of coalition politics where diversity can operate in tension. The contact zone of the conference for Asian American transnational feminism was located in discussions of whether the "comfort women" system was unique to Japan, indicated something particular about Japanese culture, or needed to be addressed for the sake of the future of the Japanese state.[56] In short, the volatile aspects of the coalition involved loyalties to cultural and political nationalisms, which are ultimately challenged by the very foundations of transnational feminisms. At risk in such discussions was, on the one extreme, a type of cultural relativism that may have excused the criminal behavior of individuals and the Japanese government, and, at the other extreme, a racism that could be used to rationalize all kinds of structures and global hierarchies of nations, including the use of atomic bombs on Japan. Rather than avoiding these obviously contentious issues, the conference organizers actually provoked or planned a space where the diversity of the coalition would operate in tension. Specifically, every speaker in the first session of the conference, as well as the keynote address by Miki Mutusko, wife of Miki Takeo, former prime minister of Japan, addressed the role of nationalism in creating the system and the role of the nation-state in taking responsibility for the system. Anticipating and even encouraging the difficult work of coalition politics, the conference organizers arranged for a text in which we could read the struggle of Asian American transnational feminism.

That the discourse of nationalism occupies the border or contact zone of Asian American transnational feminist coalition politics should not be surprising, if one recalls the politics of transnational feminisms discussed at the beginning of this chapter, the legacy of feminist critique in Asian American discourse, and Reagon's observations about the relationship between (cultural) nationalism, identity politics, and coalition politics:

> Of course the problem with the experiment [of identity politics] is that there ain't nobody in here but folk like you, which by implication means

you wouldn't know what to do if you were running [the world] with all of the other people who are out there in the world. Now that's nationalism. I mean it's nurturing, but it is also nationalism. At a certain stage nationalism is crucial to people if you are to ever impact as a group in your own interest. Nationalism at another point becomes reactionary because it is totally inadequate for surviving in the world with many peoples.[57]

Coalition is defined as the "cooperative activities of people and groups with different points of view," and the different points of view or assumptions about nationalism were the site of tension, the border area, or the contact zone for the coalition active around the "comfort women" issue and explored in the cultural autobiography of Asian American transnational feminism.[58] Connected to an earlier period of interrogation into the limitations of cultural nationalism, the transnational feminism of Asian American women rigorously insists on a critique of the modernist forms of nationalism still holding currency in postmodernity.

Finally, the conference reveals possible characteristics of the collective form of cultural autobiography that are not necessarily present in the personal form of cultural autobiography, including the sharing of a historical narrative and a bibliographic and documentary function. In several ways, the conference organizers provided fragmented bits of information that, taken together, presented a narrative that delineates, though not in precise chronological order or with a sense of unity, the activism around the "comfort women" issue as a coalition involving Asian American transnational feminism. First, everyone was provided with a folder containing the program agenda, a chronology of dates and events on "comfort women" issues, descriptions of the exhibits associated with the conference, a photocopy of a *Time* magazine article, and information on the WCCW. Other materials were also made available, some free of charge, including the United Nations Commission on Human Rights Report on the issue of military sexual slavery in wartime, and some for sale, such as Yuki Tanaka's book and WCCW's video. In addition, the conference was structured so that there were no overlapping or simultaneous presentations, which clearly contributed to a sense of shared cultural history.

The first session of the conference contributed to the sense of a common historical text, because it carefully set out the terms of the discourse of the transnational feminist coalition. Margaret Stetz began the session with the presentation "Wartime Sexual Violence against Women: A Feminist Response," which helped to set the tone for both the session and the conference. She described the long history of military sexual slavery, she outlined the effects transnational feminist analysis has had in the activism around the "comfort women" system, and she summarized how feminists have worked in various national locations and across national borders. Dai Sil Kim-Gibson's presentation, "Slaves of Sex: 'Comfort Women' in World War II," provided a critique of the Japanese nation-state's role in institutionalizing the assault and colonization of women, pointing out that schools were pressured to provide girls for the imperial army. Kim-Gibson's analysis of the ideological state apparatuses used to institute military sexual slavery suggested that other nation-states are complicit in disguising what happened: the Smithsonian Institution's Enola Gay exhibit (1995), for example, "buried Japan as a brutal aggressor" in World War II.[59] A representative from Human Rights Watch extended Kim-Gibson's analysis by summarizing how the "comfort women" system should be approached from an international human rights perspective that forces nation-states to take responsibility and denies their ultimate power to claim authority over women. Yuki Tanaka's "Why 'Comfort Women'" also analyzed the relationship between nationalism, patriarchy, and colonialism. Ending the session, Professor Chris Simpson of American University discussed the differences and similarities between mass rape and sexual slavery, which hinge on the nation-state's involvement in and maintenance of violence against women. In short, the conference's structure ensured that those attending the conference would have a certain amount of shared information and be familiar with the discourse of Asian American transnational feminist coalition politics.

As a cultural autobiography or historical narrative of Asian American transnational feminism, the conference participated in creating and preserving documents and compiling bibliographic references. While the conference showcased what might be considered numerous primary documents of the struggle for justice for former "comfort women," including Kim Yoon-shim's testimony and the "comfort women" exhibit, it also documented the history of the coalition politics of Asian American transnational feminists involved in the struggle through various sources, including the presentations as described above, the films, and the artwork. The efforts that the conference organizers made to educate those who attended included offering numerous bibliographic references for sources that simultaneously evidence Japanese military sexual slavery and the history of Asian American transnational feminism.

"The 'Comfort Women' of World War II" conference included and is itself an Asian American transnational feminist text. In it and through it, Asian American feminists worked in collaboration "to compare multiple, overlapping and discrete oppressions rather than to construct a theory of hegemonic oppression under a unified category of gender," and to "articulate the relationship of gender to scattered hegemonies such as global economic structures, patriarchal nationalisms, 'authentic' forms of tradition, local structures of domination, and legal-juridical oppression on multiple levels."[60] Further, the conference articulated a history of Asian American transnational feminism working toward the creation of new forms of community in postmodernity. Reading the conference as Asian American transnational feminist cultural production illuminates alternative modes of expression and narrative strategies that will help feminists not only identify decolonizing signification for women in different locations, but will also help feminists recognize, understand, and practice coalition politics more readily.

Notes

1. Nora Okja Keller, *Comfort Woman* (New York: Viking Press, 1997), p. 209.
2. The conference, held at Georgetown University on 30 September–2 October 1996, was organized by Professors Bonnie B. C. Oh and Margaret D. Stetz and was cosponsored by Georgetown University, the Washington Coalition for Comfort Women Issues, Inc. (WCCW), and the Korea Society. Although I understand the uneasy relationship many have with the term "Asian American," in this essay and elsewhere I use it rather than "Asian Pacific American," because the conflation of the Indigenous people of Hawai'i and other Pacific Islands with people who are themselves immigrants or whose ancestors were immigrants to the United States risks the collapse of radically different histories, cultures, subjectivities, and politics. For a discussion of problematic terminology such as "comfort woman," see Chin Sung Chung, "The Origin and Development of the Military Sexual Slavery Problem in Imperial Japan," *Positions* 5, 1 (spring 1997): 220–222.
3. My analysis of the conference is informed by research in my forthcoming book *Asian American Women's Writing: Theorizing Transnationalism*. I argue in it that Asian American women's writing theorizes a transnationalism that resists singular and static nationalist affiliation and results in cultural production that represents and can itself create alternative communities. My analysis of the conference is deeply indebted to the work of Caren Kaplan, who has been theorizing "transnational feminism" since at least the early 1990s.
4. Activism around the issue of Japanese military sexual slavery has largely involved the local and national organizations of women from Korea, the Philippines, and Japan. For an overview of individuals and national organizations, particularly in Korea, and international coalitions active in the movement to make Japan take responsibility for its military sexual slavery in the Pacific War, see Chung, "Origin and Development," pp. 239–243. For an interesting discussion of Japanese

hegemony in disseminating information about military sexual slavery, see Hyunah Yang, "Revisiting the Issue of Korean 'Military Comfort Women': The Question of Truth and Positionality," *Positions* 5, 1 (spring 1997): 54–57. For details of activism in the Philippines, see George Hicks, *The 'Comfort Women': Japan's Brutal Regime of Enforced Prostitution in the Second World War* (New York: W. W. Norton, 1994), pp. 237–275, especially pp. 242–245; Hyun Sook Kim, "History and Memory: The 'Comfort Women' Controversy," *Positions* 5, 1 (spring 1997): 94–96; and Yuki Tanaka, "Introduction," *Hidden Horrors: Japanese War Crimes in World War II* (Boulder, CO: Westview Press, 1996).

5. Feminists easily recall and often mention, for example, work by Paula Gunn Allen, Gloria Anzaldúa, Patricia Hill Collins, "bell hooks," and Cherríe Moraga when thinking of U.S. women of color feminisms, and perhaps Gayatri Chakravorty Spivak or Chandra Talpade Mohanty when thinking of Third World feminisms. But the contributions made by Asian American feminists, including Esther Ngan-ling Chow and Mitsuye Yamada, are more often than not disregarded.

6. I follow Anderson's thesis in *Imagined Communities: Reflections on the Origin and Spread of Nationalism* here to suggest that not only print culture, but also other types of texts in postmodernity participate in imagining and constructing communities, especially those communities that do not rely on patriarchal nationalisms.

7. Use and definition of the term "transnational" is contested and changes across academic disciplines. Sometimes "transcultural" is also used to describe a postmodern but resistant flow of culture. For three different discussions of the term "transnational," see Arif Dirlik, "The Postcolonial Aura: Third World Criticism in the Age of Capitalism," *Critical Inquiry* 20 (winter 1994): 328–356; Caren Kaplan, "'A World Without Boundaries': The Body Shop's Trans/national Geographics," *Social Text* 43 (fall 1995): 45–66; and Aihwa Ong, *Flexible Citizenship: The Cultural Logics of Transnationality* (Durham: Duke University Press, 1999), pp. 1–26.

8. The early formulation of transnational feminisms in the United States came, in fact, from those who recognized that feminism could be as imperialist as other modernist projects. Gayatri Spivak's work, such as the essays collected in *In Other Worlds: Essays in Cultural Politics* (New York: Methuen, 1987), has been catalytic since the mid-1980s. Cynthia Enloe points out, in *Bananas, Beaches & Bases: Making Feminist Sense of International Politics* (Berkeley: University of California Press, 1989), that women and feminists have been complicit in colonization; Mohanty, Russo, and Torres's edited collection of essays, *Third World Women and the Politics of Feminism* (Bloomington: Indiana University Press, 1991) has also been extremely influential in rethinking the challenges of collaboration between feminists in different locations.

9. See Kaplan, "Resisting Autobiography," p. 116.

10. Resistance to Asian American transnational feminism was first remarked in Asian American literary discourse. See note 12 below and David Leiwei Li, "Asian American Literature and Culture between 'Nation' and 'Transnation'" (paper presented at the MELUS Conference, Ala Moana Hotel, Honolulu, 20 April 1997). Lane Ryo Hirabayashi and Marilyn C. Alquizola also write in their essay, "Asian American Studies: Reevaluating for the 1990s," in *The State of Asian America: Activism and Resistance in the 1990s*, ed. Karin Aguilar-San Juan (Boston: South End Press, 1994), pp. 358–359, that a neglect of feminist discourses and class analy-

sis "turn out to be precisely the kinds of weaknesses that were often replicated wherever cultural nationalist agendas drove Ethnic Studies programs."

11. See Inderpal Grewal and Caren Kaplan, "Introduction: Transnational Feminist Practices and Questions of Postmodernity," in *Scattered Hegemonies: Postmodernity and Transnational Feminist Practices*, ed. Inderpal Grewal and Caren Kaplan (Minneapolis: University of Minnesota Press, 1994), p. 17; for discussion of the origins of the Asian American women's movement, see Sonia Shah, "Presenting the Blue Goddess: Toward a National, Pan-Asian Feminist Agenda," in *The State of Asian America: Activism and Resistance in the 1990s*, ed. Karin Aguilar-San Juan (Boston: South End Press, 1994), pp. 147–158; and Sonia Shah, ed., *Dragon Ladies: Asian American Feminists Breathe Fire* (Boston: South End Press, 1997); and William Wei, *The Asian American Movement* (Philadelphia: Temple University Press, 1993).

12. For a discussion on this pressure in relation to Asian American independent filmmaking, see Renee Tajima, "Moving the Image: Asian American Independent Filmmaking 1970–1990" in *Moving the Image: Independent Asian Pacific American Media Arts*, ed. Russell Leong (Los Angeles: UCLA Asian American Studies Center and Visual Communications, Southern California Asian American Studies Central, Inc., 1991), p. 11. For a discussion of it in the realm of literary studies, see King-Kok Cheung, "The Woman Warrior Versus the Chinaman Pacific: Must a Chinese American Critic Choose between Feminism and Heroism?" in *The Woman Warrior: A Casebook*, ed. Sau-Ling Cynthia Wong (New York: Oxford University Press, 1999), pp. 113–133. See Yen Le Espiritu, *Asian American Panethnicity: Bridging Institutions and Identities* for a discussion of the panethnicity of Asian American politics and identity and the first usage of the term "Asian American" (pp. 1–52).

13. For a thorough discussion of the reasons for this resistance in Asian American discourse, see "Emphasis on the Transnational" in my *Asian American Women Writers: Theorizing Transnationalism*, forthcoming. See also Cheung, *The Woman Warrior*, passim; Elaine Kim, "'Such Opposite Creatures': Men and Women in Asian American Literature" *Michigan Quarterly Review* (winter 1990): 68–93; Lisa Lowe, "Heterogeneity, Hybridity, Multiplicity: Marking Asian American Differences," *Diaspora* 1.1 (spring 1991): 24–44; and Sau-ling Cynthia Wong, *Reading Asian American Literature: From Necessity to Extravagance* (Princeton: Princeton University Press, 1993) for analyses of the Frank Chin/Maxine Hong Kingston debates or how Asian American women writers recognized the limited confines of national identity and challenged these essentializing definitions of national identity because of the obstacles they placed in the coalition politics of Asian American struggle.

14. Lisa Lowe's essay, "Work, Immigration, Gender: Asian 'American' Women" in *Immigrant Acts: On Asian American Cultural Politics* (Durham: Duke University Press, 1996) appeared in 1996 (see specifically pp. 154–173); and her essay "Work, Immigration, Gender: Asian 'American' Women" in *Making More Waves: New Writing by Asian American Women*, ed. Elaine H. Kim, Lilia V. Villanueva, and Asian Women United of California (Boston, MA: Beacon Press, 1997) appeared in 1997.

15. See Lowe, "Work, Immigration, Gender," pp. 154–173. Echoing Kaplan's essay, "Resisting Autobiography: Out-Law Genres and Transnational Feminist Subjects" in *De/Colonizing the Subject: The Politics of Gender in Women's Autobiography*, ed. Sidonie Smith and Julia Watson (Minneapolis: University of Minnesota Press, 1992), pp. 115–138, Lowe's reading "seeks to understand Asian American

124   LEGACIES OF THE COMFORT WOMEN

cultural production critically and broadly to interpret the interconnections between testimony, personal narrative, oral history, literature, film, visual arts, and other cultural forms as sites through which subject, community, and struggle are signified and mediated" (p. 157).

16. Lowe, "Work, Immigration, Gender," p. 158.

17. Of course, women of various Asian American ethnic subgroups were involved in international issues before the 1960s, but it would be anachronistic to call this activism "Asian American," since the term was not in use until the late 1960s. For a discussion of the international perspective of the early Asian American movement, the antiwar movement, and Asian American women's engagement with Marxist ideology, see Wei, *The Asian American Movement*, pp. 22–30, 37–43, and 72–81.

18. There are numerous examples of transnational feminist cultural production by Asian American women. See Lowe, "Work, Immigration, Gender," passim; and Jessica Hagedorn, ed., *Charlie Chan Is Dead: An Anthology of Contemporary Asian American Fiction* (New York: Penguin Books, 1993) for an introduction to some primary works. On the recent activism of Asian American transnational feminism, see Shah, *Dragon Ladies*, passim; Sheila Coronel and Ninotchka Rosca, "For the Boys: Filipinas Expose Years of Sexual Slavery by the U.S. and Japan," *Ms.* (November/December 1993): 10–15; Tracy Lai, "Asian American Women: Not For Sale" in *Race, Class, and Gender: An Anthology*, ed. Margaret L. Anderson and Patricia Hill Collins (Belmont, CA: Wadsworth Publishing Co., 1992), pp. 163–171; and Helen Zia, "Made in the U.S.A.," *Ms.* (January/February 1996): 67–73. Evelyn Ch'ien provides a concise introduction to the collaborative nature of contemporary Asian American feminisms, particularly in their transnational forms, in "Asian Americans and the 'New Feminism': An *A. Magazine* Roundtable" in *A. Magazine: Special Women's Issue* (1994), p. 20.

19. Kaplan points out that the six types of outlaw genres that she reviews are not "a comprehensive list or complete map of global literary production that refers to the 'autobiographical' tradition" but simply indicate "a variety of reading and writing strategies in operation as the law of genre intersects with contemporary postcolonial, transnational conditions" ("Resisting Autobiography," p. 119). Two Asian American women's texts that have been considered types of outlaw genres are Jade Snow Wong, *Fifth Chinese Daughter* (New York: Harper, 1945); and Maxine Hong Kingston, *The Woman Warrior: Memoirs of a Girlhood among Ghosts* (New York: Vintage, 1989). See Anne Goldman, "'I Yam What I Yam': Cooking, Culture and Colonialism" in *De/Colonizing the Subject: The Politics of Gender in Women's Autobiography*, ed. Sidonie Smith and Julia Watson (Minneapolis: University of Minnesota Press, 1992), pp. 169–195 for a consideration of "autoethnography" in *Fifth Chinese Daughter*; and Lee Quinby, "The Subject of Memoirs: *The Woman Warrior's* Technology of Ideographic Selfhood" in *De/Colonizing the Subject: The Politics of Gender in Women's Autobiography*, ed. Sidonie Smith and Julia Watson (Minneapolis: University of Minnesota Press, 1992), pp. 297–320, for a consideration of "ideographic selfhood" in Kingston. Recent works that may be considered autobiographical versions of transnational feminist cultural production include both the following listed texts and others by Meena Alexander, *Fault Lines* (New York: The Feminist Press, 1993); Sucheng Chan, ed., *Hmong Means Free: Life in Laos and America* (Philadelphia: Temple University Press, 1994); Le Ly Hayslip with Jay Wurts, *When Heaven and Earth Changed Places: A Vietnamese Woman's Jour-*

ney From War to Peace (New York: Plume, 1990); and Elaine Kim and Eui-Young Yu, eds., *East to America: Korean American Life Stories* (New York: New York Press, 1996).

20. Kaplan, "Resisting Autobiography," pp. 119–122.

21. Pp. 119, 122, 134, 125. See also Caren Kaplan, "The Politics of Location as Transnational Feminist Critical Practice" in *Scattered Hegemonies: Postmodernity and Transnational Feminist Practice*, ed. Inderpal Grewal and Caren Kaplan (Minneapolis: University of Minnesota Press, 1994), pp. 137–152.

22. See Yoon-shim Kim, "Testimony" (presented at "The 'Comfort Women' of World War II: Legacy and Lessons" conference, Georgetown University, Washington, DC, 30 September 1996); and Christine Choy, dir. and cinematographer, *In the Name of the Emperor*. (Christine Choy and Nancy Tong, prod. Filmmakers Library, 1995).

23. For a discussion of testimony as dialogic in nature, see Norma Field, "War and Apology: Japan, Asia, the Fiftieth, and After," *Positions* 5, 1 (spring 1997): 1–49; 28–36.

24. See John Beverley, "The Margin at the Center: On *Testimonio* (Testimonial Narrative)" in *De/Colonizing the Subject: The Politics of Gender in Women's Autobiography*, ed. Sidonie Smith and Julia Watson (Minneapolis: University of Minnesota Press, 1992), pp. 92–94. Beverley remarks that his definition should be considered "at best provisional, and at worst repressive," because testimonial is "by nature a protean and demotic form not yet subject to legislation by a normative literary establishment" (p. 93).

25. For a critical discussion of the relation between the narrator or informant and the recorder or inquisitor/scribe in testimonial, see Doris Sommer, "No Secrets: Rigoberta's Guarded Truth," *Women's Studies* 20, 1 (1991): 51–72.

26. There was no registration fee or fees of any kind for the conference. The testimony was mediated through an interpreter, Sangmie Choi Schellstede, Vice-President of WCCW and a U.S. government interpreter, according to the conference program. Carr offers, with the example of Rigoberta Menchú and Elizabeth Burgos-Debray, *I, Rigoberta Menchú: An Indian Woman in Guatemala*, a possible compromise to the problem of the consumption of testimonial in the global marketplace. In particular, Carr supports a suggestion that audiotapes of Menchú's testimonial, rather than translated, transcribed (printed) texts, be produced. See Robert Carr, "Crossing the First World/Third World Divides: Testimonial, Transnational Feminisms, and the Postmodern Condition," in *Scattered Hegemonies: Postmodernity and Transnational Feminist Practices*, ed. Inderpal Grewal and Caren Kaplan (Minneapolis: University of Minnesota Press, 1994), pp. 156–157 and his footnote 10.

27. The presence of the media is a complicated issue since, as Beverley points out, part of the purpose of testimonial is to heighten awareness of a particular group's oppression or struggle. The WCCW is a Washington, D.C. area–based, nonprofit, nonpartisan, educational organization run by "volunteers of every nationality and diverse points of view." According to the information given out at the conference, media attention has been on the WCCW's agenda since its inception. The efforts to heighten awareness have no doubt played a major role in the fight for accountability. Moreover, the kind of exposure WCCW is involved in should be distinguished from the kind of value extracted from testimonials as knowledge by First World academics, which Carr discusses, and certainly from the kind of value extracted by

journalists who pay for women's stories. For further discussion of the problem of commodification, see Carr, "Crossing the First World," passim; Field, "War and Apology," pp. 26–27; and Dai Sil Kim-Gibson, "They Are Our Grandmas," in *Positions* 5:1 (Spring 1997): 257–260.

28. Kaplan, "Resisting Autobiography," p. 123.

29. According to Beverley, the "situation of the narration in *testimonio* has to involve an urgency to communicate, a problem of repression, poverty, subalternity, imprisonment, struggle for survival, implicated in the act of narration itself" (p. 94). See also Hyun Sook Kim, "History and Memory," pp. 73–106, for a discussion of the collective and political nature of former "comfort women's" stories.

30. Beverley, "The Margin at the Center," p. 95.

31. Researchers estimate that of the more than two hundred thousand women exploited by the "comfort women" system, 80 to 90 percent were Korean, although Burmese, Chinese, Dutch, Filipina, Indonesian, Japanese, Malaysian, Manchurian, Taiwanese, Thai, and Vietnamese women were also victimized. See Chung, "Origin and Development," pp. 227–232; Yuki Tanaka, *Hidden Horrors: Japanese War Crimes in World War II* (Boulder, CO: Westview Press, 1996), p. 99; and Yang, "Revisiting the Issue," p. 57.

32. Filipinas and Filipina Americans have been very active, for example, in the collective international organization Gabriela. See Coronel and Rosca, "For the Boys," passim; Hicks, *The Comfort Women*, pp. 242–245; and Tanaka, *Hidden Horrors*, "Introduction."

33. Carr, "Crossing the First World," p. 152.

34. I recognize the difficulty of arranging for two former "comfort women" to speak at the same place and time. See Beverley's discussion of polyphonic testimonial, "The Margin at the Center," p. 96; and Carr's discussion of Sistren and Honor Ford-Smith's *Lionheart Gal: Life Stories of Jamaican Women* (London: Women's Press, 1986), pp. 163–166.

35. See Coronel and Rosca, "For the Boys," passim; Ninotchka Rosca, "Cold Comfort," *The Women's Review of Books* 8.3 (December 1995): 5–6; and Tanaka, *Hidden Horrors*, "Introduction."

36. Hyun Sook Kim, "History and Memory," p. 102.

37. For details on the establishment of "comfort stations," see Tanaka, *Hidden Horrors*, pp. 79–109; Hicks, *The Comfort Women*, pp. 45–65; and Chung, "Origin and Development," pp. 223–224.

38. Beverley also points out that testimonial "has been important in maintaining and developing the practice of international human rights and solidarity movements" (p. 99), although since Beverley's essay was published critics, especially feminist critics examining nongovernmental women's organizations, have begun to scrutinize the subject assumed and interpolated by legal discourse in international rights efforts.

39. See Tanaka, *Hidden Horrors*, pp. 79–109; Hicks, *The Comfort Women*, pp. 168–193, 194–219; and Chung, "Origin and Development," pp. 234–246.

40. Compellingly, some of Christine Choy's other films assign the viewer this juridical function, including *Who Killed Vincent Chin?* (Renee Tajima, prod. Filmmakers Library, 1989) and another film codirected with Dai Sil Kim-Gibson, *Sa-I-Gu: From Korean Women's Perspectives* (Christine Choy, Elaine Kim, and Dai Sil Kim-Gibson, prods. Cross Current Media, 1993). In *Who Killed Vincent Chin?* Choy

reviews the case of a Chinese American man beaten to death by disgruntled auto workers in Detroit; *Sa-I-Gu* deals with the interethnic conflicts following the Rodney King verdict.

41. Beverley, "The Margin at the Center," p. 99.

42. For a discussion of the erasure of the subaltern female subject between competing discourses, see Gayatri Chakravorty Spivak, "Can the Subaltern Speak?" in *Marxism and the Interpretation of Culture*, ed. Cary Nelson and Lawrence Grossberg (Chicago: University of Illinois Press, 1988), pp. 271–313.

43. For a discussion of cultural autobiography, see Reagon, "My Black Mothers and Sisters or On Beginning a Cultural Autobiography," *Feminist Studies* 8 (spring 1982): 81–96.

44. Kaplan, "Resisting Autobiography," p. 132.

45. See "bell hooks," "Writing Autobiography," in *Talking Back: Thinking Feminist, Thinking Black* (Boston: South End Press, 1989), pp. 155–156; see also Kaplan's discussion of hooks's essay in "Resisting Autobiography," pp. 130–131.

46. Ibid.

47. Reagon, "Coalition Politics," p. 357.

48. Kaplan, "Resisting Autobiography," p. 132.

49. Ibid.

50. Just as the "'Comfort Women' of World War II: Legacy and Lessons" conference is not limited to a cultural autobiography of Asian American transnational feminism, these examples may also participate in more than one distinguishable discourse of resistance.

51. For a discussion of the contact zone, community, and the classroom, see Mary Louise Pratt, "Arts of the Contact Zone," in *Ways of Reading: An Anthology for Writers*, ed. David Bartholomae and Anthony Petrosky (Boston, MA: Bedford Books, 1993).

52. See Reagon, "Coalition Politics," pp. 356–361.

53. For an analysis of the racism of Japanese military sexual slavery, see Yang, "Revisiting the Issue," pp. 60–66; and Hyun Sook Kim, "History and Memory," 87–89.

54. "The 'Comfort Women' of World War II: Legacy and Lessons" conference website was http://www.georgetown.edu/comfortwomen.

55. The various screenings included *Comfort Women* by WCCW; *In the Name of the Emperor* by Christine Choy and Nancy Tong; *Murmuring* by Young-ju Byun; *Camp Arirang* by Diana Lee and Grace Lee; *The Women Outside* by Hye Jung Park and J.T. Takagi.

56. Several of the veterans interviewed in Choy's film gave the future of Japan or Japanese political nationalism as their reason for speaking out.

57. Reagon, "Coalition Politics," p. 358.

58. Kaplan, "Resisting Autobiography," p. 132.

59. For a detailed discussion of the U.S. role in the erasure of Japanese responsibility for the suffering of non-Japanese Asians, see Field, "War and Apology," passim.

60. Grewal and Kaplan, "Introduction: Transnational Feminist Practices," p. 17.

Chapter 7

Urgent Matters

Redress for Surviving "Comfort Women"

Dongwoo Lee Hahm

Let me come straight to the point. The "comfort women" issue must not and shall not be swept under the carpet. The Japanese government today is hoping for what it calls a "biological solution to the 'Comfort Women' problem." For the present Japanese administration, a sincere apology and payment of redress to survivors of the Japanese system of military sexual slavery of World War II is not an issue of justice, but a mere public relations "problem" that it hopes will fade away, as the survivors die of old age or the lingering effects of war-inflicted injury or disease.

The Japanese government has once again miscalculated about this issue. There is today a worldwide movement for justice for "comfort women," with active organizations in Korea, Japan, China, the Philippines, Indonesia, Taiwan, the Marshall Islands and other Pacific Islands, Guam, Australia, New Zealand, the Netherlands, Germany, the United Kingdom, Canada, and at least a dozen major cities in the United States. The movement is particularly strong among Koreans, because Korean women formed the majority of those used in the "comfort women" system of military sexual slavery. But Koreans have many allies in this matter, including other Asians of many nationalities who suffered at the hands of the Japanese during World War II, veterans organizations and POWs in the United States and United Kingdom, survivors and families of victims of the horrifying biological warfare experiments conducted by Unit 731, the International Commission of Jurists, and Japan's own Federation of Bar (Attorneys) Associations, churches and temples of many different religious faiths, and especially women's organizations in almost every nation of the world.

There are, of course, many differences among any group of organizations this broad. But we are united in agreeing on one point: Japan's system of military sexual slavery during World War II was a war crime and a crime against humanity organized by the Japanese government. We urgently demand justice for survivors of this system and for the families of those who did not survive. The redress that "comfort women" survivors seek is so minimal, so much less than what was taken from them when they were trapped in the military brothels, that in any other context it would almost seem pitiful. Their demand is simply this: first, that the Japanese government make a clear and unequivocal apology to the "comfort women," an apology that acknowledges the Japanese government's role in the creation and maintenance of the system of military sexual slavery, and then that the payment of a sum of reparations be made to the women from *the government's own funds*, as a means of demonstrating that the government has accepted responsibility for these crimes.

The Japanese government and its current emperor, Akihito, have a strong moral obligation to act now. Many of the surviving women are in poor health and living in poverty. Seeking a "biological solution" of waiting for the deaths of the victims, such as some of the more foolish Japanese parliamentarians have suggested, will actually compound the crimes against these women in the eyes of the world.

As I see it, it is also crucial to set clear legal standards that recognize systems of mass rape and military sexual slavery as both war crimes and crimes against humanity, and to demonstrate that the perpetrators of such crimes will be brought to justice, however long that takes. The recent and terrible examples of mass rapes in the Balkans, in Africa, and in other areas of the world demonstrate that the "comfort women's" demands are urgent matters that must be addressed by the United Nations and other international groups today. It would be a travesty of justice, too, to accept Japan as a permanent member of the United Nations Security Council, so long as it continues to contend that its wartime treatment of the "comfort women" was not a crime.

We know today that millions of individuals suffered from Japan's war of aggression during World War II. Among them were approximately two hundred thousand Asian, European, and Pacific Island girls and women who were used as sexual slaves in "comfort stations" by Japanese military troops. Many of these "comfort women" were tricked, abducted, or drafted as teenagers and were held prisoners in military brothels for sexual service. The Japanese government established and controlled these so-called "comfort station," which spread with their invading troops throughout Manchuria, China, Burma, Thailand, the Philippines, Malaysia, Indonesia, and many other locations in the South Pacific.

These war crimes were committed almost sixty years ago. However, the facts about them became widely known to the public only as recently as 1992, when one seventy-four-year-old survivor, Kim Hak Soon, stepped forward to declare to the world that she had been a "comfort woman." Others since have come forward, one by one, to talk about their horrific experiences during World War II.

Many of the "comfort women" are dead now. Some died from torture or from diseases contracted during wartime, some committed suicide, and many were murdered by the Japanese military when World War II ended; very few are known to have survived. Most of the victims who did survive live today with irreparable psychological wounds and physical problems. None so far have received reparation from the party that was principally responsible for the crime against them—namely, the Japanese government.

I have had many occasions in the past few years to interview surviving former "comfort women." Their names and their faces were different, but their stories shared common threads. Theirs were stories of having been deceived, abducted, raped, and beaten during their imprisonment in military brothels, and then more recently of having been publicly humiliated and denounced as greedy prostitutes by the same officials who captured and enslaved them. Every one of these women asked me to take a message back to the American people and to the world: that they are not after money; their painful stories are not for sale; receiving a token of money is not the issue. Some have said, "Please don't let us die twice by throwing false charity money at us from private funds." Others have said, "Please help us to resolve this issue soon." All have said, "Please help us to restore our dignity and honor."

What all of these elderly women, many of whom are now destitute, want is a formal acknowledgment of the crime committed against them by the Japanese government and formal reparation from the government's treasury, not from the private funds that the Japanese government has tried to raise, to substitute for proper redress to these women. Neither the acknowledgment nor the reparation has been forthcoming from Japan. Indeed, the recent "private fund charity plan" has been used deliberately by the Japanese government to avoid any clear acceptance of responsibility.

This is the reason why these issues challenge those of us today who are activists. While we recognize the importance of the large issues placed before us concerning violence against women in wartime, we at the Washington Coalition for "Comfort Women" Issues, Inc. (WCCW) are focused on a more specific problem: namely, redress for the inhumanities suffered by ordinary human beings, like any one of us, at the hands of a government. We ask that the Japanese government make a clear, official apology and reparation to the victims from its treasury, not from private funds. Only by officially and openly acknowledging and apologizing for the government's own previous role in establishing the "comfort women" system can the Japanese government and its people today bring this shameful episode in their history to a close and restore honor to the Japanese nation.

In February 1996, a group of women from Okinawa Acting Against Military Violence came to the United States to discuss the well-known case of a young Okinawan girl raped by American servicemen. This Okinawan group also supported the platform of action approved at the 1995 Beijing Conference on Women that clearly states, "Rape that takes place in a situation of armed conflict constitutes both a war crime and a crime against humanity." The "comfort women" system organized by the Japanese government before and during World War II clearly falls under this definition. The definition holds as true for the crimes of more than fifty years ago as it does for those committed today.

We are now at a turning point in worldwide efforts to restore the dignity of all victims of rape during wartime. The urgency with which we approach this task is based on a simple truth: The number of surviving "comfort women" is small, and the number is growing ever smaller. The few surviving "comfort women" are mostly in their seventies. It seems that the Japanese government is waiting for the last "comfort women" to die, hoping, perhaps, that this issue will die with them. For this reason, it is crucial to redress the inhumanities suffered by these "comfort women" as soon as possible. In another place or time, any one of us could have been one of these women. To ensure justice for these women is imperative. We must show the world that no government will be allowed to perpetrate such atrocities on women without being called to account.

What follows is the testimony of Kim Yoon-shim, a former "comfort woman," whose presence at the international conference on "comfort women" (The "Comfort Women" of World War II: Legacy and Lessons) at Georgetown University on 30 September 1996 was sponsored

and arranged by the WCCW. The translation has been provided by
WCCW member, Sangmie Choi Schellstede.

Testimony of One "Comfort Woman"

I am Kim Yoon-shim from Seoul, Korea. I had just finished grade school
two months before; I was fourteen (thirteen, in American age). One day I
was playing jump-rope in front of my house when an automobile drove
up the road. Trains don't even come through my village, let alone cars.
Curious about something we had never seen before, all the children nearby
ran to it and tried to climb up. The driver shook the small children off and
let me and my girl-friend get in. There were two other uniformed men
inside. I thought it would be a short ride, but the truck rolled on with us in
it and then kept on going and going. I asked them to let me out and, with
tears, importuned them to take me back to my village, to no avail. The
truck arrived in the City of Kwangju, Cholla Namdo Province, where I
encountered twenty or so older girls. I cried all night, repeating the same
words: "Take me back to my mother!" The next morning all of us were
thrown into a cargo train; the compartment was covered with coal-soot
and our clothes got all soiled. There, I was separated from my friend from
the village. I later found out that she was sent to a textile factory. The
train travelled all day and all night, and all I could do was cry my heart
out. The next night I was put on a cargo ship that sailed for about three
days, I think. There were some soldiers and also civilians on board. My
continuous crying annoyed the guards. So they tied my hands behind me
and threatened to drown me by lowering my tied-up body to the ocean
surface if I didn't stop crying. At the port the girls were divided into two
groups and transferred to military trucks. I was put on a Harbin-bound
truck. We got to our destination, and I saw only an open field and some
dug-up shelters. All of us were confined like prisoners in cubicles called
"comfort" stations and given only a small handful of rice to eat. Throughout the evening, three truckloads of soldiers arrived at the camp. Every
evening soldiers queued up in front of my cubicle and one by one raped
me all night long. Their bodies were filthy and they didn't speak a word.
I couldn't sleep and cried all night. As punishment for crying, I had to
stand outside without any food. I could not survive, they said, even if I
escaped, because there was no place to run to in an empty open field. My
body was so young, and repeated sex caused my uterus to be inverted.
Sitting up was so painful; I could only lie down. Penicillin shots would
heal my sores and also injections called #606. Many girls got pregnant,
but still were forced to have sex up until childbirth. If a girl refused sex,
the soldiers would tie up her feet with his boot straps and force sex on her.

When she delivered a baby, a blue-uniformed woman put the baby in a sack without cutting the umbilical cord properly and carried it away. She was given no recovery period after childbirth and was forced to have sex right away. As a consequence, many girls got very ill. Suddenly, I noticed a female hand stretched straight up from a blanket. I realized later that it was the hand of the sick girl who must have been buried alive, and who must have struggled to free herself from the wrapped blanket. Many soldiers used a "saku" ["sack" or condom] which they often washed, dried, and re-used. Girls often got infected from the used condoms, but the soldiers didn't care. I lived in fear, because I knew if I got very ill, they would wrap me up in a blanket and carry me away like that girl I saw by the stream. Verbal abuse from the soldiers was constant and unbearable. They told me "Chosun" [the old name for "Korea"] people are liars, untrustworthy, sub-human, and have no ancestors. When a girl got too sick, a guard would wrap her up in a blanket and carry her away. I did not see any of the sick girls ever come back. No one cared if Chosun people were killed, the soldiers said.

Such was my life in Harbin, where I stayed for about a year until the next move. One night I was told to get on a military truck. After traveling all night, the truck arrived at another empty, open field. I later found out it was a place called "Kwang-tung." During the night, three truck loads of soldiers arrived. They queued up in front of the cubicles for sex. Girls were identified with numbers. I was simply known as "Number 27." After each soldier, I wasn't even given time to wash up and get dressed for the next soldier in line. I serviced eight to ten soldiers during the night and about seven officers in the daytime. I once tried to hide under my blanket to avoid sex, but the soldier found me, and then beat me and kicked me with boots on. Even now I can't walk straight.

One day an officer after sex felt sorry for me and gave me 500 yen. With that money, I planned an escape. That night I ran through the open field and finally reached a house I thought would be a private home. It was full of soldiers. They interrogated me and searched my body and found the hidden money. They accused me of being a spy and turned me over to the military police. The police beat my body severely and smashed my hands, weaving a stiff pen between my fingers like this. Look at my fingers now, all crooked. I was sent back to the same hell I tried to escape from, and all day long, I was left completely disrobed, with my hands and feet bound.

Another year passed like this. It was about June of 1945. A camp worker showed up at our location and whispered to us secretly to leave the place quickly; otherwise we would all die. We didn't know why, but noticed the number of the soldiers was decreasing and the remaining soldiers seemed spiritless. So when the camp seemed deserted, I escaped with two other girls and ran all night, finally reaching a shore. I found a boat and hid under the tarp. The next morning the boat sailed out to sea, and I was discovered, when the fishermen lifted up the tarp. I shamelessly pleaded, "I will do anything, anything for you, only if you will drop me off on Korean shores." So I worked on the anchovy fishing boat for about a month, cooking, cleaning, washing clothes, and servicing sex. When I found out one of the fishermen was a Korean, I was so overwhelmed and cried with joy. It was like meeting my own parents.

Early dawn the captain dropped me off. "From here on, it's Korea," he said. It was an island. I found out later that it was the leper colony. I knocked on a gate. The lepers came out with welcomes and gave me some rice. I made up stories about my past, because I simply couldn't tell them the truth. They helped me send a letter to my parents. My mother had been so grief-stricken over my disappearance that she had become very frail and developed a tumor inside her nose. My parents came for me, but I couldn't go home with them for fear I might be kidnapped again. Also, once a girl leaves home, she is not supposed to return to her parents' home, according to our custom. So I stayed with my relatives. My parents married me off as a safeguard, because the government was less likely to summon married women for work.

Completely affected by my past, I could not be happy in my marriage. Korea was liberated and all the Japanese left our land, but I couldn't be happy. All these years I have lived in secret, shame, and in pain. I resent the Japanese. How could they have done such unspeakable things to me? And to so many innocent young girls? I worry now, what if a war breaks out in the future? How do we know that the Japanese will not repeat such atrocities again? Even now, the Japanese appear to be kind on the surface, but I don't trust them. How can I trust them?

Activities of the Washington Coalition for "Comfort Women" Issues, Inc.

The Washington Coalition for "Comfort Women" Issues, Inc. (WCCW) was created in December 1992 to further research and education in the Washington, D.C., area concerning crimes against "comfort women" during World War II. It is an independent, nonprofit, and nonpartisan educational organization open to volunteers of every nationality and with diverse points of view. The WCCW is staffed entirely by volunteers. In recent years, WCCW activities have included preparation of educational videos, publications, newspaper advertisements, TV and radio appearances, speeches at public events, the staging of symposia, and the gathering and translation of scholarly research materials concerning "comfort women." The following timeline shows some of these major activities:

1992

November: Testimony by Hwang Keum Ju, a former "comfort woman," on military sexual slavery by Japan at Korean United Methodist Church. (News coverage by Channel 5 TV station.)

December: WCCW established.

1993

January: Collection of 8,000 petitions on behalf of redress for "comfort women."

April: International symposium "The Asian Women and Peace," Tokyo, Japan.

October: Publication of a WCCW open letter to Japanese prime minister Hosokawa in the *Washington Post.*

1994

February: "Forum on 'Comfort Women,'" cosponsored by Georgetown University Law Center Students Association. Speaker: Dr. Heisoo Shin, the Korea Council.

February: Address on "comfort women" at Amnesty International Regional Conference, "Treatment of Women during Wartime." Speaker: Won Kim, Esq.

March: Presentation on "comfort women" at the International Women's Day Symposium on Women's Human Rights around the World, University of Richmond.

May: Forum on "comfort women." Speaker: Kenichi Takagi, Attorney-at-Law, Tokyo, Japan.

October/   Videotaped interviewing of fifteen surviving "comfort
November: women" (South Korea) to preserve their testimonies.

1995

March: Production of the video *Comfort Women.*

April: "The 'Comfort Women'": An exhibition at the United
                Methodist Church, Washington, DC.

August/   Presentation of the video *Comfort Women* at the Fourth
September: UN World Conference on Women in Beijing.

September: Presentation of "comfort women" issues at the opening
                ceremony of the exhibition "Asian Holocaust," Old
                Dominion University, Norfolk, VA.

November: Presentation on "comfort women" issues at the Korean-
                American Women UN Seminar, New York.

1996

March/April: Attendance at the 52nd UN Human Rights Commis-
                sion, Geneva.

April: Talk show on "comfort women" at "The Women
                Connection," New York.

June: Providing of historical photos to *Time* magazine (*Time*
                magazine later featured a six-page article titled "Japan:
                The Furor Over Making Apologies to the 'Comfort
                Women'").

September: International conference at Georgetown University:
                "The 'Comfort Women' of World War II: Legacy and
                Lessons," cosponsored with Georgetown University, the
                Korea Society, and other organizations.

September: Testimony by Kim Yoon-shim, a surviving former "com-
                fort woman," at Georgetown University.

October: Scheduling of meetings for Kim Yoon-shim with the
                U.S. Justice Department and the U.S. Department.

1997

February/   Presentation on WCCW activities in the United States
March: on "comfort women" at an International Symposium in
                Seoul, Korea.

May: Presentation on "comfort women" at a press confer-
                ence, U.S. Congress.

July: Congressional Representative William O. Lipinski, joined by other U.S. congressional representatives (sixty-nine members as of May 1998), submitted House Resolution 126 to the U.S. Congress, urging the Japanese government to extend a formal apology and pay reparations to victims of Japanese war crimes.

December: Book signing by Therese Park, author of *A Gift of the Emperor*.

1998

June: Presentation of significantly expanded exhibit: 'Comfort Women' of World War II: An Indisputable Tragedy" at the Cannon House Office Building Rotunda on Capitol Hill, Washington, DC (1–14 June 1998).

June: Testimony by Kim Bok Dong, a surviving former "comfort woman" at a luncheon conference on Capitol Hill, Washington, DC.

1999

March/May: Exhibit: "'Comfort Women' of World War II" at the Free Library of Philadelphia (19 March–31 May 1999).

March: Keynote speech by Kim Yoon-shim at the Thirteenth Annual Korean American Students' Conference, co-sponsored by Stanford University and the University of California, Berkeley.

2000

September: "'Comfort Women' of World War II" event at the U.S. Holocaust Museum, Washington, DC.

September: "Year 2000 Remembrance: Women of Dignity and Honor," event at the Rayburn House Office Building, Capitol Hill, Washington, DC.

Travel Schedule of the "Comfort Women" Exhibit and the Video *Comfort Women*

The "comfort women" exhibit has been traveling around the United States:

1995

25 April–19 May:	Washington, DC: "'Comfort Women': Suffering and Dignity in Asia During WWII."
29 June–15 July:	Korean American Museum, Los Angeles, CA.
1–5 September:	Fourth World Conference on Women, Beijing.
23–26 September:	Old Dominion University, Norfolk, VA: "Asian Holocaust" Exhibition.
27 September–1 October:	Chinese Community Center, Virginia Beach, VA.
8–15 October:	Atlanta, GA: "The Forgotten Holocaust."
28 October–5 November:	St. Paul, MN: "The Asian Holocaust."

1996

May:	Metro Toronto Reference Library; sponsored by the Canadian Coalition for "Comfort Women" Redress.

1997

24–29 March:	Dickinson College, PA.

1998

1–12 June:	"'Comfort Women' of WW II: An Indisputable Tragedy," Cannon House Office Building, U.S. Capitol.

1999

19 March–31 May:	The Free Library of Philadelphia: "'Comfort Women' of WWII."

A Brief Chronology of "Comfort Women" Issues

1990

November:	The Korean Council for the Women Drafted for Sexual Slavery by Japan is formed in South Korea.

1991

August:

Kim Hak Soon becomes the first "comfort woman" to testify publicly that the Japanese military forced her into sexual servitude during World War II.

November:

Yoshida Seiji, the Japanese labor mobilization director during World War II, confirms that the Japanese military obtained the services of "comfort women" through force and deceit.

1992

January:

Japanese chief cabinet secretary Kato admits for the first time that the Japanese imperial army was involved in running military brothels.

February:

The "comfort women" issue is raised at the UN Commission on Human Rights.

August:

The "comfort women" issue is raised at the UN Sub-Commission on the Prevention of Discrimination and Protection of Minorities.

December:

Washington Coalition for "Comfort Women" Issues, Inc., is formed.

1993

August:

The Japanese government issues a carefully worded statement admitting an unspecified role in the military brothels, yet rejecting legal responsibility for them. Japan continues to contend the brothels were not a "system" and not a war crime nor a crime against humanity.

November:

Twenty-four members of the U.S. Congress write to Japanese prime minister Hosokawa urging his government to investigate the sexual slavery of "comfort women."

1994

August: Japanese prime minister Murayama announces the
                   Japanese government's first version of the "private fund"
                   plan. It stresses job-training programs for Japanese
                   companies employing Asian women, but rejects
                   payment of reparation to "comfort women."

November: International Commission of Jurists concludes in a
                   special report, "Report of a Mission," that "It is
                   indisputable that these women were forced, deceived,
                   coerced, and abducted to provide sexual services to the
                   Japanese military . . . Japan violated customary norms
                   of international law concerning war crimes, crimes
                   against humanity, slavery and the trafficking in women
                   and children."

1995

March: UN Commission on the Status of Women NGO work-
                   shop adopts a resolution supporting "comfort women."

July: The Japanese government announces the establishment
                   of the Asian Women Fund.

September: The UN Fourth World Conference on Women, Beijing,
                   adopts a resolution supporting "comfort women."

1996

January: UN Special Rapporteur on Violence Against Women,
                   Ms. Radhika Coomaraswamy, issues a detailed report
                   on crimes against "comfort women" to the UN
                   Commission on Human Rights.

December: News release by the U.S. Justice Department announc-
                   ing that sixteen suspected Japanese war criminals have
                   been placed on a "watch list" for the first time. The
                   men on the watch list are prohibited from entering the
                   United States.

1997

July: Members of the U.S. Congress (sixty-nine as of May
                   1998), headed by Rep. William O. Lipinski, introduce

H. Res. 126, urging the Japanese government to extend a formal apology and to pay reparations to all the victims of Japanese war crimes during World War II.

1998

August: UN study report by Special Rapporteur Gay McDougall calls on the Japanese government to accept legal responsibility for enslaving women in rape camps during World War II.

1999

August: UN Sub-Commission on Human Rights adopts a resolution on sexual crimes that "the rights and obligations of States and individuals recognized by international law with respect to these violations could not be extinguished by peace treaty or amnesty."

2000

December   The "Women's International War Crimes Tribunal on Japan's Military Sexual Slavery" held in Tokyo.

Chapter 8

My Own *Gaiatsu*

A Document from 1945
Provides Proof

Grant K. Goodman

In August 1993, I received a telephone call from the office of the consul general of Japan in Kansas City, Missouri, inviting me to meet the consul general for lunch at the elegant Kansas City Club. Having willingly accepted his invitation, I arrived at the appointed date and time to find that this was a luncheon at which only the consul general and I were present. He greeted me warmly, shook my hand, and said in English, "Professor Goodman, thanks to you, the Japanese government has now accepted responsibility for the wartime *ianfu*" ("comfort women" or sex slaves). While his statement surprised and, indeed, delighted me, and while I recognized that once again the Japanese government had responded to *gaiatsu* (foreign pressure), this peculiarly cathartic experience led me to think back to the grandstand of the muddy Santa Ana race track in Manila, where it all began.

At the age of eighteen-and-a-half years in April 1943, I had enlisted in the U.S. Army, having been previously selected to enter a special program for the training of Military Intelligence Service Japanese Language Officers. After a year of intensive Japanese language study at the Army Intensive Japanese Language School at the University of Michigan, two months of infantry training at Ft. McClellan, Alabama, and six months further language study at the Military Intelligence Service Language School at Ft. Snelling, Minnesota, in April 1945 I was commissioned a second lieutenant in the Military Intelligence Service. The very next month, I was sent overseas and assigned to the Allied Translator and Interpreter Section (ATIS) at the headquarters of General Douglas MacArthur in Manila, the Philippines.

This being the summer of 1945, plans for the forthcoming invasion of Japan were well under way, and among our important assignments was the gathering of as much intelligence as possible on the subject of the morale of the Japanese armed forces. To that end, I personally was engaged both in the interrogation of captured Japanese prisoners of war and the translation of captured documents.

As the title of the now famous ATIS Research Report No. 120 clearly indicates, one of the ways in which Japanese military morale was analyzed was through a study of "Amenities in the Japanese Armed Forces." This report was based on data available to ATIS up to 31 March 1945, and covered canteen stores, amusements, news, and mail accessible to the Japanese military. Under amusements, the document included athletics, movies, geisha and entertainment troupes, opportunities for leave, and brothels. The section on brothels was only twelve pages in length, plus nine pages of appendices. The subheadings under brothels covered general regulations, business operation, management, hygiene, discipline, and regulations for special clubs for officers and high-ranking civilian officials. The specific geographic sites of brothels described by the ATIS report were the Philippines, Burma, Sumatra, and New Britain. The two appendices provided fourteen forms required by the Japanese army for a brothel to be operated in Manila, plus an example of a very detailed police report of a medical and sanitation inspection of a typical Manila brothel.

My best memory is that at the time the material about these military brothels was being translated, it did not arouse any special interest, since the U.S. military intelligence knew well that the Japanese had been involved in operating brothels for their armed forces, at least since the outbreak of the war in China in 1937. Speaking personally, however, at the then tender age of twenty and being a very innocent youth from a middle-class American family in Ohio, I found these data very informative. Accordingly, after our report was published for circulation at GHQ, I managed to keep a copy and mailed it home with a request that my parents keep it for me until my return from overseas.

In January 1992, I happened to read in my local newspaper, the *Lawrence Journal World*, an Associated Press story that Professor Yoshimi Yoshiaki of Chuo University in Tokyo had found documents in the Defense Agency archives that demonstrated the direct involvement of the Japanese military in the organization and utilization of brothels. Although the Japanese government questioned the authenticity of Professor Yoshimi's documents, for the first time the chief cabinet secretary, and later the then prime minister Miyazawa Kiichi, offered public apologies for the government's role in the matter of the *ianfu*.

These news stories struck a familiar chord with me. First of all, the entire subject of Japanese government-sponsored prostitution did not seem surprising to me. Somehow, I recalled that this was something that I and many other Americans had known about nearly five decades earlier. Indeed, I remembered not only the translation work I had done at ATIS GHQ in Manila, but most importantly that I still had my own copy of Research Report No. 120!

Remarkably, in short order I found in my files the document from almost half a century earlier. Its contents were extremely specific and left no doubt of Japanese government responsibility for the *ianfu* brothels. The question then became what my next move should be.

As a scholar and a historian, of course, I especially wanted to avoid any suspicion of sensationalism. Moreover, I did not want to be in the position of a foreigner accusing the Japanese of anything. To my mind, making the document available was of far greater importance than any publicity that might come to me personally. Accordingly, I decided to make my document known to a Japanese journalist whom I knew personally, Mr. Miura Junji of the Kyodo News Agency Washington Bureau.

I had come to know Mr. Miura in November 1991, when he had interviewed me for a feature story he wrote for the fiftieth anniversary of the Japanese attack on Pearl Harbor. I had been especially impressed by him because, after the interview, he had telephoned me to recheck his facts and to ascertain the accuracy of the quotations that he was attributing to me. Indeed, when the story ran in the Japanese press, Mr. Miura had very courteously sent me copies for my records. In short, this was one of the most polite and thorough journalists I had ever known, and I felt entirely comfortable in offering to share my document with him.

When I informed him of what I had, he was tremendously excited and almost excessively appreciative. At his request, I sent him a photocopy via Federal Express, and on 5 and 6 February 1992, the story broke on practically every front page of every Japanese newspaper, as well as on every Japanese television news program. Here is the English version of Mr. Miura's dispatch as it appeared in the *Japan Times* of 5 February 1992:

> War Brothels Were Strict, Report Shows. Under Military Rules, "Comfort Women" Had One Day Off a Month.
>
> By Antonio Kamiya

WASHINGTON (Kyodo) Battlefront brothels run by the Imperial Japanese Army in occupied Asian territories were operated under strict military rules that provided for everything from prices to the prostitutes' hygiene conditions, according to evidence unveiled here Monday.

Records translated from Imperial Japanese Army documents show that the military kept a close watch and dictated rules for the brothels' operations.

Women, often under false pretenses or through force, were brought from Japan, Korea, China and Southeast Asia to provide sexual services exclusively for the benefit of Japanese soldiers and the army's civilian employees.

Compiled by the U.S. Occupation Forces in Japan, the report, titled "Amenities in the Japanese Armed Forces," details the regulations, business operation, management, hygiene and discipline of the army-run brothels. They were euphemistically called "houses of relaxation" and employed prostitutes known variously as "comfort women" or "geisha and hostesses."

The report, made available to Kyodo News Service by Professor Grant Goodman, a former translator of Imperial Japanese Army documents and now a Japanese scholar at the University of Kansas, provides the most detailed account yet on the controversial brothel operation run and abetted by the Japanese military in occupied Asian territories.

According to a section of the report detailing brothel operations in Manila, a "bound printed booklet" issued in February 1943 by a Lt. Col. Onishi at a Japanese military unit known as the Manila District Line of Communication Squad specified that the "authorized restaurants and houses of relaxation will be used only by soldiers and army civilian employees."

The regulations stipulated that prostitutes, identified in army documents as "geisha and hostesses," had to hand over half of their income to their Japanese managers, who in turn were required to submit daily and monthly business reports to the military.

Hours of operations were set, and "an army physician" was on hand to determine whether any particular illness incurred by the women was "due to overwork," the documents show.

Such a diagnosis, according to the document, would entitle the women to medical expenses paid by brothel operators. The prostitutes were given only one day off a month.

Apparently in a move to prevent transmission of venereal diseases, the army regulations stipulated that "association with the hostesses will be forbidden to those who refuse to use condoms," and that the women "will not be kissed."

Hygiene Rules Ignored

While the regulations provided numerous hygiene rules governing the operation of the army brothels, the U.S. report shows that they were often ignored.

The U.S. study cites a police report that accuses operators of army-sanctioned brothels in Manila of paying "scant attention" to hygienic rules.

"Many managers are interested in nothing beyond their own profit and do their job with no other purpose," said the police report, issued by the Manila Sector Line of Communications in February 1944.

According to the police report, there were at least 1,183 "comfort women" working in Manila at 20 brothels and "special clubs for officers and high-ranking civilian officials" at the time it was compiled.

Police inspectors gave a vivid report on sanitary conditions at one "special club" in Manila known as the "Round Pearl," run by a man identified as Shigeru Terao.

Infested by Insects

"There are numerous insects in the kitchen," the report says. "Proper care is not taken of the chopping boards. The lift to carry the food from the kitchen to the second and third floors and the beer and sake bar on the second floor (is) too close to the lavatories, with (the) result that there are numerous insects against which no measures have been taken. People are seated too close in the dining hall. The latter is not clean and insects are numerous."

Of the 1,183 prostitutes who underwent medical examination, 69 were found to be ill, according to the police report.

The U.S. report provides details on the special privileges of the Japanese military brass, noting that special clubs catering to officers and high-ranking civilian officials were allowed to hire "minors as geisha, waitresses or maids" under special army permission.

Prices at the brothels were strictly set by the Japanese military.

According to a "bound mimeographed and handwritten file of drafts of orders and bulletins" belonging to the Manila Army Air Depot and dated over a two-month period from August to October 1944, the cost of a 40–minute session was set at ¥1.50 for enlisted men, ¥2.50 for noncommissioned officers and ¥4 for civilian employees.

The price listings were classified as "secret," the U.S. report says.

In the case of regulations set by the Japanese military unit known as the South Sector Guard Headquarters, which the U.S. report says was located "probably in (the) Shanghai area," the prices varied according to the nationality of the prostitutes. The price that officers and warrant officers paid for a one-hour session with a Japanese or Korean prostitute was ¥3, while that for a Chinese was ¥2.50.

The wartime Imperial Japanese Navy also operated its own brothels but disguised them, according to the U.S. report.

For example, navy-run establishments in Rabaul, Papua New Guinea, were categorized as "special warehouses," the report says.

Testimony obtained through the interrogation of Japanese prisoners of war indicate that the Japanese military also operated brothels in Indonesia and the Southwest Pacific area, the report says.

According to accounts from a Japanese POW identified as First Class Private Kiyoichi Ishiguro, who was captured in November 1942, "two native women from Narumonda and six Chinese women served" in "an official army brothel in Belawan (Sumatra)," the report says.

As reported last week by Kyodo, the Imperial Japanese Army also ran an extensive battlefront brothel network in Burma, now Myanmar, according to statements from a Japanese prisoner of war and a civilian brothel owner who was captured with his wife and 20 army prostitutes near Waingmaw on Aug. 10, 1944.

Japan Times, Feb. 5, 1992 (Permission to reprint kindly granted by *Kyodo News*)

Reactions to these press reports were overwhelmingly positive. Phone calls, faxes, and letters to me arrived from friends, as well as from previously unknown individuals who wanted to express their appreciation. Mr. Miura himself wrote me a most gracious letter to say that in over twenty years as a journalist, thanks to me, this had been his greatest scoop ever. One response, however, was a bit frightening.

On 6 February, early in the morning I received a telephone call from the consulate general of Japan in Kansas City, asking whether someone from the consulate could meet with me as soon as possible, perhaps within an hour! Of course, I already knew that news of my document had broken in Japan, and that I had been identified in those reports as a University of Kansas professor emeritus. Accordingly, I imagined that overnight messages had probably arrived from the Foreign Office in Tokyo, instructing the consulate general to get as much information as possible about this "Goodman" and his document.

Certainly, I did not want to meet with anyone from the Japanese consulate general in a precipitate manner. My own parochial reaction to their request was that, if the Foreign Office were truly distressed by my releasing this document, I might even be barred from future travel to Japan. I, therefore, responded by saying that I had a number of prior engagements that day, but I would call the consulate back to set up an appointment.

Then, as any red-blooded American would do, I placed a call to my lawyer. His advice, which in retrospect was excellent, was (1) to set up an appointment for that afternoon; (2) to meet with the consular officials in a public place; (3) to take my lawyer with me to the meeting and identify him as a friend but not as my lawyer; and (4) to bring a copy of the document with me, as well as a copy of my curriculum vitae. The meeting took place at 2 p.m. on 6 February 1992 in the coffee shop of the Lawrence Holidome. Two persons came from the Consulate General, and I was present with my lawyer. Indeed, a copy of the document and my curriculum vitae were exactly what they wanted. Since I was prepared accordingly, the meeting took less than fifteen minutes, and no one even drank a cup of coffee.

Below is the text of the signed receipt that I requested from them when I gave them a copy of the now famous document.

> Received of Dr. Grant Goodman a copy of the "Amenities in the Japanese Armed Forces" dated 15 Nov. 45, consisting of 26 pages, including I, iii, iv, 9–20, 28–36.
> Dated February 6, 1992.
> Japanese Consulate General
> By Mitsuo Takamatsu
> Consul of Japan

What is particularly interesting about this latter encounter was its obviously strained formality. Of course, the Japanese consulate general in Kansas City knew me well, since I had enjoyed extensive and frequent contact with its staff and with successive consuls general since its establishment in 1977. However, in this instance, especially since my name had come to the attention of the highest levels in the Foreign Office, it was as though no one at the consulate general had ever heard of me before. Nevertheless, just a week later, I received an invitation to dinner at the home of the consul general and was asked by his secretary to provide the names of anyone whom I would like to have included on the guest list!

In best Japanese fashion, while the matter of the document was never specifically mentioned, it was clear that this very relaxed and pleasant event was the consul general's marvelously indirect way of letting me know how much he had appreciated my cooperation with him in providing the consulate with a copy of the document, as well as informing me that I had passed muster in Tokyo and was again in the relatively good graces of the Foreign Office. Luckily, I suppose, my half century of training and experience as an academic Japan specialist facilitated my ability to interpret this peculiar sequence of events. Moreover, some fifteen years earlier, another bizarre encounter with the Japanese Foreign Office over a reference to *burakumin* in a footnote to a scholarly paper had given me some preparation for the extreme sensitivity that was evidenced on this occasion.

The subsequent development of international and national pressure on the Japanese government to admit to its prewar and wartime participation in the recruitment—often forceful—and utilization of sex workers to service the Japanese military is well known. And, in August 1993, as its last official act, Prime Minister Miyazawa's cabinet issued its admission of guilt and its formal apologia.

Why no one could find the document that I had in my personal files for almost half a century is still a mystery to me. Not only are all of the ATIS Research Reports in the National Archives, but they were published on microfiche, as *Wartime Translations of Seized Japanese Documents: Allied Translator and Interpreter Section Reports, 1941–1946*. (Bethesda, MD: CIS, 1988), 2v. I can assume, however, that contemporary researchers had simply failed to look for *ianfu* data in a report entitled "Amenities in the Japanese Armed Forces."

I am, of course, proud of the crucial role that my own "Revelation" of the contents of ATIS Research Report No. 120 played in bringing about the Japanese prime minister's acceptance of responsibility for the so-called "comfort women." However, as in so many analogous instances, that the Japanese government only made its admission and evidenced contrition after a foreigner provided incontrovertible evidence is truly tragic. Professor Yoshimi's documentary proof was certainly as convincing, if not more so, as anything contained in the ATIS document. Yet his efforts were apparently not taken seriously by the highest levels of Japanese governance. And even after my data received worldwide publicity, it required another year and a half for the Japanese cabinet to make a full admission.

This is not the place for a lengthy examination of the reasons for the continued Japanese reticence to deal with its wartime misdeeds. Nevertheless, while Germany has demonstrated a continuing willingness to face its very unfortunate and, indeed, terrible Nazi crimes, Japan has seemingly purposefully avoided meaningful confrontation with its atrocities and iniquities.

In the specific case of the *ianfu*, the denials that preceded the August 1993 cabinet statement had many rationales, all of which certainly combined to reinforce the government's inability to face the matter squarely. Japan has been historically and still is very much a male-dominated society, so psychologically the concept of women in servitude to men must not have seemed anathema. Moreover, Western perspectives on human rights or individual responsibilities have played little or no part in Japanese society. Further, prostitution has a substantive history in Japan and, in its various forms, including such derivations as geisha or bar hostesses or massage parlor employees, is seen as simply another kind of gainful employment. Thus, through a system like that of the *ianfu*, the Japanese military saw itself as providing an opportunity for women from poor families, especially in rural areas of Korea and China, for example, to have employment opportunities that would otherwise not be available to them. Important, too, in their desire to maintain a fighting force with high morale, sexual release at government-controlled and government-inspected brothels was viewed as logical and necessary. Additionally, by maintaining such establishments, the Japanese military again viewed itself as extremely magnanimous since, they contended, this would prevent Japanese troops from molesting or even raping local women in occupied areas.

Interestingly, too, since August 1993 many articulate Japanese, including some academics, have publicly deplored the prime minister's apology, as well as the establishment of the Asian Women's Fund to try to provide some compensation to surviving "comfort women." These individuals have argued that the Japanese have nothing to apologize for, and that what they see as the abject apology of the government's leader is another example of a Japan toadying to foreign opinion. In fact, the latter explanation of the 1993 Japanese apologia may be more accurate than the scholar-observer would perhaps like to think.

In my opinion, as much as I would like to believe the Kansas City consul general's rather grandiose estimate of my particular role in the August 1993 statement, I think that the Japanese government simply felt that, whatever the consequences, there was an obvious point of diminishing returns in continued denial. And that point could be, I believe, measured in real as well as potential foreign trade statistics. In other words, there were undoubtedly those at the cabinet level of Japanese government who saw the *ianfu* problem as a pocketbook issue. That is, in the significant context of Japan's booming trade with Asia, there was surely no need to inflate a potential irritant to Japan–Asian relations. Thus, while I am happy to think that my own *gaiatsu* was crucial to Japan's acceptance of the onus for the wartime military brothel system, the real *gaiatsu* was probably the possibility that a failure to apologize could only exacerbate political differences between Japan and its Asian neighbors and, accordingly, threaten very profitable economic ties.

Chapter 9

Placing Japanese War Criminals on the U.S. Justice Department's "Watch List" of 3 December 1996

The Legal and Political Background

John Y. Lee

The Application of the Holtzman Amendment

On 3 December 1996, the U.S. Department of Justice announced that the United States would apply the Holtzman Amendment against Japanese war criminals. The Holtzman Amendment[1] provides that a person who has participated in, under the direction of the Nazi government or any other government that was an ally of the Nazi government, the persecution of any person because of race, religion, national origin, or political opinion is prohibited from entry into the United States. Additionally, the Holtzman Amendment[2] stipulates that any alien fitting the above description is deportable.[3]

Pursuant to these sections of the law, the Justice Department placed on the U.S. government's "Watch List" aliens that fall within the categories of the persons described in the manner above. Specifically, members of "Unit 731," an infamous Japanese army detachment in Manchuria that conducted inhumane and frequently lethal pseudo-medical experiments—including vivisection—on thousands of prisoners of war and civilians, were placed on the Watch List.

The other persons prohibited from entering the United States and to be deported if they are already present within the United States are those who are suspected of involvement in the Japanese imperial army's establishment, maintenance, and utilization of forced sex centers where women were taken—principally from Korea, China, and other Pacific nations—and held captive. In these "comfort stations," women were beaten and tortured in addition to being repeatedly raped day after day by the Imperial Japanese soldiers.

The Justice Department further announced that sixteen Japanese citizens have been put on the U.S. government's Watch List of aliens who are ineligible to enter the United States.

The Holtzman Amendment

The legislative history of the amendment, which was enacted in 1978, shows that the term "persecution" was intended to signify the individual act of inflicting suffering or harm, under government sanction, on persons who differ based on race, religion, political opinion, or so on, in a manner condemned by civilized government. The harm or suffering need not be physical, but may take other forms, such as the deliberate imposition of severe economic disadvantage or the deprivation of liberty, food, housing, employment, or other essentials of life.

The Supreme Court and other lower courts have consistently held that deportation proceedings are civil rather than criminal in nature, and therefore the ex post facto prohibition of the U.S. Constitution is not applicable to deportation proceedings.[4] In the case of *Artukovic v. Immigration and Naturalization Service,*[5] the U.S. Circuit Court specifically ruled that members of the Nazi faction who had persecuted people because of their race, religion, national origin, or political opinion were deportable, and such deportation did not constitute an ex post facto law. Nor was this section held unconstitutionally vague for its use of the term "persecution."

Furthermore, the courts held that neither the Holtzman Amendment nor the Immigration and Naturalization Act Section governing the suspension of deportation constituted bills of attainder or ex post facto laws.[6]

The Holtzman Amendment, as discussed above, has not been successfully challenged either in the United States courts or in other courts around the world. The right of any sovereign nation either to exclude or to deport any aliens on the grounds stipulated in this instant statute is well recognized. Further, the procedural due process requirement for each individual determination has been satisfied in the past cases developed since the enactment of the statute.

International Movements Supporting the "Comfort Women"

Report of the International Commission of Jurists

Prior to the Justice Department's decision on 3 December 1996 to implement the foregoing section of the law, the International Commission of Jurists had conducted an extensive investigation of the facts of the "comfort women" system and published its 1994 Mission Report in *Comfort Women: An Unfinished Ordeal*. Its analysis of the legal issues and its conclusions regarding the Japanese military practices during World War II are authoritative and pertinent, giving a legal basis for the Justice Department's decision to place individuals on its "Watch List" and to exclude them from entering the United States.

The report, after setting forth the facts of the "comfort women" practices, stated that since the Japanese soldiers directly or indirectly participated in the "comfort women" system, their actions must be imputed to the state. Therefore, the commission affirmatively expressed its view that the government of Japan must be held responsible for its actions under international law. The following are the commission's findings and conclusions regarding the legal issues involved in the "comfort women" system.

Imputability of Soldiers' Acts to the State of Japan

Under international law, the report reasserted a traditional rule of international law that, where officers act as officials and not as private individuals, their actions must be imputed to the state.[7] The report found that Japanese officers who regulated the "comfort stations" were acting as officials and not as private individuals, as evidenced by documents obtained by the mission of the International Commission of Jurists. One of the documents contained evidence of special requests made by Japanese field officers to commanders in Tokyo for the recruitment, as well as the transportation, of the "comfort women." This shows that field officers and high-ranking officials were both actively involved in the systematic, militarily sanctioned recruitment and placement of women in those stations. Under these circumstances, the International Commission of Jurists authoritatively decided that the state can be held responsible for their actions under international law.

The Trafficking of Women and Children

In addition to its determination that individual acts of Japanese soldiers can be imputed to the State of Japan, the International Commission of Jurists further concluded that Japan has breached the International Convention for the Suppression of the Traffic of Women and Children of 1921.[8] Japan ratified this convention in 1925. Under this convention, ratifying nations such as Japan were obligated to take all necessary steps to discover and prosecute persons engaged in the trafficking of women and children under Articles 2 and 3. Japan's systematic recruiting of women from Korea and other areas in the Pacific for its "comfort stations" clearly violated its duties under the convention, as it was heavily involved in the trafficking of women and children for sexual slavery purposes.

Geneva Convention

With regards to specific treaty law, the International Commission of Jurists has decided that the Geneva Convention Relative to the Protection of Civilian Persons in Time of War of 1949 is not applicable "ratione temporis" to acts by the Japanese military against the "comfort women." In other words, because the Geneva Convention did not exist during the period of World War II and was a postwar event, it does not apply to Japan's crimes during this period.

Customary International Law

The International Commission of Jurists has further concluded that the Japanese military has, in addition to violating its duties under the Suppression Convention, also violated customary international law. For example, its use of the "comfort women" as sex slaves has violated customary law prohibiting slavery.[9] Article 22(5) of the Covenant of the League of Nations made it a requirement for states to administer a mandate providing for the emancipation of slaves, the suppression of the slave trade, and the prohibition of forced labor. The 1924 Temporary Slavery Commission, established by the League of Nations, resulted in the creation of the Slavery Convention of 1926, which also prohibited slavery.

The Japanese military engaged in the slave trade, as it kidnapped and transported women to its various "comfort stations." Also, after the "comfort women" were transported to such stations, the Japanese military treated them as if they were owned by the military. Thus, the International Commission of Jurists has concluded that Japan has violated customary international law regarding the prohibition of slavery, as well as the convention prohibiting slavery.

In addition to prohibiting slavery, customary international law also requires belligerents to respect civilians. Article 46 of the Hague Regulations, as customary law, requires the "family honour" of civilians be protected. The International Commission has determined conclusively that, through raping the women, the Japanese soldiers violated their "family honour."

War Crimes

The International Commission of Jurists has made an important determination that members of the Japanese army who abducted and raped the "comfort women" committed war crimes and crimes against humanity punishable under international law and should be prosecuted by Japanese courts.

The Charter of the International Military Tribunal of Tokyo defined war crimes as the violation of the laws or customs of war and crimes against humanity—namely, murder, extermination, enslavement, deportation, and other inhuman acts that are the war crimes. By entering the Treaty of Peace in San Francisco, in 1951, Japan accepted the jurisdiction and judgments of the International Military Tribunal, which defined the war crimes.

Report of the Special Rapporteur on Violence against Women: Its Causes and Consequences[10]

In addition to the report from the International Commission of Jurists, the report of the United Nations Special Rapporteur has provided the U.S. Department of Justice with a legal basis to place Japanese war criminals on its Watch List. Pursuant to the Commission on Human Rights Resolution, a UN Special Rapporteur, Ms. Radhika Coomaraswamy, was sent to Asia. The Special Rapporteur's main task entailed thoroughly investigating the "comfort women" situation by collecting evidence, as well as by hearing the testimonies of various persons. Through some of her conclusions made in her report, the Special Rapporteur further substantiated most of the assertions made by the International Commission of Jurists. Although the Special Rapporteur was not as precisely descriptive as to what law was violated, she conclusively delineated what particular provisions of international law were to be applicable to the Japanese government.

Supporting the International Commission of Jurists' viewpoints, the Special Rapporteur stated in her report that the International Convention for the Suppression of the Traffic in Women and Children of 1921 was applicable to Japan, as Japan had ratified the convention. Furthermore, Japan's contention that its exercise of Article 14 to declare that it did not include Korean "comfort women" was unfounded, as the Korean "comfort women" were taken to Japan.

Additionally, the Rapporteur asserted that Japan was a party to the Hague Convention and Annexed Regulations concerning the Laws and Customs of War on Land of 1907. As previously mentioned, Article 46 of the Hague Regulations places on states the obligation to protect "family honour" and is legitimate customary law, applicable to Japan.

Overall, the Special Rapporteur clarified that not only should certain areas of international law be applicable to Japan, but Japan must also take responsibility for violations of international law. The Rapporteur's published report explicitly explains that:

> The Special Rapporteur is absolutely convinced that most of the women kept at the "comfort stations" were taken against their will, that the Japanese Imperial Army initiated, regulated and controlled the vast network of comfort stations, and that the Government of Japan is responsible for the comfort stations. In addition, the Government of Japan should be prepared to assume responsibility for what this implies under international law.

In addition, the Special Rapporteur has rebutted various denials of the Japanese government with regards to its responsibilities under international law, including its obligation for reparation under the San Francisco Peace Treaty of 1951.

The Rapporteur supported the commission's position and concluded that the San Francisco Treaty provision was not concerned with "human rights violations in general or military sexual slavery in particular," and therefore it simply did not bar further reparations for sexual slavery.

The Report of the Special Rapporteur was welcomed and noted at the fifty-third session of the Commission on Human Rights. Published and noted by the Commission on Human Rights in April 1996, just a few months prior to the Justice Department's decision in December 1996, the report became a bridge to the Justice Department's decision.

The Legal and Political Actions to Be Pursued

Expansion of the Department of Justice's "Watch List"

Now that the Department of Justice has decided to implement international laws that the Japanese military has breached, and has already placed sixteen suspected Japanese war criminals on the Watch List, investigation and identification of the war criminals to be added to the list is necessary. It should be noted that more than sixty thousand Nazi-related war criminals have been identified and listed in the Justice Department's Watch List. Although the listing of substantial numbers of Japanese war criminals on the Watch List is not expected within the foreseeable future, sustained efforts should nevertheless be made.

In order to expand the Watch List, efforts should be geared toward procuring the records and evidence of Japanese individual and group involvement in the "comfort women" system during World War II. Because the Japanese government's archives, especially those relating to military matters, are closed to the public, authoritative agencies, especially the Human Rights Commission of the United Nations, should request either production of the records and evidence or free access to the Japanese archives, as well as to witnesses and suspects in Japan. This issue should be listed and discussed as an agenda item at the next session of the United Nations Commission on Human Rights.

In fact, during its fifty-second session on "The Elimination of Violence against Women," the Commission on Human Rights requested that information be produced by states with regards to possible violations of human rights against women. Specifically, the resolution of the Human Rights Commission at its fifty-second session emphatically requested "all Governments to cooperate with and assist the Special Rapporteur in the performance of the tasks and duties mandated, to supply all information requested and respond to the Special Rapporteur's visits and communication."

Article 10, the Commission on Human Rights Resolution, 18 April 1996

Further, the commission decided to continue consideration of the question as a matter of high priority for its fifty-third session (see Article 14 of the foregoing resolution). As there were clearly more than sixteen

Japanese citizens who were engaged in maintaining the "comfort stations," significantly more information and evidence is necessary to expand the Watch List. This question must be addressed at all subsequent
sessions of the UN Human Rights Commission.

Direct UN Action

The Special Rapporteur's Recommendations

The Special Rapporteur made specific recommendations to the Japanese government, requesting that it take certain measures to make reparations to the "comfort women." Thus, in upcoming sessions, the UN
Commission on Human Rights should determine whether or not the previous Special Rapporteur's recommendations[11] have been complied with
by the Japanese.

   In her report, the Special Rapporteur specifically recommended that
the Japanese government carry out the following tasks: (1) acknowledge that the "comfort stations" set up by the Japanese imperial army
during World War II were a violation of its obligations under international law and accept legal responsibility for such violations; (2) pay
compensation to individual victims of sexual slavery based on principles
outlined by the Special Rapporteur of the Sub-Commission on Prevention of Discrimination and Protection of Minorities on the right to restitution, compensation, and rehabilitation for victims of grave violations
of human rights and fundamental freedoms—where a special tribunal
for this purpose should be set up; (3) make full disclosure of documents
and materials in its possession with regard to "comfort stations" and
other related activities; (4) publicly apologize in writing to individual
women victimized as former "comfort women"; (5) change educational
curricula to reflect historical realities; and (6) identify and punish perpetrators who recruited and institutionalized "comfort stations."

   As the commission welcomed and acknowledged the recommendations made by the Special Rapporteur, the Commission on Human Rights
has a duty to follow through and seek to ascertain the degree to which
the recommendations have been adhered to by the Japanese government. If it is determined that the Japanese government has made no
effort to carry out some of the recommendations, the commission should
strongly request that the Japanese government implement the recommendations of the Special Rapporteur during its next UN session.

Implementation of an International Tribunal Resembling the Bosnia Tribunal

Despite the UN resolution supporting the Special Rapporteur's recommendations, the Japanese government has thus far refused to cooperate with the agents of the United Nations in the implementation of the foregoing resolution. This has especially been true where the United Nations has sought to discover evidence of war crimes. Based on the Japanese government's current refusal to cooperate, the possibility of implementing more severe sanctions in the future becomes necessary. One of the most severe sanctions would be the establishment of an International Tribunal created to prosecute war crimes related to the "comfort women."

An International Tribunal similar to the Bosnia War Tribunal should be set up specifically to deal with the "comfort women" situation. In response to massive violations by Serbian troops, including wartime rape, the United Nations Security Council established an International Tribunal to prosecute war crimes. In its charter, the Tribunal specifically condemned wartime rape as a crime that could be prosecuted and punished.[12] Through Article V of the charter for the Tribunal, it was clarified that the Tribunal shall have the powers to prosecute persons responsible for a number of crimes "when committed in armed conflict, whether international or internal in character, and directed against any civilian population."[13] Along with other heinous crimes, this article listed rape as a crime that the International Tribunal shall have the power to prosecute. This inclusion of wartime rape in the Bosnia Tribunal's charter was an unprecedented action and set the stage for future precedents on prosecuting wartime rape.

Despite massive rape against women by Japanese troops, many of these atrocities went unpunished, because wartime rape was not prosecuted effectively in the Tokyo Tribunal. Therefore, as the Tokyo Tribunal failed adequately to address this area, an International Tribunal resembling the Bosnia Tribunal should be set up to prosecute wartime rape of the former "comfort women." Specifically, as in the Bosnia Tribunal's charter, a new Tribunal should be created that has jurisdiction to prosecute rape based specifically on the inclusion of rape as a prosecutable war crime in its charter provisions.

In addition to the Tokyo Tribunal's failure adequately to address the issue of rape, a key reason to create a Tribunal that resembles the Bosnia Tribunal in its prosecution of wartime rape is the similarity of the type of rape that occurred in Bosnia and in World War II against the "comfort women." Specifically, rape in Bosnia was both massive and systematic, factors that led to its prosecution by the Tribunal. The rapes were massive in that invasions of villages would be accompanied by massive levels of rapes of women after the men were killed or captured to signify conquest of a territory. The massive rapes that occurred were also highly systematic, as large rape centers were created in concentration camps where Muslim women would be constantly raped.[14] A substantially similar situation of rape by the Japanese occurred during World War II. During this period, a system of "sex slavery" was established where *over* two hundred thousand women from occupied territories were forced into "comfort stations" located in military installations throughout Asia, where they would be incessantly raped. The rapes were systematic, as evidence indicates that high-ranking government officials knew of and authorized the systematic recruitment and deployment of "comfort women" in the "comfort stations."[15]

The significance of the massive and systematic qualities of rape to prosecution should not be overlooked, for it heightens the need to prosecute such types of rape. The severe and widespread physical as well as psychological devastation resulting from massive rapes in Bosnia and World War II makes it imperative that perpetrators be brought to justice. As both the rapes by Serbian troops and Japanese troops were also systematic, in that they were sanctioned by military officers, it was clear that the rapes that occurred were not random or isolated events. Therefore, the excuse of being undetectable or unattributable could not be made, and the rapes and perpetrators could be more readily identified and prosecuted. Overall, based on these similar characteristics of rape that occurred in Bosnia and in the World War II "comfort stations," it becomes more appropriate to apply the Bosnia Tribunal's standards regarding rape prosecution to the "comfort women" situation by creating a new Tribunal.

The U.S. State Department's Report

A measure that must be taken in order to enhance the proper handling of the "comfort women" issue is for the U.S. Department of State accurately and thoroughly to report the human rights violations committed by Japan. The State Department publishes an annual report on human rights practices in countries that are members of the United Nations or that receive U.S. economic or military assistance. Thus far, the published reports of the U.S. Department of State have insufficiently dealt with Japan's human rights violations. For example, despite the fact that the State Department has published and monitored activities of the Japanese government, it has fallen short of providing a comprehensive picture of the manner in which the Japanese government has handled "comfort women" issues. Excerpts from the State Department's "Country Report on Human Rights Practices for 1996" (the Report) provides evidence supporting this point. Published in February 1997 the Report describes the Japanese government's actions with regard to the "comfort women" issue. The Report in part describes the Japanese government's establishment of the Asian Women's Fund (the Fund), which is a private fund sponsored by the Japanese government.[16] The Fund consists of three main projects. The first is to compensate former "comfort women" from private money. The second project is to assist Asian women medically and socially, for which the Japanese government is directly involved. The third project is to improve the general status of women in Asia.

Although the Fund has been generally explained, the State Department's Report refused to comment or to evaluate the efforts of the Japanese government in defusing the issue of its own legal responsibility for its wartime criminal acts and for its state responsibility to compensate the victims of war crimes. As no government money was involved in compensating former "comfort women" from the Asian Women's Fund, the Japanese government is attempting to deny its state legal responsibility for war crimes and for the compensation of the victims of the war crimes. Thus, the system of the Asian Women's Fund is consistent with the Japanese government's contention that it has no legal responsibility for the "comfort women," only a moral responsibility.

While it is true that the State Department's Report is not intended to be judgmental, its general description of the specific efforts of the Japanese government and public to assist the "comfort women" and Asian women gives an impression of crediting the Japanese government in laudable terms and paints a one-sided picture. Specifically, the State Department's Report refused to note Japan's grave violations of human rights with regards to the "comfort women" issue, as well as the Japanese government's refusal to comply with the international laws that created a legal responsibility to redress the situation of the "comfort women."

In order adequately to address Japan's human rights violations, such as the "comfort women" issue, comprehensive and accurate information with regards to the Japanese government's position must be received. Although the Report describes the efforts of the Japanese government to provide avenues of compensation through the Fund, it does not show that the Japanese government has also attempted to divert and to deny any legal responsibility for certain human rights violations through its creation of the Fund.

Legal Action in the United States

In addition to actions by international organizations such as the United Nations, various forms of legal actions can be sought against the government of Japan, as well as against members of the Japanese military who were responsible for aiding or administering sexual slavery during World War II. The 1996 Amendment to the Foreign Sovereign Immunity Act excepted sovereign immunity for acts of torture, terrorism, and extrajudicial killing. Further, in the recent case of *Kadic v. Karadzic*, a federal circuit court empowered the victims of the human rights violations to sue under the Alien Tort Statute.

The 1996 Amendment to the Foreign Sovereign Immunity Act

Under the general rule of the Foreign Sovereign Immunity Act (FSIA), foreign states were immune from the U.S. courts' jurisdiction. However, the 1996 amendments delineated several exceptions to a foreign state's immunity from suit. The most notable exceptions[17] are listed as follows:

(a) A foreign state shall not be immune from the jurisdiction of the United States . . . in any case . . . in which money damages are sought against a foreign state for personal injury or death that was caused by an act of torture, extrajudicial killing, aircraft sabotage, hostage taking, or the provision of material support or resources for such an act if such act or provision of material support is engaged in by an official, employee, or agent of such foreign state while acting within the scope of his or her office, employment, or agency.

Based on this new amendment to the Foreign Sovereign Immunity Act, foreign states can no longer claim immunity from suits in U.S. courts, where the suits are for acts such as torture and extrajudicial killing. Therefore, the State of Japan as well as its instrumentalities can be brought to justice within the U.S. court system, where such suits are based on the acts listed in section 1605 as amended of the U.S. Code. As evidence exists that the Japanese military's system of sexual slavery included "torture, extrajudicial killing, and the material support of such acts," Japan and its instrumentalities should not be able to claim immunity due to the new amendments to the FSIA.

Additionally, the amendments provide for the principles of equitable tolling of statute of limitations for the alien's torts claim. This means that, although a cause of action must be commenced no later than ten years after the date on which the cause of action arose, this does not include the period during which the foreign state was immune from suit. As Japan was immune from suit from the date on which it had committed violations against former "comfort women," up until the adoption of the new 1996 amendments barring immunity, the plaintiffs have ten years from the adoption of the new 1996 amendments to commence their causes of action against the Japanese perpetrators and their government.

Alien Tort Claims Act

As the new amendments to the Foreign Sovereign Immunity Act of 1976 have extended jurisdiction to U.S. courts over foreign states, so the Alien Tort Claims Act (ATCA) provides an important avenue by which plaintiffs can bring suit against their perpetrators. Further, a recent decision of the Second Circuit Court interprets the Alien Tort Claims Act broadly.

The ATCA was enacted in 1789 to apply federal court jurisdiction to the specific tort of wrongfully boarding a ship believed to be aiding the enemy in time of war. However, recently the Second Circuit concluded in *Kadic v. Karadzic* that, despite its original application, the ATCA would not be limited to such restrictive interpretation. Although one type of tort had prompted the creation of the ATCA, the court ruled that this did not mean that the broad terms of the ATCA should be confined to a single tort. The court explained that "statutes enacted with one object in the legislative mind are frequently drafted in broad terms that are properly applied to situations within both the literal terms and the spirit of the statute, though not within the immediate contemplation of the drafters."[18]

In supporting its decision to apply the ATCA broadly to various torts, the court cited *Filartiga v. Pena-Irala*.[19] This decision required that the ATCA be given a broad scope, and that courts "must interpret international law not as it was in 1789, but as it has evolved and exists among the nations of the world today."[20] The decision also clarified that the following enactment by Congress of the Torture Victim Protection Act codified *Filartiga*'s broad interpretation of the ATCA.[21]

Based on this Second Circuit decision rendered by Chief Judge Newman, alien perpetrators and their state can be specifically liable for their torts under the Alien Tort Claims Act. In terms of the ATCA's relevance to the "comfort women" situation, members of the Japanese military and government who participated in the sexual slavery system during World War II could be prosecuted under this act, due to its broad application with regards to torts committed by aliens.

Congressional Action

Congressional Representative William O. Lipinski (D-IL) has introduced a resolution that would require the Japanese government to make certain amends to its war victims. Specifically, the bill would express the viewpoint of the U.S. House of Representatives that the Japanese government should immediately issue a formal apology, pay reparations to U.S. POWs, and compensate all other victims of the war crimes committed by Japan, including the "comfort women." Although much of the focus is on U.S. military and civilian POWs who were subjected to cruel labor and sometimes starved or beaten to death, the bill would also seek to acknowledge "other victims of Japanese war crimes" by requesting an appropriate compensation. Thus, the "comfort women," who were raped and enslaved, would be included among those who should receive compensation from the Japanese government. (This forthcoming legislation would be an important step in assisting the "comfort women" in their rightful quest for adequate reparations from the Japanese government.)

Legal Action in Japan

On 27 April 1998, a Japanese district court rendered its decision ordering the Japanese government to pay 300,000 yen each to three Korean "comfort women" who were forced to provide sexual services for the Imperial Japanese army soldiers before and during World War II. In its opinion, the court said that the "comfort women" system was outright discrimination against women and the race, and violated fundamental human rights guaranteed by the Constitution.

Further, the court noted the legal responsibility of the Japanese government. It said that the government should have enacted laws to compensate the women after it had admitted in 1993 to being involved in their conscription for the frontline brothels. The court reasoned that, since the government neglected its obligation to implement its legal responsibility and to help the plaintiffs recover from their wartime suffering, it was awarding 300,000 yen for each plaintiff.

This decision is extremely significant in that it is the first case in which a Japanese authority has recognized Japan's legal responsibility as a state to compensate the "comfort women." Although it is not clear how the court computed the amount of the damages to the "comfort women," its opinion tends to show that it considered the neglect of the government as a factor in arriving at the specific amount. It did not rule out additional compensation by the Japanese government.

Both sides appealed this decision to a Japanese high court. Unlike the common law appeal process, the high court would hear pertinent facts de novo and could amend the lower court's decision, including the amount of the damages. From the high court's decision, an appeal may be filed with the Supreme Court of Japan.

Conclusion

Through the application of the Holtzman Amendment, the U.S. Department of Justice has created a special "Watch List," which includes those who, as allies of the Nazi government, persecuted persons based on their race, religion, national origin, or political opinion. The Department of Justice has created this Watch List specifically to exclude those Japanese who aided in the operation and maintenance of the sexual slavery system of the "comfort women" from entering the United States. The various legal determinations arising from the International Commission of Jurists Mission Report on "Comfort Women" and the UN Special Rapporteur's Report on Violence against Women have provided the Justice Department with solid legal support for the Watch List. In order to aid in the expansion of the Watch List, both the United States and the UN should pressure the Japanese government to produce evidence, as well as to provide access to information. It is most encouraging news that recently a Japanese district court found that the "comfort system" violated its domestic laws and that its government is responsible. Further legal developments in the Japanese judicial systems should be monitored.

Furthermore, separate and individual legal action should also be taken against the Japanese government, as the new amendments to the Foreign Sovereign Immunity Act and the Alien Tort Claims Act make it possible for individuals to bring certain torts actions in the United States against foreign entities. Although the pain and suffering of these women can *never* be fully compensated, the implementation of such actions will clearly be a step in the right direction.

Notes

1. Which is known as Title 8, United States Code, Section 1182(a)(3)(E).
2. See Section 1251(a)(4)(D) of the above Title of the United States Code.
3. See subsection 1182(a)(3)(E).
4. *Fedorenko v. U.S.*, 1981, 101 S. Ct. 737, 449 U.S. 490.
5. C.A. 9, 1982, 693 F. 2d 894, subsection (a)(19), 8 U.S.C. 1251.
6. *Schellong v. U.S. Immigration and Naturalization Service*, C.A. 7, 1986, 805 F. 2d 655, *certiorari denied* 107 S.Ct. 1624, 481 U.S. 1004, *rehearing denied* 107 S.Ct. 3199, 482 U.S. 921; *Rubio de Cachu v. Immigration and Naturalization Service*, C.A. 9, 1977, 568 F. 2d 625.
7. It cited the authorities of L. Oppenheim and H. Lauterpacht, *International Law* (London: Longmans, Green and Co., 1955), vol. I, paras. 153, 153(a), and Article 5 of the International Law Commission's Draft Articles on State Responsibility.
8. League of Nations Treaty Series, vol. 9, p. 415.
9. H. Lauterpacht, *International Law and Human Rights* (London: Stevens & Sons Ltd. 1950), pp. 334–335.
10. Radhika Coomaraswamy, "Report of the Special Rapporteur in Accordance with the Commission on Human Rights Resolution 1994/95."
11. Noted as Item 9(a) of the provisional agenda of the 52nd session.
12. See S.C. Res. 827, U.N. SCOR. 48th Sess., 3217th Mtg., U.N. Doc. S/RES/827 (1993).
13. Report of the Secretary General Pursuant to Paragraph 2 of Res. 808 at Art. 5 S.C. Res. 808, U.N. SCOR, 48th Sess., 317th mtg., U.N. Doc., S/RES/808 (1993).
14. Sharon A. Healey, "Prosecuting Rape under the Statute of the War Crimes Tribunal for the Former Yugoslavia," *Brooklyn Journal of International Law* 21 (1995): 327, 357.
15. Tong Yu, "Reparations for Former Comfort Women of World War II," *Harvard International Law Journal* 36 (1995): 528–529.
16. See p. 685 of the Report.
17. Listed under Title 24 of the United States Code, Section 1605.
18. *Kadic*, p. 378.
19. *Filartiga*, 630 F.2d 876 (2d Cir. 1980); *Kadic*, p. 378.
20. *Filartiga*, p. 881.
21. *Kadic*, p. 378.

Part III
Artistic Responses

Chapter 10

A Film within the Film

Making a Documentary
about Korean "Comfort Women"

Dai Sil Kim-Gibson

For almost a decade I have been an independent filmmaker, following careers in academia (teaching religion at Mount Holyoke College) and in government grant-making (as senior program officer at the National Endowment for the Humanities and director of the Media Program at the New York State Council on the Arts). Naively, I thought I knew all the inside secrets of grant-seeking. Little did I know. Three documentary films later, all broadcast nationally on PBS, all favorably reviewed, but not a single major grant. Just an understanding and a supportive (including financially) husband. When he decided to take early retirement and pursue some of his own interests, I thought my latest career might well be at an end.

But I kept applying. "Begging"—as that's what it is—can gnaw at one's soul, no matter how worthy the cause. And the waiting seems to get longer. Three days after Christmas 1996, Charlie Deaton of the Corporation for Public Broadcasting called. I held my breath. "Dai Sil, congratulations. We are supporting your 'comfort women' project." I interrupted, my mouth producing amazing variations of "Thanks." "Be quiet, Dai Sil, I have more," polite young Charlie literally ordered me. "We are giving you 25 percent more than you requested, so that you won't have to spend five years raising completion funds." I had always known that miracles occur in life. After the Korean War, I believed that being alive was a miracle. Since I started begging, though, the meaning of miracles had escaped me.

The waiting was over; the planning all but complete; the order now was to assemble the crew and equipment and head to Japan and Korea on a six-week production trip. In the midst of frenetic days exchanging faxes and phone conversations across the nation and oceans, I took two days off to visit my mother in Toronto. Confined to a wheelchair, with a hip bone broken and operated on but never healed, she now breathes with the help of an oxygen mask and suffers from neurofibrillary tangles that cause the loss of her memory. I found my mother trying to hold her grip on a rapidly vanishing self, with much of her past gone, her present in a blur, and the future becoming feebler by the minute. Such a helpless bundle of life, she recognized me. When I held her hand, she said, "Your gray hair doesn't seem to show as much as it did the last time," a radiant smile spreading across her trembling lips. The last time was three months ago, when her doctor declared: A "maximum six more months" until her breathing stops.

How can I tell her about my forthcoming trip? She might be gone to the land-of-no-return while I was away. "Mother, what are you thinking?" "I don't think much." "Do you not think of Father? Do you know where he went?" "I heard that he went to heaven." "Do you think of Grandma?" "I wonder if she also went to heaven." "I am sure she did. Mother, I am going to Korea to visit Grandma's grave. Promise me to wait for me. Don't go anywhere until I come back." "I will wait. I promise."

On 30 March 1997, holding tightly to my hope that mother would indeed wait, and strengthened by my husband's smile, sad for our parting but warm for our deep knowledge that no parting can separate us wherever we are, I got on a flight headed to Los Angeles. Michael Lim, a bright young Korean American who has a B.S. degree in physics from the University of Chicago, was with me. Also a computer wizard, Michael could have a bright future worthy of all the "sacrifices" his Korean-born parents made, but he would have none of that; he wanted to make films. Michael is not only a son of my high-school classmate, but also my right and left arm, wearing more than two hats at a time—film researcher, assistant editor, computer teacher, and production coordinator. My friends tell his mother, "You raised a son only to give him to Dai Sil."

On the morning of 31 March, Michael and I met with three other crew members: Charles Burnett—a filmmaker who is frequently referred to as "one of America's very best filmmakers" (Chicago Tribune), and as "the nation's least-known great filmmaker and most gifted black director" (New York Times), and whose work is often described as "masterpieces" (Film Comment)—agreed to come with me as director of photography, though he was in the middle of movie deals that could get him money to pay his bills. He had read some of my stories about Korean "comfort women" and found their stories compelling. Our warm friendship, coupled with the pain he felt for these women, made him juggle his hectic schedule and come to the Los Angeles airport dressed in a sweatshirt, jeans, and a cap, his face gentle and eyes deeply shining. For sure, he was not doing it for money.

Then there was Willie Dawkins, a young African American man with a master's degree in film from the University of California, Los Angeles. An excellent cameraman himself, he can always get a job in Hollywood for his hard work and versatile abilities. He started working on movies as "best boy" (I still don't know what that means). He is now the best man in any job he takes in order to make a living, while he writes scripts that he wants to direct. When I called him to come with us to assist Charles, he was working on one of those big action films, but he didn't hesitate to respond, "Money is not everything, Dai Sil. I will come to work with you and Charles. Especially given the topic, how could I think twice? Thanks for thinking of me." When he appeared with his girlfriend early in the morning at the airport, his smile was broad. He gave me a strong hug. It had been several years since Charles first brought him to work with me while directing a ninety-minute documentary, *America Becoming*, which I wrote and produced.

Despite the happy commotion of hugging and chatting, it was not difficult to notice an Asian man with a baby walk, Jon Oh. A third- or fourth-generation Korean American born in Hawaii, Jon holds an M.F.A. in film from the University of Southern California and spends his days surrounded by sound equipment in a one-room apartment, obsessed with sounds. Professionally, he records production sound, and edits and designs sound effects. It is hard to imagine Jon without earphones (which often make him look like an Eskimo) and some form of recording device. Greed must not be one of his strengths, because he seems to work on every independent film production for weeks and months without hope of getting paid. "Hi, Dai Sil," was all he said—a greeting pure and simple but heartfelt.

Now the entire crew stood in line to get on a Korean Air flight to Tokyo: a Korean-born woman with streaks of gray hair, two African American men, and two Korean American men (neither of whom speaks a word of Korean). Michael's mother, Young Sook, hugged her son with teary eyes, and Willie's girlfriend, Lisa, stood in sadness. "Lisa, I will watch Willie, protect him from Japanese and Korean women, and return him to you in one piece, sound in body and soul." Before we knew it, we were airborne.

The Tokyo airport was crowded. We stood in a long line to pass through Japanese customs, exhausted but excited. I went through the line before Charles and Willie. Japan allowed tourists with American passports to stay a month without a visa. I had told Charles and Willie that they didn't have to obtain "work" visas. Suddenly, I was worried that Japanese Customs might become suspicious of their "tourist" status, linking them with the heavy equipment, should we all have the same address. So on their customs form, I had them write down the address of my Japanese researcher, Yang Ching Ja—not the actual address where we were all booked to sleep. Ms. Yang is a Korean born in Japan and active in the movement on behalf of "comfort women." Suddenly, I noticed that Charles was walking away from the line, and Willie was following behind, going with a Japanese official to a small office. He was being taken to a supervisor. I followed.

Inside, a number of uniformed Japanese officials were buzzing around, talking in rapid Japanese. Charles and Willie were taken to a desk where a short, chubby Japanese woman in white top and black skirt sat. I shuddered; she reminded me of my Japanese teacher in the elementary school in north Korea, who punished me for speaking Korean on the playground. I went to the desk as well and sat down by them. She inspected their passports, looked at Ms. Yang's address, and then her eyes went across their faces. Finally, she spoke: "Who this is?" Her finger pointed at Ms. Yang's name. "A friend." Charles's voice was low. "What friend?" "A friend," Willie chimed in. "What friend?" The same question. "A friend is a friend," I said, repressing anger and frustration. She looked up at me, acknowledging my presence for the first time. "Who are you?" "I am their friend." "What kind of friend?" "We have known each other for many years. We have been friends for a long time," explained Charles.

She moved on to the next stage of interrogation. "Why you in Japan? And why [do] you stay there?" "We are here to see your country, and we are staying there because she is a kind lady who lets us stay," said Charles. "The name is not a Japanese. Right?" This time she looked at me. "She is a Korean born in your country. Is that a crime?" By this time, my voice was becoming dangerously squeaky. Her eyes just glared. Ignoring me, she directed her next question to Charles: "She your friend?" By that time, I had opened a proposal that I always carry in my shoulder bag. In it was an article from the *New York Times* with a huge picture of

Charles. I shoved it under her nose and asked, "Do you recognize this? The *New York Times*. And do you recognize this picture? You are insulting one of America's great filmmakers for no reason at all. What is your problem? Is there a rule that a Black man can't have a friend in Japan?" My voice, which started an octave higher than usual, was escalating by the second. "Why you so angry?" this Japanese woman asked me. "You want to know why I am so angry?" I was just a second away from saying, "dumb bitch!" but caught Charles's warning signal deep in his eyes. My shoulders drooped, ashamed of this Asian woman. I wanted to kneel down in front of Charles and Willie and beg for forgiveness.

By the time we walked beyond the customs area into the lobby, Ms. Yang was at the Korean Airline desk, trying to page us. That night, as we gathered for supper, struck by a thought suddenly, I exclaimed, "I should have told the bitch that Charles and Willie were both my husbands! I was such an idiot. Besides, we should have given the address of the most expensive hotel in Tokyo." In the midst of laughter, I still felt anger.

The first day of our filming in Tokyo was at Yasukuni Jinja, the shrine established by the imperial command in 1869 for the worship of the divine spirits of those who had died for their country. The term "Yasukuni" was bestowed by the Emperor Meiji and signifies "peaceful country." Thanks to all those spirits (made into deities), the country enjoys peace. I closed my eyes. Images of the Nanjing Massacre, which I had seen many times, thanks to Michael's archival research, flew over the cherry blossoms in full bloom. I felt a chill going through my spine.

In the early morning on a weekday, the Yasukuni Jinja was crowded with people—young and old, male and female. Ms. Yang introduced us to an elderly gentleman, dressed in a modified Japanese costume with a cane, Mr. Tokuda Masanori, a former soldier. While Mr. Tokuda told me how he lost many of his friends in the battlefields, Charles moved his camera to film cherry blossoms and white doves. Charles must have had the same feelings and thoughts. "We promised to see each other in the Yasukuni Shrine. I come here every day to worship those who died for Japan." As calm as he was, his voice betrayed intense emotion.

"I can completely deny recent reports that 'comfort women' were forced to work for the imperial army, since I myself was a witness. Because 'comfort women' could earn more in battle zones than in their home towns, there were many applications to work near the fronts. Thus, the imperial army set up the limited term for the women, and after their terms were up, they had to go back to their hometowns.

"So, compared with Japanese farmers, 'comfort women' could enjoy more affluent lives." Asked about discrimination against Korean women, he asserted calmly, "There was no discrimination against Korean or Taiwanese 'comfort women.' The army provided equal treatment for those women. At that time, Koreans and Taiwanese were Japanese nationals. Therefore, it was nonsense to discriminate against them." We parted with bows and good-byes.

A woman in her seventies, her back slightly stooped but covered with a knapsack and her face still retaining a girlish charm, Ms. Ikeda Masae traveled from Nara to Tokyo to talk with me on camera. Polite to a fault, she relayed this story:

> I was teaching sixth-grade children at Housan National School in Seoul. The principal told us that in Japan even small kids were working to win the war. He said, "Korean children also have to work. I have received a request from the Board of Education to send Korean children to Japanese military factories. We have to send female junior high school pupils and sixth-grade students." That was the command. Every day, I tried to persuade girls to volunteer. The school principal asked me about volunteers every day, but he insisted that I not force them. I had to induce them to volunteer. By letting them apply for the job, the Japanese government and the Japanese army could insist that they were volunteers. One day, five students volunteered to labor in Japan. I suspect that those who volunteered were forced to become "comfort women."

Ms. Ikeda's talk was a confession to absolve her sin. As she parted to catch her train, her eyes were filled with tears.

On 4 April, the day we were scheduled to go see Grandma Song Shin Do, my heart throbbed with excitement. In July 1995, I had talked with her for a couple of hours at a Tokyo inn, where she was brought to appear in court. She was the only former Korean "comfort woman" living in Japan who was suing the Japanese government. When I called Ms. Yang to arrange an on-camera interview, her response was negative. She said, "As far as I know, she never gives interviews with anyone at her home. She would be willing to travel to Tokyo. She does not like her neighbors to see her being filmed. We also worry about revealing where she lives. Her life is sometimes threatened." "In that case, perhaps you can arrange for her to go to another town, where she first landed from China, for instance." A few days later, however, Ms. Yang called and informed me that Grandma Song had agreed to talk to me at her home.

"When I presented your request, she remembered you. She said, 'Ah, that woman from America who was born in Hwang Hae province in Korea. I remember her. You can bring her here.'"

At ten o'clock in the morning, Mr. Park, another Japan-born Korean, drove our van packed with equipment and crew through the crowded streets of Tokyo onto a highway headed to Grandma Song's home. When we arrived at the small fishing village where she lives, it was eight o'clock in the evening. Grandma Song was waiting. "You must be starved. I know a Korean barbecue place. Let's go there."

The next morning, we drove along a narrow, winding road, watching a few villagers on bicycles and a few others on foot. When our van stopped almost at the end of the road, we found her standing in front of a small house—what looked like an addition to another house. In the misty morning, unmindful of gentle sprinkles from the sky, this Korean grandma stood outside to greet us. When we got out of the van, she fussed over us to get inside, lest we get wet. Following her, we heard, "Japanese son of bitch!" in English. Laughter broke out. Now, with her eyes playful, "Japanese son of bitch." She repeated it a few times until it became almost a tune.

From my previous encounter, I had known that she was moody, but she proved to be even more so with the crew. It was difficult to get her to tell her story. "Grandma, why are you suing the Japanese government?" "The war made us like this. So I want them to compensate us. I want them to say, 'We committed crime' and apologize. That's why I am suing." "What would you do with the money?" "I will buy something delicious!" Then, she laughed. "Please be serious!" I pleaded. "Because I am totally alone, I could not sue the government by myself. So people helped. If I had money, I would give money to them. They saved me, and I cannot die until I repay their kindness."

In the narrow hallway, I saw a birdcage with two birds. I stood her in front of it. Charles was ready to shoot with a camera on a tripod, and Jon was holding a microphone high enough not to get into the shots. "Grandma, why do you raise birds?" "Because I don't have kids. They are like kids." "So you are lonely." It was a mumble, not a question. "But I am all right, because of these kids." "Do you think of your babies whom you left in China?" I asked, remembering the story she had told me about her babies at the Tokyo inn in 1995. "Because I don't have kids, I raise these birds," was all she said to my question at the time, but she said more later.

"Grandma, do you have friends?" "No, no. no." "Why not?" "Why do I have to tell you about not having a friend? People whom I don't like, I don't like to be friends with." I kept my mouth shut, waiting for her to say more. "I guess I am just exhausted by people. People tell lies, and people are treacherous. I don't even want to talk with them.

"Why did I not go back to Korea? When Japan lost the War, and we were abandoned in China, I knew no one in Korea. I had no one to rely on in Korea. There was this Japanese soldier—he took me here, and as soon as we arrived in Japan, he abandoned me. No words of explanation. He just abandoned me. And I had no place to go. I tried to kill myself by jumping out of the train, but I just hurt myself."

In bits and pieces, she recollected the time when she was first taken to a place called Moo Chang in China. "All the Chinese had run away from the War. So no Chinese could be found. Only soldiers. I had no idea what was happening. When the soldiers heard that women came from Korea, they came. When I arrived, I saw a corpse. It was a Chinese man. No one was going to do anything. I found a straw mat, wrapped the corpse, dug a grave in the mountain behind the house, and buried it.

"A baby got into me. I didn't know. The baby died in my belly. The dead baby would not come out easily. The Chinese midwife didn't know if the baby was dead or alive." At that point, Willie signaled that the film had run out, but I was afraid that she might not go on if we stopped. So I just recorded the sound. "I was hungry. So I ate a couple bowls of seaweed soup and then put my own hand inside and pulled it out. Thinking back, I don't know how I could have done such a thing. The baby was dead. I also buried the baby myself." To this day, I curse myself for not filming her. Viewers should see her when she says this, but I guess it was better to have the sound recorded than nothing at all.

She told me how she gave birth to a baby boy, after the time when she pulled out a dead baby. "This time, he was alive." "Do you remember his face?" "I had his picture, but what's the use of having that picture? One day, not long ago, I tore the picture in pieces. You know the baby was given to a Chinese family." On camera, she said, "Japanese, son of bitch," before we left, but it wasn't nearly as good as off-camera, half-teasing and half-serious.

From this grandma who shared her loneliness and sorrow with the two birds in the cage, we came back to face two Japanese professors in a small office in Tokyo.[1] Prominent leaders of a surging conservative force in Japan who claim that all of this is nothing but "Japan bashing,"

they greeted us with caution and arrogance. They both spoke some English, but chose to speak in Japanese. While we were setting up, one of the two spoke to his colleague in Japanese: "You can't trust her. The less we say, the better. She will manipulate in the editing room." Jon Oh, always ready to record, dutifully put all this on his tape.

The smaller of the two spoke first. "This Korean 'comfort women' issue is fabricated by other countries to bash Japan." Thus begun, they preached how the whole "comfort women" issue rested on groundless assumptions and unsubstantiated evidence. Anger rising inside, I interrupted Ms. Yang, who was talking in Japanese, and asked in English, "So you deny that Japan institutionalized sexual slavery?" "All of the countries of the world have administered sex in their armies. But you have just stated that only Japan had an institutionalized, military-operated system of 'comfort women.' Japan actually did not do it. It was the United States that institutionalized prostitution in the military. And Germany. And other countries. Don't misunderstand this point. You are wrong. That's what I have been arguing. I really ask you to tell people that it was a lie!"

One of the two wanted to be philosophical about it. "The liaison between prostitutes and the military has existed from ancient times to the present. Even today, no matter how hard you preach moral lessons, the problem of prostitution in the army is never solved. So I believe that it is unnecessary to compare the level of morals among countries. Human beings are neither lofty nor low. Human nature is more or less the same. The issue of 'comfort women' is a problem humans have not solved."

My favorite claim was this: "Unless they had given Korean women the opportunity to become 'comfort women' and thus earn good money, it could have been said that the Japanese government was discriminating against them. At that time, they had to treat both Japanese women and Korean women equally. Therefore, the same policy was imposed equally. In that sense, the 'comfort system' was fair. They were paid equally." After this, there wasn't much else to say. Wow. Koreans should be grateful for this fair system! Why was I surprised to hear this? Similar arguments were advanced to defend slavery in America.

There were others whom we met in his small office, as he talked at length about the systematic involvement of the Japanese government in the institutionalization of sexual slavery on a massive scale. A former soldier, Kawakubo Toshio, told us that his job was to build barracks at the front, much like MASH units, for these women to be transported ahead of the soldiers like military supplies. He was remorseful for what he had to do by order. Then there was an army doctor, Yuasa Ken, who had dissected live Chinese people in medical experiments.

On 10 April, we were on our way to Seoul. At the Kimpo International Airport, a sturdy young man, Do Keun Kim, stood holding a piece of paper with my name on it. Because of our equipment, we could not all ride in the same van that Mr. Kim had brought. After Michael took off with Mr. Kim, the rest of us got into a cab. Thank goodness the traffic actually moved. In half an hour, we arrived at Yonsei University, where I had negotiated rooms through a faculty member. Allen Hall, designed to accommodate visiting professors and others related to the university, was comfortable but had no elevator. As in Tokyo, we had to carry our equipment to the second and third floors. The first night, I treated the crew to beef barbecue and *soju*, Korean wine made from potatoes. We were ready to fight the Seoul traffic and meet my grandmas.

Finally alone in my room, as I stretched my worn-out body on a clean bed, the faces of those grandmas with whom I had sat for hours while interviewing them for my book, *Silence Broken* (Mid-Prairie Books, 1999), appeared one by one. Would we be able to catch on camera the deep hurt of their souls, and the courage to fight for justice for the horrendous crimes committed against them and humanity? Would we be able to personalize the faceless atrocities through these grandmas? Would we be able to reveal the singular spirit of these women? I was excited but fearful.

The first grandma to whom I took the crew was Bae Jok Gan, a slight woman with zingy laughter, whose image made me think of Yun Dong Ju's poem, "Sorrowful Tribe":

> White kerchief around black hair
> White rubber shoes dangling on rugged feet
> White top and wrap covering her body
> White cloth knotted around her slim waist.

Ever since I had met her, I was often invaded by the image of a woman following a man, soon to become her husband, through the fields and valleys, deeper into the mountains in Kang Won province, not knowing the fate awaiting her. "My legs didn't feel like they belonged to me; at first they hurt and then they were numb. On top of everything else, it started to rain and I became soaking wet," she had told me. Then there was her story about how she had to support her "scholar" husband (who sat around all day smoking a long pipe and drinking rice wine) and six stepchildren. "All day, from dawn to night, I worked in the fields, in the kitchen, and in the mountains digging medicinal plants. By the time, I was able to lay down my small body, I was so exhausted. I didn't know if my body belonged to me. But you know what? My husband wanted to do it, not just once but again and again." When I asked if she had a wedding ceremony, she yelled, "What wedding!? He didn't buy me a pair of rubber shoes, not one dress!"

The security guard at the apartment building dialed her number and handed the phone to me. A voice rang out, "I am on my way down. Stay put. I can't wait to see you." She didn't bother to find out who I was. After my call that morning, she must have been glued to the phone. Charles and the crew were in the yard already filming establishing shots of the apartment building. Almost a year since I saw her last, she was the same. We hugged over many "*aigu*'s," a Korean phrase, an expression of both joy and sorrow. Only then did I notice a woman, shorter than Grandma Bae, standing behind her. "Oh, I brought a friend of mine to meet you, Grandma Hwang Keum Ja. You know, she also went." No need to ask "where."

When we stepped out of the elevator, the smell of soybean soup welcomed us. "I prepared lunch for you all. You must eat before you do anything. Nothing good will come from an empty stomach," she declared firmly, as we entered her apartment. The two grandmas started putting out little plates and bowls on the table that had been set in the middle of the room. Charles leaned against the wall and, responding to my worried look, said, "The sight of food makes me feel nauseated. I ate too much last night." Now sitting on the floor, leaning his back against the wall, Charles said, "A little rest will cure me. Just go ahead and eat. I'll be all right."

The food Charles missed! The two women would not join us, too busy making sure that every plate and bowl was refilled. Grandma Keum Ja, her face shadowed with worry, surprised us. "You sick?" she asked Charles. "You speak English!" I exclaimed. "A little." She went to Charles, put both her hands on his shoulders, and began massaging. "His muscles are tight," she explained in Korean, then said to Charles, "Relax. Let your body rest in my hands." In Korean again, "From his eyes, I can see that he is a man of gentle soul. You know, I like these people," now with her eyes sweeping from Charles to Willie, who was busy enjoying the soup, "They know suffering. They would understand us." Here I had been secretly worried about how they would receive African Americans. I was almost in tears. Then Grandma Bae sat by Charles, a needle with a long thread in her hand. "Ask him if I could go to work on him. I need to twitch his finger tip to get bad blood out, and I will do something for him that should help his sickness." "Of course," I said to myself, remembering her story about being a Shaman, when she returned from China. "Charles, Grandma Bae would like to help you. Will you trust yourself to her?" "Of course," is all Charles said with smile. What a sight—what the grandmas were doing to Charles! The image of my mother, young and beautiful, stroking my belly whenever I complained of pain in my stomach, swirled in front of my eyes and made my lids wet. Amidst the noise of chewing and swallowing the food, I heard my mother's chanting like a distant drum: "Mummy's hands are medicine hands, Mummy's hands are medicine hands." Charles did not eat food with us, but after the table was cleared, he did film them, looking remarkably better, as they told wrenching stories.

Still vivid from the time when I had wrestled with Grandma Bae in that room, while she repeatedly told me that she had wanted to see Japan win, I spat out my first question. "You said you wanted to see Japan win the War. Tell me why." "We went there with the Japanese. We were the same as the Japanese. I didn't know anything about Korea and Japan. I was too young and ignorant. I was blindly on the side of Japan. I am being honest. I am not lying. I was happy to see the Chinese lose and happy to see the Japanese win. I had no idea that the Japanese and Americans would fight each other. When the Chinese and Japanese fought, I believed that we could live only if Japan won. We had been thoroughly contaminated by Japan." "You also told me that you would rather marry a Japanese than a Korean. Do you still feel that?" "I like the Japanese, because it was to a Japanese that I gave my feelings first."

While I sat with the camera rolling but unable to ask the next question, Grandma Bae volunteered. "When I was about eight or nine, the monk—you remember my mother's lover I told you about—he would tell me to come in, take off my clothes—whenever my mother was not there—you know, he would make me naked and do that thing and then I would bleed. He tried to do that thing whenever my mother was gone. So whenever my mother was going out, I would follow her, crying. I yelled to my mother that he was trying to kill me. Then my mother would throw stones, so that I couldn't follow her." My chest felt tight, as if a thousand knots were tied around it. What right did I have to yell at her for liking the Japanese? A Korean monk, her mother's lover, had molested her, and her mother didn't care for her enough to see what was going on. Or did she see it and ignore it?

After that, I didn't ask any questions, but just let her talk with the camera rolling. All my good intentions of saving on film stock went down the drain. She was as adamant as before when she insisted that she blamed Korea before she did Japan. "We were taken because Korea was powerless. I want to know if the current Korean government realizes that. The way they are behaving, I am afraid we are going to be stepped on again."

Grandma Keum Ja, asked how she feels about men, threw forth words with such force that I felt almost startled. "I never think of men; I am too sick of them to miss them. What was inflicted on me by men was so terrible; I can't possibly think of men. When I see them, my mind goes blank. No desire of any sort. If I did, I would have married a long time ago. Those bastards ruined it all for me." "If I could be born again, how would I like to be born? I want to be born in a family rich enough to allow me to study. I want to study, because I was never able to learn. Can you imagine that I can't even write my own name? I want to learn, so that I can shake the politics. I want to shake the whole world. The big-headed ones, they devour the big ones. Those with smaller heads, they devour the smaller ones. Politicians take what they can, and the President does the same thing. Everybody is out for themselves, blind with greed. Our politics are so rotten. That's not governing. I want to rule the world."

Grandma Bae wanted to give me a jar of homemade *kimchi* for me to take back to my husband. That I could not take, but I did accept a black polyester blouse with a glittering zipper, which she had bought for me as soon as I phoned from the States. That filled me with sorrow.

The next day was for Grandma Hwang Keum Ju (a.k.a. Hwang Kum-ju), a woman directly responsible for my being involved with "comfort women." In November 1992, I was asked by a group of concerned Korean Americans in the Washington, D.C., area to interpret for one of the surviving "comfort women," Hwang Keum Ju. For over an hour, I had sat beside this seventy-year-old Korean woman and translated her story for Fox television. As she talked, I had felt tremors going through her body, caused by the pain from her past, so remote and so close. Then, her voice tainted with a southern accent, shook, pulling my muscles tight. She said, "This Japanese officer took his thing out and wanted me to lick it like a dog. I yelled, 'I would rather die than do that, you son of a dog!'" Her anger and pain, after half a century, was electrifying. I was drawn to her, feeling her pain in my veins.

When we entered her apartment, there was a framed picture hanging on the far side of the sitting room of me standing with her on a platform in front of the White House. Beside it was a picture of her with President Clinton in front of the White House, a cardboard cutout of the president! I laughed, pointing out that picture to the crew. Grandma Hwang sat me down, ignoring the crew. "Listen, if you are going to make a film, do it right, not like some other ones already made. You have to do your research right. For instance, in my case, you must stress that I went with an officially drafted notice. This is important because it means Japan's deceit was official and systematic—the draft notice was from the government, just like an army draft. With some other women, it is not always clear how they went. Don't make a film that will bring shame to you, you understand?"

She relayed her story again, which had become images as vivid as if they were my own flashback:

> *A proud, young woman traveling down a dark train corridor to a car full of frightened Korean girls and women. Looking out the window through the cracks of black oilpaper blinds. Glints of brilliant sun. A neighborhood official exchanging rolled papers with a Japanese military policeman. Sounds of the wind whipping and the clack of train wheels.*

"I got on the train at Ham Hung station. When the train whistled, I looked out of the window through a small crack. You know, the windows were all covered with black oilpaper, because of the bombing. I saw the neighborhood official and a military policeman exchanging rolls of paper. At that moment, it struck me, '*Acha,* they are exchanging papers about drafts.' I felt my chest trembling loud. I didn't quite know what that roll would do, but when I was going through that dreadful experience, I knew that the list was a killing roll. No doubt, our names in those papers turned us into sexual slaves. When I saw the exchange of those papers, I felt that we *Chosun* [Korean] people were being cheated. I felt that I would not come back alive."

Asked if she had been back to her hometown, she said, "Don't you remember my story about how I left home at age twelve to help buy medicine for my sick father? How I stood on a hill under a huge tree and swore that I would never step on the soil of my hometown again, unless

I made something of myself? Until this day, I have never been back. I would have gone back, if I had made something of myself. I didn't go, even when I heard about my mother's death. The only way I will go is if Emperor Akihito—ya, ya, it was his father, but now he is responsible—officially apologizes. Then I will go to my parents' graves and tell them, 'Here is his apology.' That's the only way I will go. If Akihito says, 'It was a crime committed by my father. Please forgive me.' Then I would say, 'I understand,' and receive his compensation. If not, I will never, never receive a penny. Instead, I will ask him to give my youth back. I would like to get married, give birth to children. I'd like to know what life is all about."

Before we took a long trip to the countryside, I managed an afternoon off for the crew. A relative of mine, whom I had not seen for a long time, wanted to buy us dinner. He asked about the crew. "I brought them from America. So, other than a young man who drives the van for us, the crew is all American," I told him on the phone. In the restaurant, after I introduced Charles, Willie, Jon, and Michael, he was still looking around, a little bewildered. "Are you waiting for someone else?" I asked. "Where is your crew?" It hit me! Of course, he saw no Americans—only three Asians and two Blacks—no Americans! We had similar experiences as more days went by in Korea.

We drove to Ulsan, a harbor city in the south, best known for Hyundai automobiles. It was a Saturday morning when we arrived at the government-subsidized apartment complex where Grandma Yun Doo Ri lived. Reluctant as she was, she had given me permission to come, but when we arrived, she was in a foul mood. "Why did you have to come on Saturday? I told you that I am usually frantic on Saturdays with all the things I have to do for the Church. It would have been so much better if you had come on Wednesday, like I told you." "Grandma, I am sorry for imposing on you, but I thought you understood my difficulties as well. Largely because of financial restraints, I cannot spend too many days in Korea. Because Ulsan is so far away from Seoul, it gives me added difficulties. Please forgive me for the inconvenience. I beg of you. I will need only a couple of hours of your time." I was practically on my knees, pleading. I knew that she had the right to be disgruntled—it is true that I had pushed pretty hard for Saturday, in order to schedule this interview with other activities in the area. Angry as she was, she told the crew to bring the stuff up and unpack.

Michael Lim moved around silently, setting things up. Grandma Yun took one look at Michael, turned her head toward me, and said, pointing to Michael, "Who's he? He looks Japanese. If he is, I don't want him here. Tell him to get out and stay out." "Grandma, he is not Japanese. His parents are both Korean. He was born in America. He is a Korean American." "You are pulling my leg. I am sure he is Japanese. He looks like one."

Then Jon walked in. "There, he is a Korean. I can tell." Jon, not knowing what was going on, stood looking more bewildered than usual. "What's wrong with him? Why is he standing like that? Can't he say 'hello' or something, instead of standing like a borrowed barley sack?" I could no longer hold back my laughter, not even with my guilt and fear of Grandma Yun. Bursting into laughter, I said, "Grandma, he does not speak a word of Korean. He was born in Hawaii and never learned Korean." "How stupid can he get? If he came out of the belly of a Korean woman, he should speak Korean!" Then, glaring at Jon, "Look here, what's wrong with you? How come you can't speak Korean. You certainly look like one. You should live up to your looks." I translated this into English to Jon. He immediately assumed a Buddha-like expression on his face, standing on two feet parted wider than usual. Grandma Yun was not done with him. "Are you married?" she asked him, refusing to believe that he could not understand her. "He is a bachelor," I answered. "What's wrong with him? He has a nice enough face. Is he a cripple or something? Why is he not married?" By that time, Jon had already turned around, put on earphones, and was testing sounds in the room. I saw a Buddha-like smile on his face, but no words came from his mouth.

By this time, Willie had taken over the camera work because Charles had been summoned by Oprah Winfrey, who wanted him to direct a television series. Willie, with his large eyes dancing, went to Grandma Yun, greeted her with a smile, and gently sat her close to the kitchen. Not a word was exchanged between Grandma Yun and Willie, but the tight muscles around her lips had disappeared and she even looked tamed. Willie the Charmer. When we were on the street, people stopped and stared at Willie, but for the grandmas, Willie's ebony skin warmed their hearts. With Willie's camera rolling, she recollected the fateful night when she was captured.

"My father was in the construction business. We lived in a fabulous house with a large courtyard and a tiled roof in the port city of Pusan. But the Japanese confiscated our house, and my father was unable to get any business. My father died when he was forty-nine, bottled up with anger. My mother had kidney troubles, and our family was in a pitiful condition. So I had to get a job to support my family. I was fourteen.

I had a job at a glove-manufacturing company. One night, after a long day's work, I was walking home. I was passing a police station, when I heard a voice calling me. I asked in Japanese what he wanted. He told me to come near him. I did not budge. He suddenly ran toward me, grabbed me, and took me to the station. Inside, without a word, he opened the door to a room where night guards normally slept and threw me in. There were seven girls there, sitting with their faces hidden between their knees.

About eleven at night, they took us out of that room and ordered us to get into a truck. I kicked and bit anybody who came near me. One of them tried to hit me. I kicked his balls hard. He put one hand on them and jumped around and around, with only one foot on the ground. Another slapped me hard and said, 'Look what you did to him, you bitch!' I hit him back and yelled, 'You have no right to come to our country and detain us!' I grabbed his neck and tried to bounce him with my head. I wouldn't get in the truck. Then, suddenly, I saw a pistol in front of me. 'Get in,' he said. I just wanted to die right there and then. 'If I die, who is going to feed my mother and brothers and sister?' That thought made me climb into the truck. That's how I was taken away by them."

I would give up half of my grant money if I could find pictures of this feisty young girl kicking and fighting the bastards. Alas, no such pictures exist.

Once she had started, I didn't have to ask questions. She told of her experience at the "comfort" house pretty much the way I had remembered from my previous interview. However, I had to prod her a little, to make her repeat the following story:

"One of my friends became pregnant. On top of that, she had venereal disease. She was treated, but nothing seemed to work. The disease got worse by the day. Her bottom was a mess, and her stomach looked like a balloon. She was in the eighth month of pregnancy. The soldiers stayed away from her. One day, on my way to the toilet, I saw two soldiers taking her away. I thought she was taken to have a baby. I followed them quietly. They took her to the barn. I stood by the window and looked in.

There was a wooden bed there. They tied her to that bed, both her arms and legs. Then those soldiers put on gloves. One of them took out his sword and cut her stomach. I saw her intestines dropping out of her open stomach. I fainted. I was caught and beaten until what felt like the end of the world."

Once when film ran out, Grandma Yun said to me, "If you think I have a temper now, you should have seen me when I was young. I feared nothing." I understood it to be her way of saying, "I was kind of rough to you, huh?" That was good enough for me. Needless to say, she ended up giving us a lot longer than two hours, and as we drove off from her apartment complex, I felt the tight knot in my stomach finally relaxing.

My next stop was at Jin Hae, where Grandma Chung Seo Woon lives. I had met her in Beijing in August 1995, where she came to give public testimony at the NGO Forum held in conjunction with the UN Fourth World Conference on Women. Alas, the schedule was so tight that it was virtually impossible to drive five to six hours from Ulsan. In desperation, I called her and asked if she would be kind enough to travel halfway to meet me. "Gladly," was all she said. I arranged to meet her at Pusan. One of my cousins, a longtime resident of Pusan, offered his garden for filming. It was a perfect place; among a variety of evergreen trees stood stone sculpture pieces, some of which were gathering green moss. Grandma Chung, seated by a garden table, as she poured tea from my cousin's antique pot in a graceful Korean costume, looked as refined as royalty, without a trace of her unimaginable past.

Born as the only daughter of a well-to-do landowner in southern Korea, she was deceived into going to work in a Japanese factory with the promise that her imprisoned father would be released as soon as she left home. She relayed her experience in a low voice, often repressing the pain deep in her chest. But when I asked if she felt ashamed, suddenly her face darkened and her voice rose. "No way. Why should I be ashamed? When I returned home, my parents were not there for me to tell them what happened. My father, never released, died in prison. My mother killed herself with a piece of iron in her mouth, when Japanese tried to rape her. But I told everything openly to all of my friends and neighbors. Those who dragged us and made into sexual slaves, they are the ones who should feel shame, not us. It is the Japanese government that should feel ashamed, not we. Now I am old and don't know when I will die. I want to die as a daughter of Korea, not as a prostitute. I will accept nothing but a legal compensation." Until this day, I remember her saying, "The Japanese defiled my body, not my spirit."

When we visited Grandma Kim Hak Soon, the woman who became the first public witness, she coughed constantly and was short of breath. I offered to come back but she said,

Stay. I am rarely free of this kind of attack anyway. This pain is *han*. From the time when I was little, what the Japanese inflicted on me— that's what makes knots in my chest and that *han*—how can it be untied? You can't untie it. Then, all the time when I have been fighting in the open since 1991, this knot of *han* has become even tighter. It is completely blocked now, so that I can hardly breathe. That's my trouble.

How did I become a public witness? When I came out, I had had it in my chest for a long time. The War ended in 1945, and it was in the 1990s when I gave public testimony. So it was over half a century. When I read newspapers and watched the news, Japan kept denying it. They said it was trade done by Koreans. They took us forcibly, put us directly in the military compound, and made us comfort women. I felt my breathing blocked. Here I was myself alive, determined all my life to talk about it before I die.

I don't want any apologies in words. The Japanese like official documents with signatures. Even if it takes rifles and swords, that's what they do. I want the Japanese Emperor to give a document to our President in which he offers absolute apologies.

At the time of my production trip in Korea, there were three grandmas who had been brought from China through the commitment, money, sweat, and time of a man of faith, Mr. Kim Won Dong, an elder of a Holiness Church in Seoul. To me, it was nothing less than a miracle, because it was a near impossibility for me to travel to China. In 1995, I was almost arrested as I tried to film Korean "comfort women" in Wuhan, China. My last day in Korea was at the bedside of Grandma Chung Soo Jae, who was hospitalized. One of three women brought from China, she had lived in China for fifty some years, counting the days until she could step on the soil of her homeland and see her beloved mother. I was literally afraid that, no matter how careful we were, the commotion of filming might hurt this feeble grandma. However, the interpreter assured me that she wanted to talk. I didn't understand a word of the Chinese she spoke, but my heart was swept with such sadness. I could not concentrate on what the interpreter said. According to her doctor, her remaining days were numbered. Her lung cancer was so advanced that there was no way that she would recover. Yet she enunciated clearly in Chinese, "My last wish is to become healthy enough to join this movement to right the long-delayed wrong committed against us and to bring justice to this issue."

Back home in New Paltz, New York, I struggled to make a one-hour documentary out of the countless hours of interviews I had gathered on camera. Alas, the paucity of direct visual material drove me to make an agonizing decision to dramatize some of the stories. It was agonizing for two reasons: In general, I had resisted the idea of mixing in dramatic re-enactments in documentaries, and I was fearful of the inevitable budget problem. In the end, however, I went back to Korea with funds that my husband, Don, once again secured through loans and whatnot. Whenever I see a dark cloud hovering over his face about financial worries caused by my films, I say, "Don, go do it. After all, it is the White Man's Burden." Then we both laugh. An Iowa farm boy, whose upbringing and background are as different from mine as black from white, Don is not only my husband; we feel as if we were "shoulder friends," a phrase often used to refer to friends who grew up wiping their tears and blowing their noses together.

Once again I secured help from Charles Burnett, because my experience in drama was limited. In Korea, I was able to get help from a young man, Kim Chong Kyu, the head of Production Vista. Chong Kyu, his staff, and others, including actors, gave me their labor of love that I would cherish for the rest of my life. The Korean sky and soil, which I had carried in my soul during my life in America since 1962 when I came to pursue graduate studies, were now mixed with the overflowing devotion and love from Koreans who worked long hours on this film. Other than Charles, the only person who accompanied me from the United States was Woo Ilyon, a woman born in America and a graduate student at Columbia University in English literature. Speaking fluent Korean and English, Ilyon became a natural bridge between Korean young people and us, especially Charles. Ilyon and Charles came dangerously close to a major conflict when we were given an outdoor supper after a long day's labor in a village in Cholla Province. They were in fierce competition to see who could devour more crab, noisily sapping juice and chewing meat, raw crab seasoned with all kinds of spices and the specialty of the house. Most Koreans love this dish, but to watch an African American sitting under a tent, with his legs stretched under the table, savoring this Korean crab was a sight to behold!

In making this film, I often felt my entire personal history becoming entangled with the history of my land of birth, coupled with that of humankind. In rare moments when my self was stretched beyond the focal point of my consciousness, my ego, I felt I had a vision—not of mine, but of an unborn work to which I was to give birth. Yet those were fleeting moments that disappeared as soon as they came. Clearly, then, in one sense the completed work is as shallow as I am. But I hope it is more. I rely on the power of the collected voices of the women who tell their stories and all those who suffered the insufferable, living or dead. If there is even an echo of those voices, the film will have a power surpassing the maker. By the time I moved to the dramatized scenes, it no longer became important for me to keep track of who said what. I began to feel the power of their stories as a common experience, their collective story becoming aglow with a pain that touched my heart. The women's voices narrating the stories actually belong to individuals—Yun, Chung, Song, Hwang, and Kim—but they are also telling their stories for all other women who suffered the same fate. The individual grandmas in the first part of my film are, in a way, sitting together, remembering their common past in composite characters.

The film, now titled *Silence Broken: Korean Comfort Women*, was completed in January 1999. Since then, it has had trial screenings across the country. More than two thousand people saw it that way. In May 2000, it was also broadcast nationally on television by the Public Broadcasting System (PBS). It has stirred controversy not only for its content/topic, but also for its format of using extensive dramatization in a documentary.

Of all the people who appear in the film, only Grandma Chung Seo Woon has seen the film. I invited her to a screening in Flushing, New York, that was held in conjunction with the commemoration ceremony of the fifty-fourth year of Korean independence from Japanese colonialism. After the screening, I brought her home. In the private setting of our own home, sitting at the kitchen table, I asked her, "Grandma Chung, you have seen the film. I am afraid to ask, but I must know what you thought of it." A faint smile appeared. Then silence followed. Finally, Grandma Chung opened her mouth. "You did a good job. It is a wonderful film." I sat still, waiting for more. "Everything was pretty accurate, but one thing. You know, I went by boat, but in the film my character rides a train." Sighing with relief, but still nervous, I explained how I combined her story with that of Grandma Hwang Keum Ju. "You know, for dramatic structure and stronger impact, in some cases I made composite characters, but I would still say it is a documentary based on facts. Do you think the dramatic license distorted facts in a fundamental way?" "No, not if you look at all those stories as our stories—you know, the common experience of so many young girls and women."

I have yet to show the film to other grandmas. I think of Grandma

Hwang Keum Ju with fear and trembling. I made her stories live through the character of Grandma Chung! I would consider myself lucky, if I am alive after she has seen the film. Her warning words are still ringing loud and clear, when she told me not to make a film that would bring shame to me.

Of the women who appear in this documentary, two have died: Grandma Chung Soo Jae and Grandma Kim Hak Soon. Of the 190 grandmas who have registered as former "comfort women" in South Korea, more than 40 have passed away, but Japan is still unwilling to acknowledge its legal responsibility, the least they could do for the "crimes against humanity." What was inflicted on these women was far beyond moral, intellectual, and legal wrongs that can simply be condemned in sermons, lectures, and courts. It was a violation of human spirits, both individual and collective. The evil performed with the shameless justification of "comforting" soldiers in a brutal war is the common grief of humanity that should be felt and mourned. What happened to these grandmas is not just unspeakable atrocities, but loss of lives by the waterfalls, in mountains where the spirits roam, by azalea blossoms where maiden love sprouts, and in the hometown where life on earth was claimed with a cry. It was a willful interruption in the natural flow of life that comes with birth and returns to earth in death, with all the joys and sadness in between.

If I survive Grandma Hwang Keum Ju's scrutiny, I will carry the film to the end of the earth, sustained by the resilient spirits of these women and the labor of love of all those who helped me.

Note

1. It is not specified in the release form they signed that I could use the interviews in a book or an article, only an unlimited use in video, film, or radio format. Hence I choose not to reveal their names.

Chapter 11

Making *In the Name of the Emperor*

Christine Choy

My work on the documentary film *In The Name of the Emperor* (1995) began in the spring of 1992. A woman with whom I had never spoken, "Jennifer," called me out of the blue to see if I were interested in doing a film on the Nanjing Massacre, as she had obtained some interesting documents. I said that I had heard about the incident from my grandmother while I was a child, but it really did not affect me much. She showed up in my office with a crate full of research material, which I flipped through. Much of it was interesting, but I did not think it was something I could use to make a film, because there was so much written material. I asked her if she had anything visual, photos or the like. She said that yes, in fact, a film had just been discovered: footage of the Japanese invasion shot by the Reverend John Magee, a missionary stationed in Nanjing. This film, which was in the process of being restored, had been sitting in the basement of David Magee's (his son's) house.

In 1939–1940, the Reverend Magee had cut the film together—a half hour of the material with intertitle silent film—and toured with it around churches in England and America. But when the European war took over the whole consciousness of what World War II was about and so much attention was paid to Italy and Germany, Asia was forgotten. After 1938, the film was never shown again. In 1986, a Japanese politician, Ishihara Shintaro, was interviewed by *Playboy* magazine and said that the Nanjing Massacre had been fabricated by the Chinese. David Magee contacted the Alliance in Memory of the Victims of the Nanjing Massacre in New York City about his father's film. The Alliance subsequently contacted Peter Wang and had him use the footage with a newly added interview with David Magee. They released a videotape about the incident.

I looked at the footage and saw that this could be the cornerstone of a film. Magee had secretly filmed the devastation of Nanjing: the flight of the people, the rubble of the buildings; he had gone into hospitals and filmed patients who had been badly and deliberately burned, patients whose bodies had been riddled with bayonet wounds. Nancy Tong, my coproducer on the film, went rummaging through the archives at Yale University and amazingly turned up great material: boxes and boxes of diaries of missionaries and educators—a daily record of the invasion. Now we had not only the facts, but also the eyes and voices of what had happened in Nanjing, and we set to work.

In 1992 you couldn't go into China without an invitation from a host institution, so I contacted the Beijing Film Academy, which has a quasi-relationship with the NYU Film School, and asked permission for two projects: one about Shaoling Martial Arts, and the other about Nanjing. They approved the martial arts project, but said that the Nanjing proposal might have problems, although they never really clearly gave me a yes or no. So I said, all right, since China is so far to go, let's push ahead with both films and kill two birds with one stone (a typical independent film tactic). So in order to raise money and get visas, we went forward with the Shaoling film project and figured that once we were actually in China, it would be easier to negotiate with Beijing. The crew was very, very small. Elia Lyssy, a Swiss national, did the sound, lighting, and assistant camera, and took still photographs; Nancy Tong was the producer and production manager, took care of money exchange in the black market, and did location scouting; I was the director, cinematographer, and interviewer.

I had permission to go to my hometown of Shanghai. I had not been there since having left about thirty years ago. After Shaoling, we took the train there, checked into a hotel, and went to visit some of my former childhood girlfriends to see if any of their reactions to the Nanjing Massacre might be interesting; we spoke to college students for the same reason. We went to great lengths to sneak these students into our hotel room, but they didn't have much to say; it was all hearsay: "I heard this, I heard that," and ultimately we weren't able to use any of it.

Nancy went to Nanjing ahead of time, without a crew, and attempted to set up interviews with people whom our friends had referred to us. All four told her that if we wanted to interview them, we had to go through the proper authority, because the last time they had talked to journalists who just went in without the proper authority, the survivors were arrested. These women were in their seventies, very weak, and they had suffered a lot. They had been arrested, and then they were interrogated by the police for about eight hours, standing up, without a drink of water, without anything to eat. A daughter of one of the survivors kept saying, "My mother's in Mongolia. She had to go to Mongolia, because she's still trembling, she's still shaking from the last time they interrogated her."

Now an ethical issue had arisen, and we had to make the kind of choice with which filmmakers are often confronted. If it's for the sake of a film in which they truly believe, some filmmakers will do it. But because this film was really about suffering, we did not want the survivors to suffer more for the sake of the film. It became clear that we couldn't interview survivors without official permission. At the end of July 1992, we received word that we couldn't film in Nanjing; the Emperor of Japan was visiting in September, and they did not want to do anything to enrage the Japanese, because the Japanese have investments all over China and especially in Nanjing. They were building hotels, the infrastructure, and a lot of people at the governmental level didn't want to do anything that might anger Japan.

We then went to Japan to film a conference on "comfort women," where we met a woman from Beijing who represented them. She told us that in China, the government does not want her to speak about these women. So she had to sneak out of the country, telling the government officials that she was going to Japan for a women's conference, not one about "comfort women." She attended the conference, where she told us that there are a lot of "comfort women" who stayed in China after the war, Koreans too, and they have wanted to come out to seek reparation just like the other Korean women and Filipinas. The Chinese government has refused and has silenced them. I asked her why China was still so reluctant to talk about the past, since I thought that China was the victim country. She responded by pointing out that after what happened in Tiananmen Square, the Chinese realized that any kind of grass-roots movement could very easily explode. So they didn't want any kind of organization from the people, knowing that seeking reparation from the Japanese is a big explosive issue because so many people would be able to suddenly get together and demand reparation. Then China would not be able to control this group at all, and it might get out of hand. They were afraid of allowing any filmmakers like us to work on projects there, because we could encourage the victims to organize themselves to seek reparation. At this time, China's economy was changing from a so-called socialist state to a semicapitalist state, which caused a lot of confusion. In order to have the transition take place smoothly with the foreign investors, they supposedly had to tighten up a lot in terms of democracy. That meant also limiting freedom of expression, for the sake of the transition.

We applied a second time to go to Nanjing and were flatly refused. In fact, our inability to interview the survivors led to a much more interesting film, some sort of aesthetics of an emergency. Ironically, a group of Japanese journalists were allowed to videotape several survivors. However, an official stood behind them during the entire interview, and their stories were very subdued, confined to statements such as "I was running from the fighting and I injured myself," and "Sometimes the invading army lost their composure." Everything was allegedly due to the mishaps of war. The stories were told without expression. At the end of every interview, each woman said, "Now we have nothing but forgiveness for the Japanese." It was the official rap. To get the truth, I realized that you had to go to the victimizers.

We decided to try to talk with those who had actually participated in the atrocity. I thought it would be fascinating to look at that psyche, which I think of as being the psyche not so much of a murderer as of a follower. How is it that normal young men participate in acts of such abnormal cruelty? Is it that they want to be normal, that they want to be accepted like most young men? They join the Nazi party, Mussolini's fascist groups, the Japanese emperor's army, and a month later, are they capable of anything? One soldier said that he found himself, at age seventeen, in a Chinese village where, for no reason, he picked up a gun and shot a Chinese man. Blood gushed out of the man's mouth, and he died instantly. Nearby was an infant baby held by its grandfather. They were both crying, and he shot them so there would be no witnesses. He said that he thought to himself, "A month ago I was home, with my family, and I had never killed anyone"; the desire to kill the Chinese just came to him.

We went to Japan with very pessimistic attitudes, although locating the perpetrators was far less difficult than you might imagine. The assault on Nanjing, the capital city, was highly celebrated in Japan, and many of those soldiers came back highly decorated and honored. We met a remarkable Japanese woman (who was very helpful, but wanted to remain anonymous) who was very concerned about the right-wing movement in Japan, which is on the rise, as well as the sensitivity of this topic. She agreed to be our researcher and to locate the soldiers; this was something she had always wanted to do, so that she could find out more about what the Japanese had done to the Chinese. She said that the Japanese knew all about Hiroshima, about what had been done to their own people, but that they have remained very ignorant of what they themselves have done to other Asian-Pacific nations. She contacted the Peace Movement people, and they contacted two soldiers who had come out to speak at the Kyoto Peace Museum, to talk about what they did. Many Kyoto-based troops were involved in the Nanjing Massacre.

We were the first people able to interview the soldiers on film. These soldiers had refused other requests, but they trusted our Japanese contact after they watched my film, *Who Killed Vincent Chin?* (about the racially motivated slaying of an Asian American in Detroit), which they liked a great deal. So they agreed to be interviewed.

I met them and found people in their seventies, grandfather figures. We shook hands. They didn't look at all like the young soldiers who had committed these brutal rapes and killings. Recently, I read an article about how many current healers are former criminals, who had engaged in the battle zone and actually killed other people. One of the people we interviewed, Nagatomi, actually became a doctor, after he realized that he had an energy in his palms that could relax patients or heal their illnesses, something beyond modern medical comprehension. He was just sitting there—very old, bald. Not much energy. But he had this energy in his hands. I shook his hand, and his hand was very, very warm. From it, I could feel the *chi;* though I believe in *chi-gong,* it was just a bit too spooky to ask him to fix my smoking habit!

Obviously, we didn't understand a word of Japanese. Our coordinator did all the interviewing, because we completely trusted her approach and did not want to interrupt the personal stories and emotional feelings that were being conveyed. Therefore, there was no simultaneous translation into English. I had given her the questions and specified the general areas that she should discuss. During the first interview, one of the soldiers took ten minutes to answer the opening question. Even though we did not know what he was saying, I let the camera keep rolling, because he just kept going, with hand gestures and everything. It was difficult for us to access their emotions; in general, the Japanese do not use many facial expressions. What further interested me was that their wives just sat there and listened to their whole stories, with no reactions. When their dinner came, the wives did not eat, but disappeared into the kitchen. After dinner, I asked the wives to sing their favorite songs from wartime, and two of them did. It was amusing to see the contradiction; the men were discussing horrible atrocities that they had committed, and yet everyone was partying at the same time, in a two-hour duration.

Later, I was sitting in my office at New York University. It had been an extremely busy day, and it was freezing, because something was wrong with the air conditioner and no one knew how to turn it down. I finally shut the door and read the transcript from the Japan trip. I read the words of Nagatomi, the healer, and I realized that he had killed something like three hundred people. I thought about that handshake, about the murderer's hands. I realized that I had a very strong story.

There were stories we were not able to use, either because they did not take place in Nanjing, or because we did not think that an American audience would be able to sit through the vivid brutality. I remember one interview with a priest, who described having witnessed Japanese soldiers killing two Chinese men and then cutting their chests open and pulling out their hearts. They dangled the two hearts in front of the priest and made him say a prayer for them, so he did just as he was told.

Song, the Korean "comfort woman" stationed in Nanjing whom we were able to interview, had gone through several pregnancies. She was unable to keep the children—psychologically, she just couldn't bring herself to raise a half-Japanese baby; one child she gave away to a Korean family, one she gave to a Chinese family, and one she killed in the womb. She ate a lot of hard rice, and the baby was stillborn in the color of a grape; then she wrapped the dead baby in a little towel and buried it herself. When Song met with us, she was very warm toward us and hugged us, but she was very cold toward our Japanese interviewer. At a certain point, when our interviewer asked her questions about her children, about what had happened to those she had to give away, she stood up and said, "You should ask your soldiers. It's your soldiers who did all this to me. It's the Japanese people who did this to me. If you ask me one more question about this, I'm going to walk out of this interview."

In the film, Song talks about the resistance she still encounters, when she tells her story. People think she's a troublemaker or that someone has put her up to it. She says, "I'm so indignant about it, I could die." It's only now that the Japanese government is starting to discuss the topic of proper reparations, yet their insistence that the money not be given anonymously, but that individuals be required to come forward and admit what the society still largely regards as a tremendous shame, indicates that there is still a real reluctance to come to terms with the truth. When the issue was finally officially acknowledged, the attitude toward the women was still ridiculous. The survivors were asked, "How can you possibly remember something that happened fifty years ago?"

Of course, a very interesting question is, why did these Japanese men choose to come forward? Why did they choose to tell their stories? Some of them probably were motivated by very real feelings of guilt, by a genuine desire to make reparations and to bear witness. For others, they simply want to go to "Heaven."

The experience of making the movie, of listening to these men, confirmed for me that human psychology is very complex, and yet at the same time very simple. A person is easily conditioned to act without questioning, to commit acts that are completely beyond those of which they are normally capable, when it is systematically done from conceptualization to execution. In Japan, you had an emperor who, because he was a deity on earth, was able to lead the entire military institution and to turn a good man, a good son, a good husband, a good brother, into literally nothing more than a killing machine. At the same time, the part of human nature that is equally fundamental is our curiosity, our desire to disobey, to poke and tear away at systems and at order, to question and challenge; unfortunately, it took fifty years to reveal this part.

For example, there was a Hong Kong filmmaker who went to the National Archives and obtained footage of the atrocities that occurred in China. He cut this footage into a ninety-minute documentary that depicted all of the terrible things the Japanese did, and he added narration, from Day One, of what they did in Shanghai and then Nanjing. After the screening, I heard people in the audience saying things such as, "Let's kill all the Japanese," "Look at the power of a film like this," and "The worst thing an enemy can do is to make you hate as much as they did." I didn't want just to make a film that demonstrated the violence and atrocities and who was the guilty one; I wanted to frame the film in a context of why and how, in an international perspective as well as from my own personal point of view.

Whether or not these men were truly repentant, they could never make up for what they did. And as for the "comfort women," no matter how brave and outspoken they are, they have a pain of which they can never rid themselves. As individuals, we can never escape our past, but it is only when individuals come forward as a group and engage with the past that we can cause society to examine it. When a society is able to acknowledge its past, it is a little bit more able to proceed honestly with its present. I believe that is our only real hope.

Today in America, women's groups, scholars, and activists are beginning to address issues and to search for multiple answers and an alternative to the restricted world history. They are doing so not by using selected moments of official presentations, but rather a cohesive hybridity from many voices.

Chapter 12

Tomiyama Taeko's
A Memory of the Sea

Margaret D. Stetz and Bonnie B.C. Oh
With three illustrations of work by Tomiyama Taeko

For some of the women who survived the Japanese military "comfort system," giving voice to their experiences has been fraught with pain and difficulty, yet has also provided a way of expressing an anger that has never diminished and of turning that rage into political activism. For some, it has also been a means of coming to terms with the past and of striving to reach a plane of personal peace. As the late Maria Rosa Henson wrote in her memoir, *Comfort Woman: A Filipina's Story of Prostitution and Slavery under the Japanese Military* (1999), "If Jesus Christ could forgive those who crucified Him, I thought I could also find it in my heart to forgive those who had abused me. . . .Telling my story has made it easier for me to be reconciled with the past."[1] For all the survivors, finding a means of recording what was done to them and to others has been a crucial part of their own sense of revising and changing history, by documenting what no one had wished to document before as part of the official record of World War II.

Many of the survivors have used words to create and to share their testimonials, whether oral or written. But others have turned to the visual arts. Through paintings and drawings, in particular, they have made art bear witness to the events that they remember. Maria Rosa Henson, for example, interspersed her published narrative of rape and torture with line drawings of the same experiences, with the spare images and the dreadful descriptions echoing and reinforcing one another.

But what is or should be the role of visual artists who were neither the victims of the "comfort system" themselves nor direct witnesses to it? In an earlier era, Käthe Kollwitz, the great German printmaker, stated conclusively why she used her art to support the efforts of "an international group working against war." Writing in the 1920s, she said, "Everyone must work as he can. I agree that my art has purpose . . . to be effective in this time when people are so helpless and in need of aid."[2] It was, she believed, the responsibility of the artist to document suffering and injustice and to protest against such actions.

This sense of responsibility is one felt keenly by artists, such as Tomiyama Taeko, who have brought the subject of "comfort women" into their paintings, collages, installations, and prints. As Tomiyama herself has asked in an essay, "Shadows from a Distant Scene," that appears in the catalogue *Silenced by History: Tomiyama Taeko's Work* (1995), "Should the artist be a passive observer of the times?"[3] For artists using "comfort women" themes and images, the answer is a clear "No." Their art has been a form of political, as well as aesthetic, intervention in the present, as well as a contribution to history. Yet, as the critic Hagiwara Hiroko has noted of another Japanese artist, Shimada Yoshiko, who has combined visual images and protest, "Shimada's intention is not to expose and exhibit the dreadful daily life of Korean "comfort women" in military brothels. She knows she must be circumspect in dealing with the issue so as not to encourage the Japanese audience's pitying gaze on the victimized."[4]

Hagiwara's point is an important one. Even for women artists, the danger of turning the "comfort women" into a mere spectacle—and especially an erotic spectacle—is great. Those who have dealt explicitly with the depiction of images of battered and violated female bodies have had to be especially careful not to reduce those bodies to objects.

One of the most brilliant examples of a painter who has managed both to create figurative images of raped and tortured "comfort women" and to keep them present as subjects, not objectified bodies, is Miran Kim, a Korean American artist who works in New York. In her 1993 *Chongshin-dae* series, Kim has produced large canvases in which portraits of "comfort women" are fused with self-portraits—thus, in which the body in pain is her own and the face is that of the artist, confronting and challenging the spectator. Her images deny and refuse distance, whether the artist's from the legacy of the "comfort system" experience or the viewer's from the horror of that legacy.[5]

Among the professional artists who have been dealing longest with the legacy of the "comfort women" and, in particular, with Japan's responsibility for the crimes against them is Tomiyama Taeko, who produced her series of oils and lithographs on this subject, *A Memory of the Sea*, in 1986.[6] Tomiyama (born in 1921), a socially committed artist of contemporary Japan who has won international acclaim, was profoundly influenced by her youthful impressions of the sufferings caused by militarism, which she witnessed while living until 1938 in the former Manchuria, a Japanese-controlled territory. Even as a girl growing up as a privileged subject of Imperial Japan, she empathized with the peoples—especially the women—who had been colonized. She became conscious very early of the disparities between the lives of the colonizers and of those who were oppressed and enslaved under imperialism, dedicating herself to recording and to ending such injustices.

As a young artist in postwar Japan, she used her observations and memories to produce work on subjects ranging from the lives of the laborers in coal mines to the fates of political dissidents to the sexual exploitation of women. Irresistibly, too, she was drawn to depicting the plight of Korea, as a former Japanese colony that had suffered the ravages of conquest. Bearing a sense of personal guilt, as a Japanese citizen who had benefited at least indirectly from the long occupation of Korea, she returned hesitantly to South Korea in 1970, for the first time since the end of World War II. There she saw the lingering signs of economic and cultural devastation—the aftermath of decades of Japanese colonial rule—at the very moment when Japan itself was enjoying a postwar financial boom.

During this visit, Tomiyama recalled hearing about the tragic fates of earlier Korean literary figures who had participated in the resistance movements of the colonial period, and she also became acquainted with contemporary South Korean poets, such as Kim Chiha, who were using their art in the service of antigovernmental political statements in the 1970s. She embarked on a series of political images and established *Hidane Kobo* as a new art movement, producing slide presentations that used the mixed media of poetry, pictures, and music for the purpose of appealing widely for the release of political prisoners in Korea and elsewhere in the world. Some Japanese audiences, still in denial about their nation's responsibility toward Korea, shunned her and rejected her art. Tomiyama began sending her work to Amnesty International, to progressive religious groups, and to grass-roots human rights movements in various countries. She decided that she would have to reach out to a worldwide people's culture of resistance, different from the national culture of capitalism.

While researching life in South Korea and using her findings to paint images that revealed the continuing influence of the past on the present, Tomiyama realized that deep and permanent scars had been left by Japanese militarism on the people of Korea, most especially on those who had been used as "comfort women." In 1986, she turned to the horrors of the "comfort system" in a series of pictures and brought the subject to the forefront of public discussion, through her staged performances, exhibitions, and slide shows, under the title *Umi no kioku* (A memory of the sea).

A Memory of the Sea was dedicated to the women, especially those of Korea, who had been sent to the Asian battlefront by the Japanese military as "volunteers" during World War II, in numbers ranging up to two hundred thousand. The stories of so many of these women, as Tomiyama reminded her viewers, were forever lost in the depths of the South Pacific; their drowned voices, echoing back from this dark night of history, had never been heard. Tomiyama created the series of pictures called *A Memory of the Sea* to tell the story of this dreadful past and to make visible the lost lives of the military "comfort women." She also linked their plights to those of the earlier *karayuki*—Japanese women who had been sent as prostitutes, in the first decades of the twentieth century, to support the colonial enterprise, and who had also vanished from the world's consciousness.

A Memory of the Sea, which has been reproduced in the catalog *Silenced by History: Tomiyama Taeko's Work,* consists of six related images: a depiction of a lotuslike flower; an untitled mixed media piece (60 x 50 cm); an oil titled *Java, Island in the South* (100 x 72 cm); an oil called *At the Bottom of the Pacific* (162 x 130 cm); a third oil painting, *The Night of the Festival of Garungan* (162 x 130 cm); and a final, untitled stencil on rice paper (65 x 55 cm). Together, these images compose a narrative of terror, suffering, futility, and inhumanity that lingers through time. With *At the Bottom of the Pacific*, Tomiyama has produced a haunting painting of the symbols of war, submerged and lost on the floor of the dark sea. In this picture of the grim human remains of the Japanese war efforts of World War II, both the victims without any trappings and the victimizers with their emblems of glory are together for eternity, hardly distinguishable from one another, except through the presence of the helmets that remain on a few skeletons. At the rear of the blackish green background are the silhouettes of three sunken battleships. Central to the composition is an image of mourning: a large eye with a teardrop, which stares at the viewer as though begging for compassion. Around the eye are strewn pearly white, almost iridescent skulls, their mouths opened in mute cries of anguish; the whitened bones of

At the Bottom of the Pacific

hands; the tiny corpse of a nude woman, no bigger than a bone; and enormous shells. Also visible through the murky waters, though, are the garishly colored symbols of Japan's imperial war machine: a huge gold chrysanthemum (an emblem of the empire); a navy flag with its bright red Rising Sun; an officer's badge and hat; and soldiers' helmets, along with the other eerie souvenirs of an invading army. Through this sinister landscape of the carnage of war, fish of different shapes, colors, and size swim unaware, by themselves or in groups, as uncomprehending witnesses.

Quite different in mood is *A Night of the Festival of Garungan* (*The Day the Ghost of the Dead Returns*). Here, Tomiyama has brought to life the cliché that "war is hell," for if there is a hell, then this would surely be one of its tableaux. Between two red columns at the center of the painting is a monstrous head with protruding eyes, a smaller middle eye, and a terrifying mouth with fangs, huge teeth, and a long, flaming-red tongue. The head sports a red-and-white beard and a mop of hair like that of a lion's mane. Above it is a red umbrella, from which red, black, and white crinkled streamers hang. In the foreground stands a colorfully costumed and rouged female figure, positioned as though to

A Night of the Festival of Garungan (The Day the Ghost of the Dead Returns)

lead a group of people of diverse ethnic features and complexions to welcome the squatting skeletons to their left. The skeletons are flanked by a Japanese naval flag and sheltered by two red umbrellas, obviously indicating they are the dead who have returned and are being feted. Also arranged before the monster's head are giant shells: one has a skull at its center; from another, disembodied legs dangle; the third holds three female bodies, piled atop one another, with their legs spread-eagled and their genitalia cruelly displayed. There is also a headless nude woman, with a tray of skulls where her head should be. In the lower right foreground, naked women huddle, two of them bearing colorful platters of food for this celebratory "feast." Arranged from left to right across the image are a row of emblematic figures, including an outsized trumpet with the imperial chrysanthemum, several squatting soldiers, a Japanese military flag, additional groups of soldiers, and three older women in an attitude of prayer. Tomiyama depicts a chaotic scene, a human world that is also monstrous, where there is no evidence of reason or of humanity. The living and the dead, the various races, the beastly and the human, all come together in a nightmarish environment of violence and

Untitled Stencil

its aftermath. Here, the emperor's war has produced a giant maw, a thing of horrifying appetites—the very opposite of that orderly, hierarchical system that Imperial Japan claimed it was fighting to preserve and to expand.

The last work in the *A Memory of the Sea* series is an untitled stencil on rice paper. For the catalogue of her work, Tomiyama has provided the following remarks above this image: "*In 1945 the war ended and the soldiers returned home. But though almost half a century has passed since then, we have no news of what became of those Korean women. Some died, some were abandoned on southern islands, never returning to their homes, where the chastity of women is treasured.*" Looking at the stylized and abstract stencil, which has been done in stark colors, the viewer is confronted by the realization that some of the women who never returned home—who were murdered, who committed suicide, or who died of the effects of disease and injury—must have served as food for the creatures who live in the water; some might even have become, through cycles of reincarnation, such creatures themselves. The picture features two crocodile-like heads pointed in opposite directions. These heads have bodies that appear to be composed of assemblages of figures, humanlike and female, in crawling or swimming postures. Many of the "comfort women" of World War II who never returned home may indeed have fallen prey to such sea monsters, their bodies digested as mere feed. But their souls might now roam the ocean in the form of sea creatures, too.

The image, like all those in Tomiyama's works inspired by the sufferings produced by militarism, is one of a grotesque horror that haunts eternity and that inspires neither rest nor peace, only an endless unease. In her art, Nature itself bears living witness to the crimes of the past, which human history has tried unsuccessfully to shut out. But ultimately, the impetus to take responsibility and to take action falls back on the living spectator, who is never allowed to view these images from a comfortable or aestheticized distance.

Notes

1. Maria Rosa Henson, *Comfort Woman: A Filipina's Story of Prostitution and Slavery under the Japanese Military* (Lanham, MD: Rowman and Littlefield, 1999), p. 91.

2. Quoted in Mina C. Klein and H. Arthur Klein, *Käthe Kollwitz: Life in Art* (New York: Schocken Books, 1975), p. 82.

3. Tomiyama Taeko, "Shadows from a Distant Scene," in *Silenced by History: Tomiyama Taeko's Work*, ed. The *"Asia eno Shiza to Hyogen"* Organizing Committee (Tokyo: GendaiKikakushitsu, 1995), p. 58.

4. Hagiwara Hiroko, "Comfort Women: Women of Conformity: The Work of Shimada Yoshiko," in *Generations and Geographies in the Visual Arts: Feminist Readings*, ed. Griselda Pollock (New York: Routledge, 1996), p. 261.

5. See Miran Kim, "Paintings," *Muae: A Journal of Transcultural Production* 1 (1995): 216–218.

6. Hagiwara Hiroko, "Silenced by 'History'—Tomiyama Taeko's Harbin Series," in *Silenced by History: Tomiyama Taeko's Work*, ed. The *"Asia eno Shiza to Hyogen"* Organizing Committee (Tokyo: GendaiKikakushitsu, 1995), p. 62.

Chapter 13

"Unsuspecting Souls"

Art Evokes History at
the Isabella Stewart Gardner Museum

Jill Medvedow
With two illustrations of work by Mona Higuchi

In the summer and fall of 1996, the artist Mona Higuchi lived and worked at the Isabella Stewart Gardner Museum in Boston. Ensconced in a four-room apartment in a former carriage house on the museum's grounds, with twenty-four-hour access to the museum, Higuchi was asked to participate in a relatively new artist-in-residence program that invites several artists each year to spend time at the Gardner. In the case of Higuchi, she was also asked to create a new work for public exhibition that responded to some aspect of the museum and its permanent collection.

Bamboo Echoes: A New Work by Mona Higuchi Dedicated to the Comfort Women was the result of that residency and took many by surprise. Tourists anticipating Renaissance masterpieces, members with long familiarity with the courtyard and collection, students walking over from nearby schools, staff and board who had been watching the progression of the piece, marveled as they entered a special exhibition gallery transformed by pyramids of open bamboo cubes and dangling squares of shimmering gold. Abstract and geometric in its structure, *Bamboo Echoes* drew its viewers in through a narrow doorway of form and shape and light. Once there, they began a quiet journey that connected them to history, awe, and Asia.

Mona Higuchi was the fourth visual artist to create a new work that directly responded to the permanent collection and history of the Gardner Museum. This practice of supporting new work and important artists is a direct legacy from the museum's founder, Isabella Stewart Gardner, and continues the museum's tradition as a vital patron for contemporary art and artists. Left "for the education and enjoyment of the public" by

Bamboo Echoes: Dedicated to the Comfort Women **(View One)**

Isabella Stewart Gardner at her death in 1924, the museum is prohibited by her will from any changes in the arrangement of objects and from any new acquisitions. Thus, many of the strategies used by other museums to pursue new ideas, engage audiences, and reinvigorate collections—acquisitions, "blockbuster" shows, and reinstallations—are unavailable to the Gardner Museum. Instead, the museum chose to resurrect Gardner's own support of the artists of her day and her passion for travel and art as a viable new strategy and direction.

The artist-in-residency program was created in 1992 to infuse the museum with new ideas and energy. It was established with three main goals: to give artists time and space to work; to reinvigorate the museum through the work and presence of practicing artists; and to encourage fresh approaches to the museum's permanent collection.

Born of Japanese and Korean descent, Mona Higuchi is an American artist whose work, poised on the borders of pain and beauty, speaks quietly of dislocation, identity, and history. I first saw her work at the Cambridge Multicultural Center where *Threading History*, an evocative piece on the experience of Japanese–American internment, was on view.

Bamboo Echoes: Dedicated to the Comfort Women **(View Two)**

Neither didactic nor confrontational, *Threading History* was a room-sized work that explored the personal stories of two Japanese Americans during World War II. The first story, symbolized in the piece by one thousand seven-inch stainless steel needles hanging from long threads, told of a Japanese American soldier who was among the Allied troops who liberated the concentration camps in Dachau in 1945. His mother, who herself was interned in a camp in Arkansas, had sewn a cloth sash for him with a thousand stitches, a tradition to bring him protection, courage, and strength in battle. The second story was of one individual who learned that her mother had been interned at Tule Lake, where she had collected hundreds of tiny shells and made them into a necklace. Years later, her mother still kept the necklace at the bottom of her jewelry box, never taking it out or wearing it. Higuchi individually glued one thousand shells onto wooden dowels and, together with the hanging needles, created a thin, vertical field of poignant, feminine, and evocative associations.

After tracking down the artist, I gathered slides and information on her previous installations and was struck by the consistent strength of her work. Rather than recreating moments of total loss, Higuchi's work spoke of survival and of the artist's role as a healer and a mediator. Out of the events of the past—Japanese–American internees, Holocaust victims, and the "disappeared" in Chile, she made sculptural worlds that had a tactile weight, a moving lightness, and an evident presence of hand, labor, and repetition. This world was sometimes gritty, sometimes elegant; it was both ordered and familiar, and uncomfortably "other." I was also struck by how little known her work was by my peers and colleagues.

When, several months later, I still found myself visualizing and thinking about *Threading History*, I proposed Mona Higuchi as a resident for the Gardner Museum, in the hope that she would connect to some aspect of the Asian collection and create an equally compelling piece of art. Only one previous resident, artist Constance de Jong, had chosen that aspect of the museum, and it was an area rich in history, much of it untold.

Both Mona Higuchi and Constance de Jong before her stumbled onto Isabella Gardner's relationship with Asia through her travel journals, now housed in the museum's archives. Both of the artists found a deep and personal connection to the travels described. And they found themselves immersed in a little-told history of the former Buddha (or Chinese) Room created by Isabella Stewart Gardner for her museum. The first Chinese Room opened in 1903, simultaneous to the opening of the museum's doors, and was located on the second floor in what is now the Early Italian Room. The room was an eclectic combination of Chinese and Japanese art, Venetian chinoiserie furniture, and other Western objects. It was a dramatic room bursting with gold and color, marked by portraits of Gardner herself and her husband and filled with hanging Chinese embroidery, statuary, wooden carvings, temple fittings, and cabinets brimming with curios and bric-a-brac. It was a room in which she shared many confidences with her dear friend, the renowned Japanese art critic and educator, Okakura Kazuko.

After the sudden death of Okakura in 1913, Gardner relocated the Chinese Room, creating a two-story Buddha Room in a back corner of the museum. More than a quarter of the Asian objects in the original room were moved there, as were objects from other galleries in the museum. The relocated Chinese Room was windowless and sober, containing only Asian objects, with her Buddhist statues arranged along the east, west, and south walls. It now had the character of a small, provincial Buddhist temple. According to memoirs and interviews, it was used by Gardner as a private space for "communing with her Buddhas" and meditation.

The Chinese Room remained intact, albeit ignored, until January 1961, when the space was needed to repair the second-century Roman mosaic pavement in the central courtyard. Room views were then photographed, objects inventoried and numbered, some artworks were even treated. Never open to the public during Gardner's lifetime, it was considered by the museum administration and trustees to be a private space. In 1970, the trustees of the museum authorized most of the contents of the Chinese Room to be "sold by order of the Trustees of the Isabella Stewart Gardner Museum from Storage." On 16 April 1971, the objects were sold at public auction. After the sale, the space was renovated for use as a guard's room on the basement story and a textile workroom in the first floor. In 1979, the workroom was converted to a café.

The history and disposition of Isabella Stewart Gardner's collection and two installations of Asian art, and her long and apparently passionate association with its history, philosophy, and religion, became the subject of Mona Higuchi's study and research during her residency. For her, the story embodied two key issues: the lack of parity between Western and Eastern art in America; and loss of personal, cultural, and institutional memory and history.

Bamboo Echoes, which evolved after weeks of research at the museum and outside it, was a major work of art that was on view from September through December 1996. The installation was dedicated to the "comfort women" and was informed by two distinct and unrelated histories: that of the Asian "comfort women," and that of the museum's former Buddha or Chinese Room. A wall text provided both the dedication and the context.

Bamboo Echoes was the first time that the creation and dismantling of the Buddha Room was publicly presented. Juxtaposing a piece of museum history with the horrific piece of modem history invoked in the dedication disrupted the preconceived notion of the museum as a calm and peaceful place for reflection and meditation. And disclosing Gardner's passion and serious involvement with Asian artwork, philosophy, religion, and references shook up the predominant association of Isabella Gardner with Italian Renaissance and American turn-of-the-century art. Altogether, it was an exhibition that subtly and effectively addressed uncomfortable, and unspoken of, periods of time.

In *Bamboo Echoes*, Higuchi, whose mother is Korean and father Japanese, explored the Japanese–Korean tensions from a political and personal perspective. Although Higuchi is quick to assert that neither her mother nor any of her female relatives were "comfort women," and equally clear that her childhood was not marked by racial tension, her dedication of *Bamboo Echoes* to the "comfort women" was a departure from her previous focus on Japanese–American issues.

Bamboo Echoes made a startling impression, one that was both quiet and haunting. A roomful of bamboo poles were tied together to form a three-dimensional grid that filled the Museum's gallery, gradually stepping up from the floor to just below the ceiling and forming a corridor between two mirrored halves. Passing through it, the bamboo symbolized a living tree, a time-honored and cross-cultural metaphor for growth and regeneration. It also spoke of torture, imprisonment, and a rigid social order. Hanging from the bamboo cubicles were hundreds of small, gold squares, gently dangling inside the arbor, gold-leafed on both sides to catch and reflect the light. The intensity of the shimmering gold punctuated the deep shadows cast by the cubes. The precarious balance and atmospheric lightness of the installation belied the resiliency of its materials and its subjects.

For most visitors, the bamboo symbolized a cage or a site for torture and imprisonment. Seemingly uniform and utilitarian to the Western eye, it exposed a host of cultural associations, bias, and subtle racism. The cheapness of most of the bamboo imported into the United States is one of its best-known features. Consequently, most of us know little about either the hundreds of varieties of bamboo in the world, their natural growing habitats, or the wages and working conditions of the rural poor who harvest or transport it. Yet with the orchid, chrysanthemum, and plum, bamboo was one of the Four Noble Plants of Chinese Garden lore. And with the Plum and Pine, it was among the Three Friends, a plant trinity representing Lao Tze, born beneath a plum tree, the Buddha who died in a grove, and Confucius. The phrase to "trim bamboo" was a Chinese expression, meaning to become a Buddhist. Perhaps because of its hollow core and flexible emptiness, bamboo embodied many of the principles of Zen and was an apt material for an artwork that at once evokes the spirit of Buddhist art and the "comfort women's" story of containment and enslavement.

Compassion for the "comfort women" was explicitly represented only through the inclusion of a late-eleventh- or early-twelfth-century sculpture of Kuan Yin, the Buddhist bodhisattva of compassion, which was evocatively placed at one end of the gallery, outside the bamboo structure. Borrowed from the permanent collection of the Gardner, Kuan Yin is a polychrome gilt wooden statue, which depicts the bodhisattva seated in repose, one leg hanging down, the other bent at the knee with the foot resting on top of the pedestal. Kuan Yin provided the bridge between the two histories from which Higuchi drew and linked their disparate histories.

The eerie image of the cubicles, some empty, some filled with gold, elicited perceptive, often precise associations, connotations, and responses from viewers. Eighth-grade students from three neighborhood public schools came to the museum prior to the opening to study the installation, and later to meet the artist. The participating schools—A City on a Hill Charter School, Boston Latin School, and the Lawrence School—were each participants in a four-year partnership with the museum. Without the benefit of title or accompanying wall text, astute students from A City on a Hill had the following comments to make: "The gold squares are like souls," said one girl. "And the empty boxes are lost souls," said another.

When students from the Lawrence School arrived two days later, the title and text were installed. Their observations and reactions made astounding connections between the abstract and formal structure and its psychological and historical associations.

Myung (m):
1. I felt when I first came in that the piece contained many ideas compacted into one.
2. I also felt that the women were trapped inside the bamboo cage.
3. The red in the background signified anger to me.

Vanessa (f):
My interpretations of this piece were not of anger or hate, but of the women who are trying to reach up to the light and finish what was started before they died or die. Maybe that's why the squares at the top of the sculpture spin so quickly, because they want to die in peace.

Another is that those who told and took a risk are represented by the squares on the edge. Because they took a risk in that if they fall nothing supports them. But they shine through the most and though they remember they are still happy.

It looks like the squares echo on and on and on.

A.J. (m):
1. The bamboo reminded me of a cage, or small cages, which the former "Comfort Women" are trapped in all of their life because of the painful memories that they have.

2. The structure reminded me of steps that can lead the "Comfort Women" to the top of the structure and to almost total bliss, but because of their horrible memories they can never totally escape.
3. The lights shining on the structure represented a ray of hope from heaven shining down on the women.

And finally, Kassandra (f):
I thought "wow!" it would take me 300 years to do this.

As many of these young people noticed, the dedication of *Bamboo Echoes* found its most direct expression in the gold-leafed square shapes that hang from the interstices of the bamboo panels. Subtly irregular, the approximately 1,800 paper squares were cut by hand, with Higuchi then applying a thin layer of gold leaf to each surface. The repetitive, laborious, and slow process provided the framework, structure, and time for Higuchi to meditate, contemplate, and reflect on the "comfort women." This ritual was, by its very nature, a private one. There are no overt images of enslaved women or sexual abuse. Rather, there is an environment for understanding, compassion, and healing. Writing about the artist Michelle Stuart, whose colors and processes recall those of Higuchi, the critic and author Lucy Lippard wrote, "Ritual-like processes, hour after hour of grinding and polishing . . . frees the mind to remember, the women have always remembered while working at such monotonous tasks."[1]

The sculptural aspects of Higuchi's installations played with scale, space, and the relationship between the viewer and the work. Her use of interior and exterior spaces was less about negative space than it was about drawing us into a space beyond our experience and tying us to the experiences of others who have come before. Overlapping planes, a combination of seemingly fragile or delicate materials with sturdier, even abrasive ones, moved us between formal concerns of abstraction and structure to concrete associations and narrative history. Ultimately, and when it was most successful, this heightened our awareness of both the visual and the historical landscape—a landscape characterized by women's work, vernacular materials, endurance, and reclamation.

Individual works of art rarely change social policy or affect political choices. Rather, they make change through the transformation and transfer of materials, associations, and perspectives. They can invoke close observation and inspire the imagination. Mona Higuchi brought to the Gardner Museum a previous and ongoing interest in the history and fate of the "comfort women," a history unknown to most of the museum's visitors. It was one that included national politics, gender politics, and the politics of war. She took from the Gardner Museum a new interest in the history of one arts institution and its relationship to Asia and Asian art. And in *Bamboo Echoes*, she combined both interests in an obsessive and original way that took unsuspecting viewers through time, loss, and history to survival, memory, and beauty.

Note

1. Lucy Lippard, *Strata: Nancy Graves, Eva Hesse, Michelle Stuart, Jackie Windsor* (Vancouver: Vancouver Art Gallery, 1977), p. 18.

Chapter 14

To Give a Voice

Therese Park

When Anne Frank's diary was published shortly after World War II, the world grieved for one young teenager, as well as for the lives of six million Jews, crushed by Nazi atrocities. Her innocent voice pulled readers into the attic where a dozen Jews lived together in hiding and reverberated throughout the world with a single message about how cruelly we humans treat one another.

Often, the feeble voice of the powerless turns into a thunderous roar when our inner ears are open to it. This happened to me in the summer of 1993, at the Harry S. Truman Library, while I watched a documentary film about World War II in which three former "comfort women" testified that the Japanese government had forced them into prostitution. After scenes of intense battle filmed in China during the war, the camera moved into a courtroom in present-day Tokyo, and I was looking at three old Korean women standing before a roomful of Japanese men and women. As each woman told of her abduction, torture, and repeated rapes in a military brothel, most of the men in the courtroom showed contempt and disgust. Only a few Japanese women wept with the plaintiffs.

I was disturbed—two hundred thousand teenage girls, mostly Korean, had been forced, coerced, and tricked into prostitution! I couldn't dismiss this tragedy as a misfortune that had merely struck some women, but realized instead that it was a serious crime perpetrated by one nation against another. How absurd that the Japanese government still denied its involvement in thousands of military brothels all over Asia, for the written documents had been discovered and victims had testified! I couldn't believe it. (Three years later, in August 1996, Japanese prime minister Hashimoto Ryutaro finally apologized to President Kim Yong-Sam of South Korea for Japan's use of Korean women as sex slaves during World War II.) As the days went by, the images of the three old women, testifying before abductors, rapists, and murderers, urging them to admit their crimes, grew in my mind and merged with my own childhood memories.

I was born in Korea in 1941, a few months before Japan attacked Pearl Harbor. In the middle of the night, ear-shattering sirens would go off, and we would have to move, crying and shivering, to an underground shelter. Mother told us that the American Yankees, who were Japan's enemy, were going to bomb our towns and villages. If we didn't stay in the shelter, she said, we would all die. I hated that damp, underground place, which amplified my voice to a monstrous howl and chilled my bones. I was afraid of the darkness, the whispering, and the American Yankees, who were going to kill us with their bombs.

I also remember the chaos that postwar liberation brought to the people of Korea—confusion, unemployment, starvation, and rioting, then Communism and the 38th Parallel.

Years later, I learned in school about Japan's treatment of Korea. At the dawn of the twentieth century, Japan had taken over our land by force, and its emperor had abolished the Yi Dynasty and enthroned himself as our king, without our permission. This was shortly after the Russo–Japanese War, in which Japan declared victory over Russia.

In the fall of 1905, Prince Ito Hirobumi, Japan's elder statesman, had marched into Kyongbok Palace with armed troops, demanding that King Kojong affix his seal to the so-called Protectorate Treaty, which Japan had prepared without the king's consent. King Kojong refused; he did not want Japan to "protect" or control Korea for an unlimited time. Hirobumi ordered his troops to drag the Korean prime minister to the courtyard and to beat him, which they did. King Kojong still would not consent, so Hirobumi and his troops went to the Foreign Ministry and ordered the Minister of Foreign Affairs to stamp the Protectorate Treaty with his own seal. Threatened with death, he did so. Four years afterward, Ito Hirobumi was assassinated by a young Korean activist named An Jung-Gun.

Decades later, in 1937, Japan's successful invasion of Nanjing, China, not only brought Emperor Hirohito blood-scented glory and honor, but also a nightmare as well; venereal disease began to spread among his imperial soldiers, threatening their ability to fight. After careful consideration, the emperor made a royal decision and ordered the military to use young women from Japan's colonial holdings as sex slaves. He preferred Korean girls for this purpose, because he knew that Korean society emphasized the preservation of female purity and chastity. His soldiers had a field day combing Korean towns and villages, hunting virgins. What Korean culture valued, the emperor stole and gave to his soldiers to defile.

Two hundred thousand lives! I couldn't picture that many human beings in my head. The largest number that I could actually see all at once would be at a local baseball stadium that held forty-six thousand seats. So one Sunday afternoon, I drove to the stadium, parked my car on a curve overlooking it, and pretended that the huge pool of people below were young women destined for Japanese military brothels. I imagined that the buzzing noises of the baseball fans buying soda, popcorn, and beer were the muffled cries of girls forced to provide sexual service to soldiers—thirty or forty times a day! Though the immense crowd represented only one-quarter of the number of human beings used in brothels by the Japanese, the visual picture and the silenced cries of women remained with me for a long time.

By now, I wanted to write a book about these women. I wanted to become a channel between them and the Western world, so that their voices could be heard loud and clear and would echo in every corner of the globe. I wanted to demolish the thick walls supporting the Confucian belief that women were supposed to be quiet about their "shameful" pasts—although they were victims—and that it was their fate that brought tragedies on them.

I began my research. I gained valuable insight into Japanese society by reading *Casting Stones: Prostitution and Liberation in Asia and the United States* by Rita Nakashima Brock and Susan Brooks Thistlethwaite. Their book explained how the inferior status of women in Japan (and in most parts of Asia) enabled the Japanese military to undertake without guilt such actions as using women as sex slaves. From the twelfth century through the Meiji Restoration in 1868, a warrior class of men, called *samurai*, had dominated the Japanese government and ruled in outlying provinces. *Samurai* were supposed to be stoic warriors, who followed a rigid code of honor and practiced obedience and self-discipline, but their long separations from wives and families undermined such resolve, especially in their sexual conduct. To make matters worse, inns, geisha houses, and brothels mushroomed everywhere. Despite their rigid Confucian moral standards and spiritual enlightenment, the warriors helped the huge sex industry in Japan. For centuries, then, the value of a Japanese woman was equal to the amount of money that a man was willing to spend at a brothel or at a live sex theater. The term *mizu shobai*, or "water trade," was a metaphor for the floating sex trade that allowed men a transient, impermanent, swirling lifestyle.

I also learned much about Japanese soldiers by reading a work called *Samurai* by Saburo Sakai, a pilot who had fought in World War II. In his book, he revealed the utmost fear, devotion to the emperor, and sense of honor that he had felt as a Japanese fighter. Meanwhile, *Philippines Diary*, by Stephen Mellnik, also enriched my knowledge and understanding of some American soldiers and of their strength while captive. The author, a former American POW, had survived a "Death March," during which ten thousand men had perished on the road, and had later escaped with nine other inmates. His depiction of prison life under heartless Japanese guards intensified my conviction as a writer.

My Wartime Crime, the published confession of Seiji Yoshida, a former Japanese military officer, validated what I was writing about and fueled my imagination. Had I not known so much already about the issues of "comfort women" and of Japan's cruelty to Koreans, I would have thought he was a good storyteller. His tale of rounding up more than two thousand girls from Korean towns and, without any guilt, of sending them to brothels was simply mind-boggling. What was his purpose in confessing his crimes fifty years later? To comfort his victims or himself? Obviously, he was worried about his redemption after death.

Another resource for me was a hand-bound, unpublished manuscript, "Victims of Pacific War," by Dr. T.H. Lee, a retired Korean physician. Since 1990, Dr. Lee had been corresponding with an organization in Seoul, Korea, which encouraged former "comfort women" to come forward and eventually to sue the Japanese government over their forced slavery. The text was loaded with information about "comfort stations" all over Asia, including their house rules, statistics, and sanitary measures.

The heroine of my novel, Soon-ah, came to me during a long walk. It seemed that she found me, rather than that I created her. "I was one of them," she told me. "I'll tell you how it happened, if you'll trust my voice." Not only did I trust her voice, but I embraced her with compassion as well.

Wittingly or unwittingly, a writer also portrays herself in her "characters." Soon-ah's determination to survive throughout her daily torture came from my own struggle as an Asian woman transplanted to American soil, which is harsh to nonwhites. "Go back to China!" Americans had yelled at me often. Life is a thorn thicket, my mother used to say. I learned that it's wise to find my own path by walking through a "thorn thicket," rather than to search for a "rose garden." In spite of her intolerable ordeal, Soon-ah trusts her own inner voice and tends her spirit by telling herself, "Never despair. Flowers can bloom in a desert."

Finally, my own purpose in writing *A Gift of the Emperor*, which was published by Spinster's Ink in 1997, was not to condemn a particular nation or its people, but rather to give a voice to those women of my own native land who, in spite of daily degradation and abuse, clung to life, even when death was an easier alternative and despair was inevitable. It is time for the world to listen to their resounding voices, telling how the men of a stronger nation treated them, when their country was poor and powerless. It is time for the Japanese government to comply with their demands, too, which are so small in comparison with the magnitude of what they lost, due to forced sex slavery. It is time.

Index